STEVE HO[DEL]

New York Times Bestselling

THE FURTHER SERIAL CRIMES

THE

EARLY

OF GEORGE HILL HODEL, M.D.

YEARS

Part II — The 1940s
Before "Black Dahlia Avenger"

The Early Years - Part II
Copyright 2021 - Steve Hodel

ISBN: 13-9780996045780

Printed in the United States of America 5432109876
Cover design: Hannah Linder

Thoughtprint Press Los Angeles, California

Dedication:

For the victims, living and dead

~

When I despair, I remember that all through history the way of Truth and Love has always won. There have been tyrants and murderers and for a time they can seem invincible, but in the end they always fall. Think of it, always.

—Mahatma Gandhi

Contents

About the Cover Image

The cover's image is of George Hodel circa 1936.

~

TEY Part 2 - 1930s Crimes Map of California

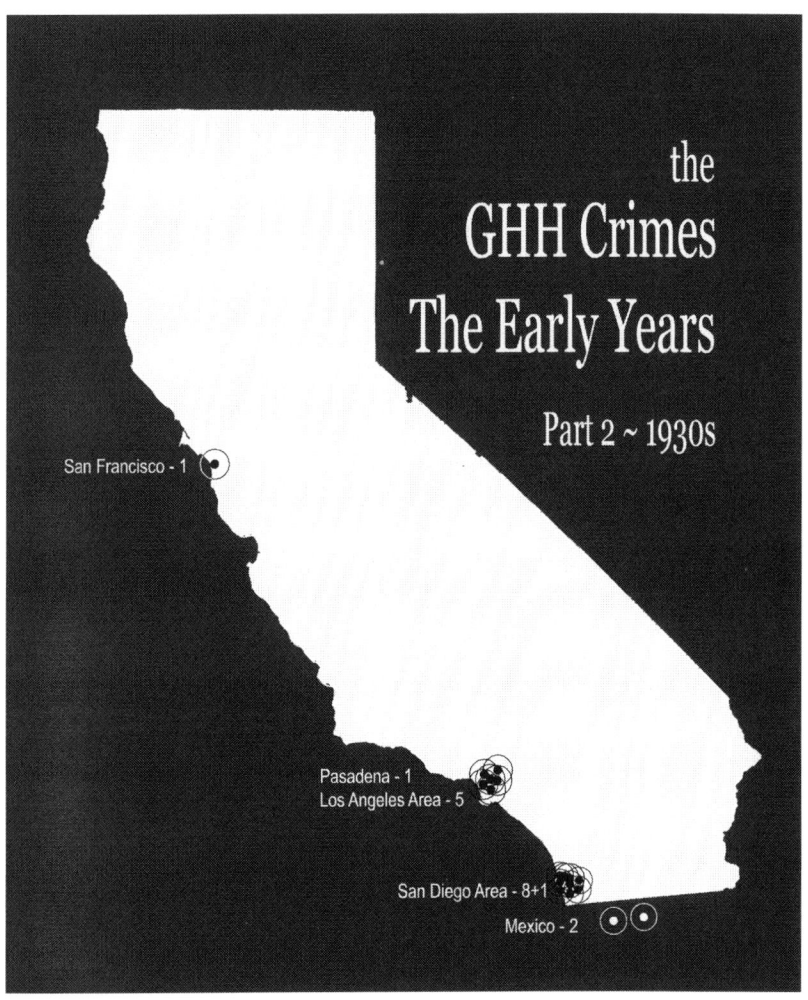

Introduction

In writing about George Hill Hodel: "The Early Years," my original intent was to present all of my father's *suspected* crimes from the 1920s and 1930s in one book. Due to the extent of these crimes one book was not enough.

Therefore, I have concentrated and collated "The Early Years" into two parts, two books.

The GHH Murders: The Early Years Part 2 (*TEY P2*) presents my investigations of George's **suspected** crimes during the **1930s**.

Note that I said, "***suspected* crimes**."

I want to be crystal clear on this point. My two-part, "Early Years" investigations are just that—a search for the truth.

Investigation - {dictionary.com]

Investigation is the noun form of the verb investigate, which derives from the Latin verb ***investigare***, meaning "to follow a trail" or "to search out."

...

The ***vesig*** part of the word can be traced back to the Latin word *vesigium*, meaning "footprint." (This is also the basis of the English word *vestige*, meaning "a trace or visible evidence of something.")

In the presentation of these crimes from long ago (the first one goes back *one hundred years*), I make no claim as to a "solution." I do not and am not saying that my father, George Hill Hodel, committed any of these crimes beyond a "Reasonable Doubt"—which would be the legal requirement to find him guilty.

Several of these crimes, without the introduction of hard physical evidence or DNA, are not solvable.

Others have been claimed "solved" by law enforcement, and are considered, "Case Closed."

In several of them, it is my position that 1) the wrong man was convicted or 2) the suspect committed the crime, but had an unidentified accomplice(s) or 3) the suspect has never been identified, and the case remains an *ice-cold whodunit* that was filed and forgotten long ago.

I can hear the hardcore skeptics' voices now—their minds made up—even before the books are published:

"Jesus, now Hodel is saying his dad killed _____ and ____! What? Does Steve think his dad is responsible for every famous unsolved murder in California and beyond? Where is he going next, 'The Grassy Knoll' in Dallas?"

To be clear:

These crimes from the Twenties and Thirties did not present themselves to me post *Black Dahlia Avenger* published in 2003. (See **Author's P.S.** pages 423-428.)

I was aware of them and his possible involvement in them as early as the year 2000, *a full three years* before I presented my father to the world as the killer of Elizabeth "Black Dahlia" Short and the perpetrator other LA Lone Woman Murders.

Back then, I thought these two books would be my second and final book presenting these crimes as *suspected* offenses committed in his youth, i.e., "the early years."

I had no idea that by "following the evidence," I would be led to George Hodel's crimes as: Chicago's "Lipstick Killer" and Manila's "Jigsaw Murder" and then to his pre-retirement serial crimes in the San Francisco Bay Area as "Zodiac."

So, here we are, some twenty years and six books and twenty-five murder victims later.

What I thought would be "Book II" has now become **Book VII** *(TEY P1)* and **Book VIII** *(TEY P2)*.

For those who are coming across my investigations for the first time, I would strongly urge you to read the pre-"early years" books in the below-recommended order.

Steve Hodel's: 6 True-Crime Books (in reading order left to right)

In truth, the above six books plus *TEY P1 & P2* represent *one ongoing investigation* very much like an actual Homicide Progress Report, which chronologically updates new findings and linkage as the new evidence is uncovered.

This is where "The Early Years Part 2" begins:

Chapter 1

1933

The Sphinx Murder - Dr. Leonard Siever

ONE OF TWO SPHINX AT THE ENTRANCE TO THE
SCOTTISH RITE TEMPLE - PASADENA , CA.

The Crime
December 13, 1933 - 5:00 a.m.

Light rain continued to fall as milkman Harold Fox
walked up the driveway on his route to deliver milk to

Peter Bennett, the caretaker of Pasadena's Scottish Rite Cathedral, located at 150 N. Madison Avenue in that city. Harold Fox initially thought the male body lying on the ground near an expensive car was a transient asleep. Still, in taking a closer look, he saw the blood coming from a head wound and realized the man was shot and immediately called the Pasadena Police Department.

Detectives responded to the crime scene, and their on-scene investigation revealed the following:

Evening Herald Express **photo showing the position of Dr. Leonard Siever's body sprawled next to his vehicle in parking space adjacent to the Pasadena Scottish Rite Cathedral**

- On the previous evening, December 12, 1933, at approximately 7:00 p.m., neighborhood witnesses heard what sounded like two gunshots fired but did not call the police.

- Officers were unable to locate any witnesses who may have provided a physical description of the shooter.

- Based on the position of the victim's body, detectives believed that the victim had approached and was about to enter his parked personal vehicle when the suspect, believed to be lying in wait, approached from behind and shot him in the head. (Based on later autopsy examination, *the coroner speculated that the second shot, which penetrated the heart, was not fired for some "five to ten minutes after the first shot."* This finding corresponded to additional witness statements that there was a seemingly long delay between the two sounds of gunshots.)

- Powder burns were noted on both the head wound and the chest wound, indicating the gunman fired at a very close range.

- Recovery of the spent slugs from the body during the autopsy and analysis revealed the murder weapon was a .32 cal Iver Johnson revolver. The handgun was not recovered at the crime scene, and to my knowledge, was never found.

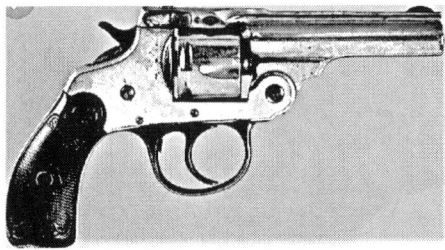

**IVER JOHNSON .32 Caliber revolver
of the type used in Siever murder**

- The key to Dr. Siever's automobile was found hanging from the door lock, indicating to detectives that the victim was about to enter his vehicle when distracted by the gunman, then shot.

- Dr. Siever's dental office was located approximately one block from where he had parked his car at the Scottish Rite Cathedral.

- The victim's pockets had been turned inside out. An expensive platinum watch had been removed from his wrist. Also, his wallet had been taken. Even so, authorities proffered the belief that the motive for the murder was likely *not robbery*, but instead based on later information, most probably "revenge or jealousy involving an unknown woman."

Pasadena P.D. detective points to where victim Siever's body lay next to his touring car's estimated parking space adjacent to Scottish Rite Cathedral for ten hours before being found by milkman, Harold Fox, at 5:00 AM the following morning.

Front of Pasadena Scottish Rite Temple showing two Sphinxes guarding the entrance. Based on this location, the 1933 local Pasadena and Los Angeles newspapers quickly dubbed this "THE SPHINX MURDER."

The Victim

Dr. Leonard Siever DDS

Dr. Leonard Siever was a prominent Pasadena socialite and dentist. Born in Russia, in 1890, his parents reportedly brought him to America when he was sixteen. He attended the University of Michigan in 1916 and became a naturalized citizen that same year.

After relocating to Los Angeles, he attended and obtained his Doctor of Dentistry degree at the University of Southern California and opened his practice in Pasadena where he founded the Artist-Student League, a benefit foundation for music students, to which he contributed several scholarships.

Dr. Siever was a bachelor and shared a Pasadena residence with a Dr. Francis P. Weston, a former Pasadena police surgeon.

Dr. Siever's friends described him as "a mystic and an aesthete. A man who played the violin and loved both art and nature. Friends described him as a person with a strong desire for knowledge."

He also had a reputation as "a ladies man" and was known to woo scores of women and reportedly had serial engagements, none of which resulted in marriage.

The doctor's murder became headlines in both the Los Angeles and Pasadena newspapers for a month straight with the main speculation by reporters being an "affair of the heart murder" portraying the victim as "the Don Juan Dentist" with their sensational interviews centered around and with his prior girlfriends along with publishing love letters from and to his ex-fiancée.

***Santa Cruz Evening News*, February 17, 1934**

A Mystery Witness?

Within days of the murder, a mystery witness, "a beautiful dark-haired woman," is reported having been seen with Dr. Siever at his office just one hour before his murder.

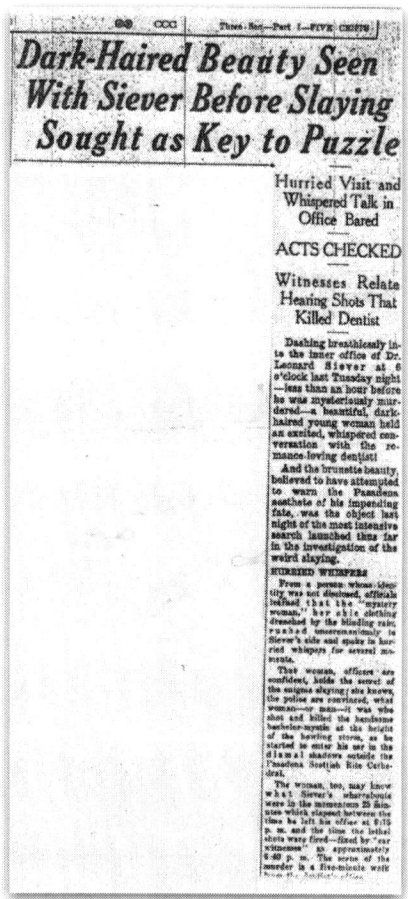

Los Angeles Examiner Dec 15, 1933

Here is how it was reported in the *Los Angeles Examiner* just two days after the body was found—shot on the 12th:

Dark-Haired Beauty Seen
With Siever Before Slaying Sought as Key to Puzzle

Hurried Visit and Whispered Talk in Office Bared

...

Dashing breathlessly into the inner office of Dr. Leonard Siever at 6 o'clock last Tuesday night—less than an hour before he was mysteriously murdered—a beautiful, dark-haired young woman held an excited whispered conversation with the romance-loving dentist!

And the brunette beauty, believed to have attempted to warn the Pasadena aesthete of his impending fate, was the object last night of the most intensive search launched thus far in the investigation of the weird slaying.

HURRIED WHISPERS

From a person whose identity was not disclosed, officials learned that the "mystery woman," her chic clothing drenched by the blinding rain, rushed unceremoniously to Siever's side and spoke in hurried whispers for several moments.

That woman, officers are confident, holds the secret of the enigmatic slaying; she knows, the police are convinced, what woman—or man—it was who shot and killed the handsome bachelor-mystic at the height of the howling storm, as he started to enter his car in the dismal shadows outside the Pasadena Scottish Rite Cathedral.

The woman, too, may know what Siever's whereabouts were in the momentous 25 minutes which elapsed between the time he left his office at 6:15 p.m. and the time the lethal shots were fired—fixed by "ear witnesses" as approximately 6:40 p.m. The scene of the murder is a five-minute walk from the dentist's office.

(**SKH Note**: In separate articles, the unidentified mystery woman's name is mentioned as possibly being "Dorothy," with no further information.)

Two days later, In a separate newspaper article in the *Los Angeles Examiner* on December 17, 1933, the witness who spoke briefly to "the mystery woman" is identified and provided a more detailed description.

Los Angeles Examiner Dec. 17, 1933

MYSTERY GIRL DESCRIBED

A description of the "mystery woman" who rushed breathlessly into the office and conversed in excited whispers with Siever shortly before he was slain Tuesday night was given yesterday by pretty Ena Sylvester, the elevator operator who directed the mysterious visitor to the doctor's suite.

"She was a woman about 25 or 26," Miss Sylvester said. "She had dark hair and dark eyes, and I would say that she was chic, smart looking, rather than outstandingly beautiful.

"She wore a swagger coat of brown tweed and carried herself as, I should imagine, a society girl would. She stayed in Siever's office but a few minutes and then dashed out and left the building, alone.

"It was only three or four minutes later that the doctor, appearing nervous and upset, went out into the rain after hesitating and exclaiming, 'Well, I guess I've got to go.'"

Miss Sylvester said she had never

MYSTERY GIRL DESCRIBED

A description of the "mystery woman" who rushed breathlessly into the office and conversed in excited whispers with Siever shortly before he was slain Tuesday night was given yesterday by pretty Ena Sylvester, the elevator operator, who directed the mysterious visitor to the doctor's suite.

"She was a woman about 25 or 26," Miss Sylvester said. "She had dark hair and dark eyes, and I would say that she was chic, smart looking, rather than outstandingly beautiful.

"She wore a swagger coat of brown tweed and carried herself as, I should imagine, a society girl would. She stayed in Siever's office but a few minutes and then dashed out and left the building, alone.

"It was only three or four minutes later that the doctor, appearing nervous and upset, went out into the rain after hesitating and exclaiming, "Well, I guess I've got to go."

Miss Sylvester said she had "never seen the woman before."

...

SKH Note - Based on the joint witness statements in the above two articles, I am compelled to make the following observations:

My mother, Dorothy Jean Harvey, after seven years of marriage to film director, John Huston, separated from him in January 1933. Huston legally filed for divorce in Los Angeles Superior Court on August 18, 1933, some four months before the Siever murder.

In his filing for divorce, Huston alleged that his wife, Dorothy, of "being extravagant and of keeping him in debt and of making no effort to become a good housekeeper." (This included her extravagant need to constantly buy expensive and very chic clothes, at a time when John was just a struggling Hollywood screenwriter.)

John Huston, Son of Actor, Seeks Divorce

John Huston, 28 years of age, a film writer and a son of Walter Huston, actor, yesterday filed a suit for a divorce in the Superior Court here against Mrs. Dorothy Huston, 27, formerly Miss Dorothy Jeanne Harvey, an actress.

Huston accuses his wife of being extravagant and of keeping him in debt continually. He also accuses her of making no effort to become a good housekeeper.

Under a property settlement filed with the complaint, Huston promises to pay Mrs. Huston $50 a week for three years.

The couple, married October 17, 1926, and separated on January 10, last, according to the complaint prepared by Attorney Mark M. Cohen.

Los Angeles Times August 19, 1933

At the time of the December 13, 1933, witness description of the "mystery woman." provided above by elevator operator/witness Miss Ena Sylvester, could very well have been my mother (to be, I won't be born for another seven years). The description was as follows:

> "Dorothy," age 27, dark brown eyes, dark brown hair, normally very chic dresser, was and carried herself as a society girl having lived and associated with top film actors as well as being close friends to Ira and George Gershwin and the New York theatre society.

Whether or not she was the "mystery woman" who may have warned Dr. Siever of his imminent danger, just an hour before his demise, I cannot say. However, no question that in name and physical description, Dorothy Jean Harvey fits it "to a T."

I do not possess a photograph of my mother in her mid-twenties. However, the following two pictures (top of page 20) show her at age 19 and 36.

The photo on the left was taken in 1926, in the year she married a fellow teenager, John Huston.

The photo on the right was taken by my parents' good friend "Man Ray," who was our family photographer for a decade in the 1940s.

"Man" took the photograph of my mother "Dorothy" in 1944, a decade after Dr. Leonard Siever's murder.

 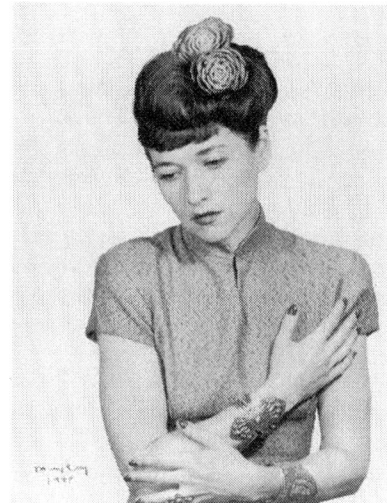

Dorothy age 19   Dorothy age 37
(1926)   (1944)

In viewing the two photographs above, one must "age" the photo on the left by some seven years and then "youthen" the image on the right by ten years to get an accurate picture of "Dorothy" as she would have appeared in December 1933.

The Initial Investigation

As the high-profile headlines continued in the early days of the investigation, then-Deputy District Attorney Buron Fitts wanted to make sure the press and public knew that he was the man in charge.

Rest assured, people; he had his Chief Investigator, Blayney Matthews, working directly with Pasadena P.D. and its detectives who insisted that indeed "an arrest was imminent."

Pasadena Post January 5, 1934

-HEADS PROBE

BURON FITTS REVIEWS MURDER CASE PROGRESS WITH DETECTIVES HERE

District Attorney Declares Investigation Results To Date Satisfactory; Much Uncovered Held Of Real Value

District Attorney Buron Fitts came to Pasadena yesterday afternoon to review the work of representatives of his department in the investigation of the murder of Dr. Leonard Siever. Before leaving for his ranch near Duarte last night he consulted not only with his own department men but also talked with Chief of Police Charles H. Kelley and Chief of Detectives Charles A. Betts. He went over with them in detail the results of the protracted investigation and, before departing, told newspaper men that he is well satisfied with the progress made. "You may say for me, if you wish, that, as the result of a lot of hard work covering a long period of time, the investigators in this tough case have secured much information which is of value. This does not mean at all that we are about to

BURON FITTS

District attorney, who, yesterday, assumed charge of the investigation attempting to determine the slayer of Dr. Leonard Siever, Pasadena dentist.

Cutting
It Short

DA Buron Fitts takes command of the "Sphinx Murder" on January 4, 1934, just two weeks into the investigation and assigns his DA Chief Investigator, Blayney Matthews, to oversee and coordinate all aspects of the crime.

AIDS PROBE OF SPHINX MURDER

Photo shows Dr. Carl Wagner aiding authorities in their attempts to solve the mysterious "sphinx murder" of Dr. Leonard Siever, Pasadena society dentist. Dr. Wagner, who has offices in the same building where Dr. Siever worked before his death, said: "I knew Dr. Siever only casually, but I would like to see the mystery cleared up." Left to right, are Dr. Wagner, Chief Investigator Blayney Mathews and Detective Lieut. Harry Thomas.

DA Chief Investigator Matthews (center) to spearhead Dr. Siever's murder

A Primary Witness Dr. Carl Wagner (on the left) is seen in the above photograph being interviewed by DA investigator Blayney Matthews and Pasadena Detective Lt. Harry Thomas.

Dr. Wagner, of Pasadena, was a highly respected, skilled surgeon who had an office in the same building as Dr. Siever but claimed only to know him casually.

From my reading of the published materials, it appears that Dr. Wagner had no real "hard" information but the substance of what, if anything, he knew was never publicly revealed.

In what may well have been a tragic coincidence, Dr. Wagner, after attending a movie preview in which his date, the beautiful young actress, Miss Dorothy Dell, had acted in, was returning her to her residence in Beverly Hills at the time of the murder.

SHOOT THE WORKS with Jack Oakie, Ben Bernie, and Dorothy Dell, a Paramount Studios picture, 1934

The couple had just viewed a private screening of her film, *Shoot The Works* (Paramount Studio 1934). The couple was on the way home from Pasadena when the car driven by Dr. Wagner, traveling at high speed, spun out of control, struck a large boulder and light post, and both Dr. Wagner and Miss Dell were killed.

The accident occurred in June 1934, while the Siever "Sphinx Murder Investigation" was still active and unsolved.

Without wanting to sound "paranoid," still one must wonder why Dr. Wagner would risk his and Miss Dell's lives by traveling at such a high speed.

Were they being threatened and chased by a second car?

It was very public knowledge that Dr. Wagner was a prominent witness in Dr. Siever's investigation. (So much so that he had complained: it was negatively affecting his business and professional life.)

How strange, that just as in the case of the earlier referenced Aimee Semple McPherson investigation, where an essential witness in the kidnapping case, the blind attorney McKinley, and two other individuals, were in a high-speed accident (that some suspected involved foul play) that resulted in the death of all three passengers.

Absent any additional evidence, we must consider that the Wagner/Dell accident was a mere coincidence, but still, to my mind, very hinky, and I would not exclude the *possibility of foul play*.

Spectacular Accident Costs Two Lives

Less than twenty-four hours after she had seen a studio preview of her first starring picture, Dorothy Dell, screen actress and former beauty contest winner, was killed in a spectacular automobile accident in Pasadena early yesterday. Miss Dell is shown in the upper picture, with her sister, Miss Helen Dell, left, and their mother, Mrs. Lillian Goff. In the lower right-hand picture is Dr. Carl Wagner, Pasadena surgeon and driver of the car, who died several hours after the crash. Below at the left is a view of the wrecked car.

Actress Dorothy Dell won the Galveston, Texas, "Miss Universe," in 1930 and went on to star in the Ziegfeld Follies, then on to Hollywood and a film contract with Paramount Studios.

Mrs. Frances Coen Cooke

Mrs. Frances Coen Cooke . . . she waited in vain for Dr. Siever to call for her on the fatal evening.

Wealthy Divorcee Mrs. Frances Coen Cooke

Inarguably, Mrs. Frances Coen Cooke would turn out to be the most crucial witness in the Siever murder investigation.

On the night of his murder, December 12, 1933, Siever left his office in the Professional Medical Building in downtown Pasadena. He was then to drive to a prescheduled meeting with Mrs. Frances Coen Cooke.

Mrs. Cooke never received a call from the doctor and was upset that he didn't even have the courtesy to call and inform her of his "no show" until discovering the following morning that he had been shot and killed.

The Killer Sends a Note – Taunts Police

In the first week of January 1934, Mrs. Cooke received a letter from the killer. It was postmarked "January 2" and mailed from Pasadena to her residence in that same city.

The envelope contained Doctor Siever's missing platinum-plated wristwatch and a crudely handwritten letter demanding $5000 in trade for the gun and additional information on the identity of his killer.

Los Angeles Herald-Express, January 8, 1934

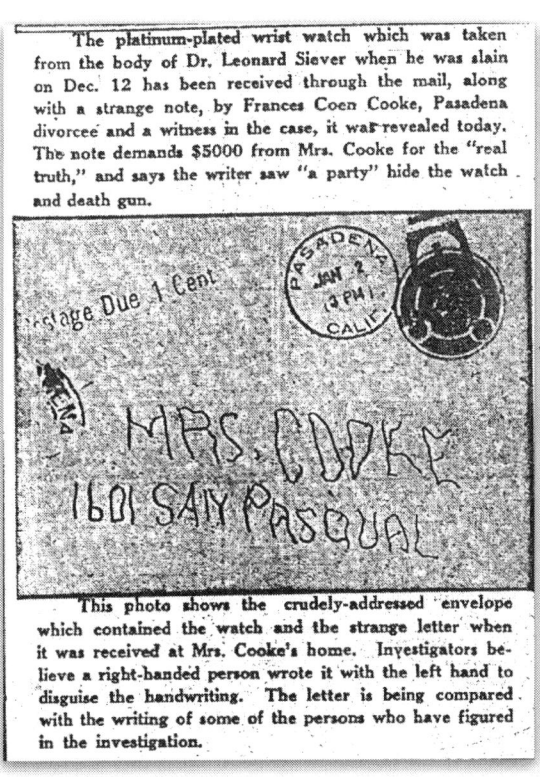

The platinum-plated wrist watch which was taken from the body of Dr. Leonard Siever when he was slain on Dec. 12 has been received through the mail, along with a strange note, by Frances Coen Cooke, Pasadena divorcee and a witness in the case, it was revealed today. The note demands $5000 from Mrs. Cooke for the "real truth," and says the writer saw "a party" hide the watch and death gun.

This photo shows the crudely-addressed envelope which contained the watch and the strange letter when it was received at Mrs. Cooke's home. Investigators believe a right-handed person wrote it with the left hand to disguise the handwriting. The letter is being compared with the writing of some of the persons who have figured in the investigation.

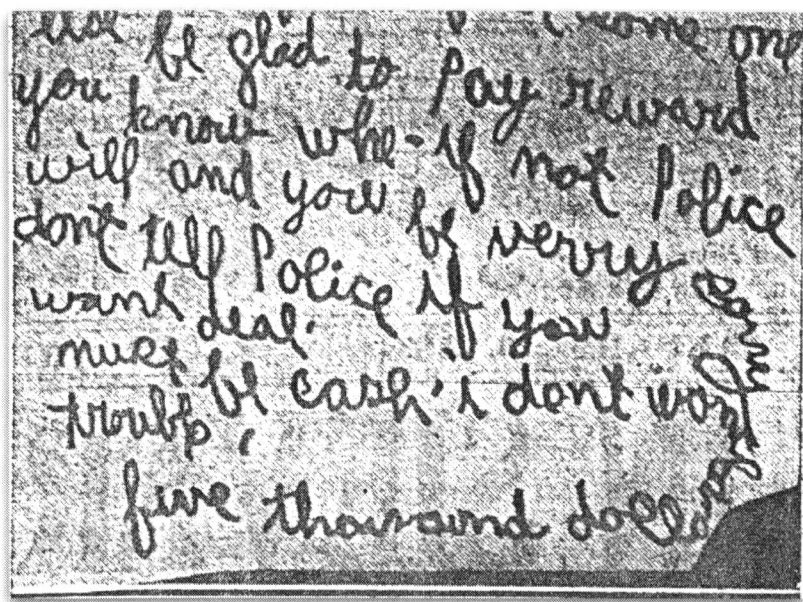

The handwriting expert opined the **letter was written by a right-handed person using his left hand to disguise his writing**. Below is the same image inverted.

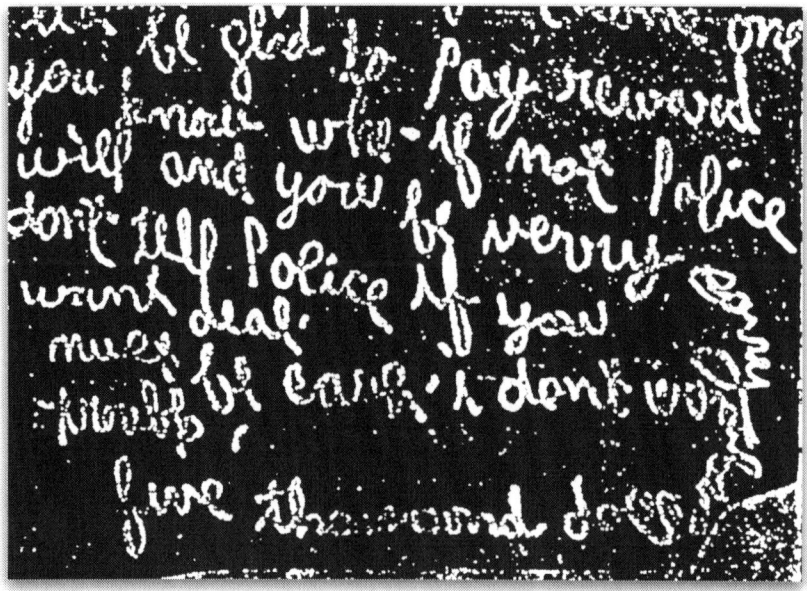

Excerpted from the *Los Angeles Herald Express* article of January 8, the mystery letter sent to Mrs. Cooke read:

"You are in a hot spot. You want to know real truth. For $5000 I give complete information, also pistol .32. I think pistol has finger marks on it. I swear this is truth before Gott. I was in brookside park Wed. December 13 and saw a party hide these evidence. Answer L.A. examiner Class 120 sign Mabel if you want to deal I will be very happy to accommodate you. If not someone else be glad to pay reward. You know who. If not police will and you be very sorry. Don't tell police

if you want deal. Must be cash. I don't want trouble. Five thousand dollars."

QUIZ CONTINUED

While the handwriting in the strange note was being enlarged and studied under powerful microscopes, with the writing of other persons also under the same study, the investigators were continuing with their questioning of various witnesses.

...

One of the interesting ironies of the mystery letter was the fact that it had been addressed to 1601 San Pasqual Street, Pasadena, where Mrs. Cooke's parents formerly resided, but where none of the members of the family had lived for a considerable time.

A postman detected "the error" and took the package to Mrs. Cooke's home at 1575 San Pasqual Street.

RUSE THEORY

What puzzled the investigators about this irony was the question of whether the note writer was some person who had no knowledge whatsoever of Mrs. Cooke, or if the writer was some clever person who actually had followed the murder case investigation closely and sought to throw the investigators off his trail.

Carrying out the instructions to Mrs. Cooke in the note to insert an advertisement in the personal column of a newspaper, police inserted the notice and then waited for a reply, hoping the note writer would arrange a meeting for the $5000 money payment and fall into a police trap. The only reply was the mysterious telephone call made from the Pasadena public park last Saturday night. Since then there has been nothing—silence.

Above article was headlined in the *Herald Express* as:

LINK EDUCATED PERSON TO SIEVER NOTE

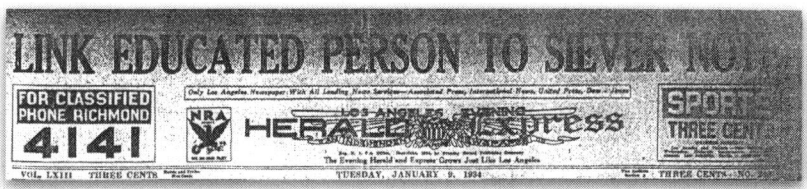

Investigators of the murder of Dr. Leonard Siever seek a "mystery m⸝ " who made a strange m⸝ ᵍⁱᵗ phone call to the home ⸝: Frances Coen Cooke, witness in the case.

After Mrs. Cooke received a letter demanding $5000 for the "real truth" of the murder, investigators were stationed at an extension phone in her home and the phone exchange was on the alert to trace calls. When the man phoned, asking for "Frances," a policewoman answered and he rang off. The call was traced to a public phone booth in the Tourists' Club quarters, above, in Central park, Pasadena. Officers rushed there, but the caller had fled.

After mailing Mrs. Frances Cooke the demand for $5000, the suspect then telephoned her at her private residence.

Detectives anticipating the call had a woman (police officer) answer the ring and the suspect asked for "Frances" but then immediately hung up. However, police were able to trace the call, and it showed the caller telephoned Mrs. Cooke from a public telephone booth in Pasadena's Central Park, inside the Tourist Club.

> **Author's Note** - 1) Did the suspect/caller expect Mrs. Cooke to be alone when he called? 2) When the police woman answered the call and the suspect asked for "Frances," could this mean the suspect knew Frances's voice, thus the reason "he hung up" was because he knew the woman answering his call was not Frances Cooke?

Officers immediately responded to the location, but the suspect was gone on their arrival. A park employee came forward and described a male seen in the area at the time of the call; however, the description and information were not released to the public.

In the weeks that followed, a second handwritten note was sent; however, it proved to be written by two teenage boys, who were arrested and admitted the "prank."

After the boys' arrest, someone mailed two additional notes to Mrs. Cooke, one handwritten and the second cut and pasted, but police opined that these were probably "crank notes" also and they were not published in the press or followed up.

(**SKH Note**: I would question the efficacy of this decision, claiming they were "crank letters" as that is what occurred in the later 1947 Black Dahlia mailings, and the subsequent letters/notes proved to be legitimate and written by Dr. George Hill Hodel.)

This photo shows Mrs. Cooke, wealthy divorcee, with whom Dr. Siever had a social engagement on the rainy night of tragedy — an engagement he could not keep because he was shot down. Mrs. Cooke has been assisting in investigation of his death.

This photo shows the beautiful mansion where Mrs. Cooke lives with her parents at 1575 San Pasqual street in Pasadena. Into this setting of beauty came a note of sinister mystery with the phone calls and the previous delivery of the letter containing, along

with the demand for $5000, the platinum-plated wrist watch which Dr. Siever is supposed to have been wearing when he was murdered. Deputy District Attorney Hugh McIsaac says the letter indicates it was written by the killer, who feared arrest and tried to create a false trail.

Mrs. Cooke's Pasadena private residence at 1575 San Pasqual St.

As the joint investigation by Pasadena P.D. and the L.A. D.A.'s investigators moved forward into 1934, by their count, at least eighty personal friends and acquaintances of Dr. Leonard Siever were contacted and interviewed.

Scores of .32 caliber Iver Johnson handguns were tested, and the ballistics compared to the evidence slugs with no match.

In my early review of all the documented evidence, it became apparent that not only did the numerous crime signatures and *modus operandi* of this killer match those of my father in his later identified murders, but as we can see, they are also consistent with those we have recently examined in ***The Early Years Part I- The 1920s***.

As I close out this chapter, I want to end with what I discovered early in my initial review of this crime in 2001.

I believe that this documented information, when taken with what we have already learned about the murder of Dr. Leonard Siever, is the most telling clue and may indicate that they identified Siever's killer by name and that person was their prime suspect.

Though his name was never publicly released, I believe that the suspect they identified as the possible killer could well have been—a young twenty-seven-year-old man who was currently home for the holiday break from his medical studies in San Francisco.

A man who would have been temporarily residing at his South Pasadena home, at 6511 Short Way, just five miles and a ten-minute drive to the crime scene at the Scottish Rite Cathedral.

His name? GEORGE HILL HODEL

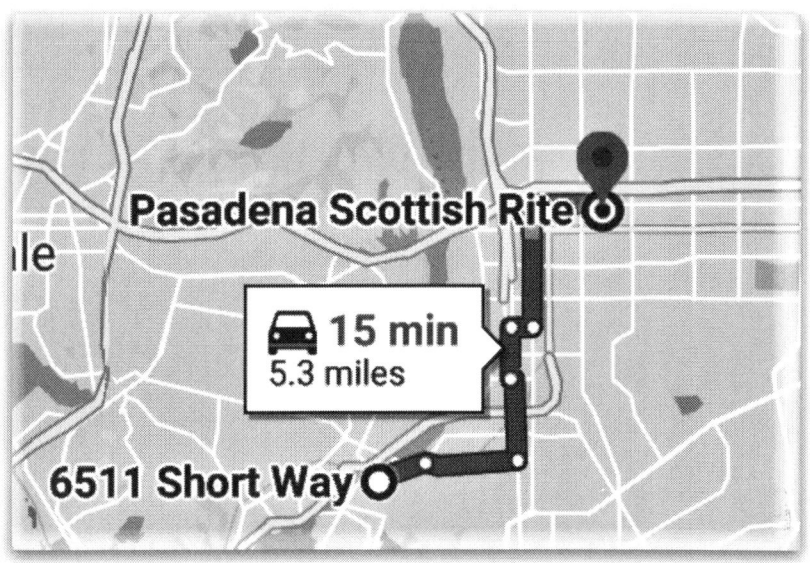

**1933 residence of George Hodel
just five miles south of the crime scene.**

Read the detailed description, attributed to DA Chief Investigator Blayney Matthews, of the man detectives called "The Perfect Villain," a man they had identified by name and believed was the jealous assassin of Dr. Leonard Siever as published in the *Los Angeles Examiner* on December 16, 1933, just four days after the murder.

See article, "SOCIETY 'FRIEND' POTENTIAL VILLAIN" on page 36 and the bullet points that follow.

SOCIETY 'FRIEND' POTENTIAL VILLAIN

Moving through the mystery-shrouded drama of the murder of Dr. Leonard Siever, there is, it was learned last night from an authoritative source, a potential "perfect villain."

Unlike the procession of women attracted to the slain aesthete, the "villain" had no love for the brilliant fellow who graced salons so well.

There is reason to believe, it was pointed out, that he had a jealous hatred for Siever, even though pretending friendship for the man he may have marked for death.

This suspect is believed to be a dope addict. It is known that he has flown into frenzies, apparently under influence of morphine or some other narcotic.

Among his intimates, his "analytical mind" has often been mentioned. He is possessed, some say, of a native cunning, which with real or imagined reason, might be turned into diabolical shrewdness in concocting and carrying out a plot such as had its denouement in the cold-blooded murder of Leonard Siever.

The finger of suspicion has not yet been pointed directly toward this man. It is felt, however, that should he have written Siever's death warrant, he would almost certainly have provided himself with a "perfect alibi."

Intelligent and suave, victor in many a battle of wits in Pasadena drawing rooms, able to disguise his suspected dope addiction, the man is a dabbler in criminology.

Phlegmatic enough normally, he is said to have become passionately fond of a woman—a woman among the scores with whom Siever was acquainted.

Did his passion flame to fury because he believed Siever had won the woman's heart? Did this amateur of criminology become a ruthless slayer?

- **GHH would have to have known Dr. Siever as both men moved in the same Pasadena society circles and had for many years.**

- **GHH could well have been known and praised by the older music and art lover, as Dr. Siever** would have been seventeen years George's senior when both were associated with Pasadena "high society."

- GHH was known to "fly into frenzies while apparently under the influence of morphine or some other narcotic."

- GHH was known "among his intimates for his analytical mind."

- GHH was known for his "native cunning and diabolical shrewdness."

- GHH was "Intelligent and the suave victor in many a battle of wits in Pasadena drawing rooms."

- GHH was "able to disguise his dope addiction and was a dabbler in criminology." (As we know, George Hodel considered himself much more than a "dabbler" and instead perceived himself as a "Master Criminal.")

Just thirteen days after The *Los Angeles Examiner,* December 16, 1933 "SOCIETY 'FRIEND' POTENTIAL VILLAIN" article appeared in the newspapers; the *Los Angeles Times* headlined the following on December 29:

Dr. Leonard Siever Mystery Murder Solution Believed by Investigators to Be Near

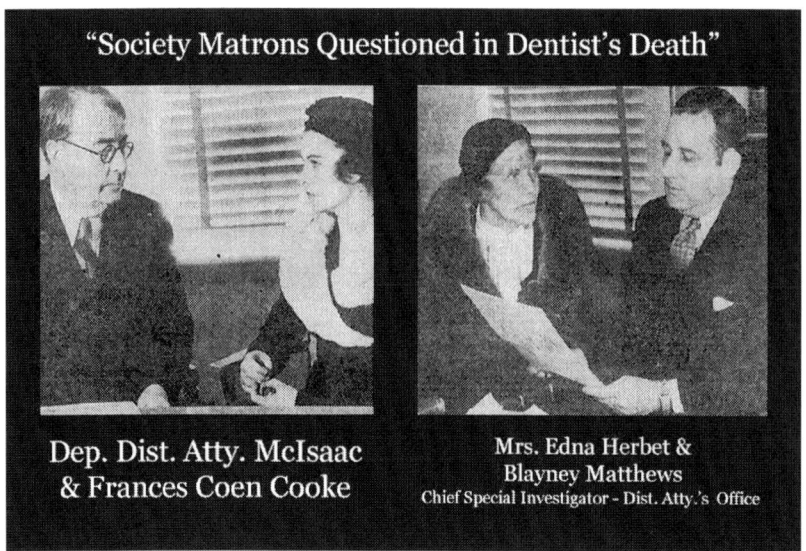

"Society Matrons Questioned in Dentist's Death"

Dep. Dist. Atty. McIsaac
& Frances Coen Cooke

Mrs. Edna Herbet &
Blayney Matthews
Chief Special Investigator - Dist. Atty.'s Office

Excerpts from that article:

ARREST LOOMS AS POSSIBILITY

Action May Be Taken in Thirty-six Hours

...

PASADENA, December 28.

The murder of Dr. Leonard Siever, prominent dentist and art patron, will be solved within thirty-six hours and an arrest made if the finger of suspicion continues to point as steadily toward the man in question as it does now, Blayney Matthews, chief special investigator of the District Attorney's office, said here today.

...

"If leads developed since we began an exhaustive questioning of persons who knew Dr. Siever stand up a little longer, we will soon have the slayer in jail," Matthews said.

SECRET INQUIRY GOES ON

The chain of circumstance now being forged was built up by a thorough, secret questioning of friends and associates of the slain dentist. This inquisition has been carried on several days in a Pasadena hotel and has developed the additional facts that gave Matthews basis for his confident assertion.

•••

Every possible clew and every shred of evidence has been investigated by Matthews since the inquisition of witnesses began.

The questioning continued tonight and will again tomorrow, Matthews said, unless an arrest is made within the next few hours.

So confident was I that the "Perfect Villain" prime suspect investigated by Pasadena P.D. and DA Investigator Blayney Matthews and named in the original 1933 murder investigation was, in fact, George Hodel, I decided to try and conduct a modern-day follow-up some eighty years later.

In 2015, I contacted the Pasadena P.D. and was fortunate enough to be able to make an appointment to meet with current day detectives with the promise of offering them what I believed was a factual based "lead" to one of their most infamous ice-cold cases, "The 1933 Sphinx Murder."

Much to my surprise, upon arriving at the police station, expecting to meet with the current homicide detectives, I was instead met by Pasadena Police Chief Phillip Sanchez, who greeted me warmly and directed me to an interview room.

As it turned out, it was a "one-on-one" meeting with Chief Sanchez in which I presented an hour-long PowerPoint slide show using graphics to summarize the facts showing that George Hodel was a serial killer in the Black Dahlia and other LA Lone Woman Murders from the 1940s, and then transitioning to how and why I believed he was connected to their 1933 Pasadena murder of Dr. Leonard Siever.

Pasadena Police Chief Phillip L. Sanchez
(Star News photo)

This is the cover of the twenty-page summary with printed graphics, which I provided Chief Sanchez after conducting my PowerPoint talk.

Chief Sanchez was impressed by the potential linkage and advised me he would "brief his detectives and have them conduct a follow-up to ascertain if George Hodel was the

'Perfect Villain' named and if not, to see if his name appeared elsewhere in the original investigation."

After several months of not hearing back, I recontacted the chief. I was informed that "His detectives were unable to locate the reports, and he was unable to confirm or provide any information."

Despite my hopes that, at the very least, I would be able to confirm that George Hodel was a named suspect in the investigation—that did not happen.

Based on Chief Sanchez's response, I am unclear if all the reports (P.D. and DA) like those in the Black Dahlia investigation "have disappeared" or if the department is simply "exercising their right to remain silent."

Chief Phillip Sanchez retired from the Pasadena Police Department in 2018.

This concludes our examination of the Pasadena, California, "Sphinx Murder."

Sadly, this likely "jealousy-based execution" is just the beginning of what I believe was George Hodel's decade-long "reign of terror" in the 1930s.

Chapter 2

1935

Thelma Todd- The Monoxide Murder

A Prelude to Murder?

The northern California paper, *The Sacramento Bee*, on October 5th, 1935, carried the headline, "Former Actress Is Found Dead In Garage Of Home."

Former Actress Is Found Dead In Garage Of Home

SANTA MONICA, Oct. 5.—(P)— Clad in a thin white kimono and partially burned, the body of Mrs. Doris Schwuchow Dazey, formerly a widely known actress, was found yesterday by her husband, Dr. George Dazey, in the garage at their home.

Coroner's Surgeon F. R. Webb said after an examination death was caused by monoxide gas from the exhaust of an automobile.

Dr. Dazey told the police the doors and windows of the garage were closed and the motor of the car was running. His wife's body was lying at right angles to the machine when he found it. The upper portion was seared, apparently by the hot fumes from the exhaust.

The mother of an infant son, Mrs. Dazey had been in ill health for several months, and had been despondent over the fact. Nevertheless, Dr. Dasey believes she did not take her own life.

"I believe she was going to take the car out of the garage, started the motor, and then realised she hadn't opened the doors," he said. "She must have fainted as she went around to the back of the car."

Dr. Dazey is a prominent physician in Santa Monica and Beverly Hills and widely known in the film colony. His first wife was Mrs. Frances French Dazey of Honolulu. He married Doris Schwuchow at Boulder City, Nev., last November. Her father is Dr. Walter Schwuchow of Los Angeles.

Doris Schwuchow Dazey, daughter of Dr. Walter B. Schwuchow, starred as Ramona, the title role, at the Ramona Pageant at Hemet-San Jacinto before marrying Dr. George K. Dazey in November 1934.

...

"Clad in a thin white kimono and partially burned, the body of Mrs. Doris Schwuchow Dazey, formerly a widely known actress, was found yesterday by her husband, Dr. George Dazey, in the garage at their home."

...

"Coroner's Surgeon F.R. Webb said, after an examination, death was caused by monoxide gas from the exhaust of an automobile."

~

The *Los Angeles Times* coverage read:

WOMAN DIES OF AUTO GAS

Found Lifeless in Garage
Death of Doctor's Wife at Santa Monica
Declared Accidental

SANTA MONICA, October 4th. (Exclusive)

After completing their investigation[1], police here today expressed belief the death of Mrs. Doris Dazey by carbon monoxide poisoning was an accident.

Dr. George K. Dazey, her husband, who last night found the body on the floor of the garage of the home at 255 Twenty-Third Street, said she was subject to fainting and apparently collapsed while the motor of her car was running.

---

[1] Ed.: Original text (After complete investigating) & (garage at the home 255) changed for clarification.

LYING ON FLOOR

The attractive 31-year-old mother of a 4-months-old child was lying on the floor, her face about eighteen inches from the exhaust pipe of the machine with the garage doors closed. Investigating officers said she may have been about to open the doors when overcome.

An autopsy, determining the cause of death as carbon-monoxide poisoning, was performed at the Gates, Mendenhall & Gates mortuary.

Dr. Dazey told officers he found the body when he returned home from his office. He said his wife, whom he married a little less than a year ago, was subject to fainting. This was corroborated by Mrs. Dazey's father, Dr. Walter B. Schwuchow of Los Angeles.

THEORY TOLD

Investigating officers said they believed that Mrs. Dazey may have gone into the garage by a side door, gotten into the car and started the motor, and then discovered that she had neglected to open the door through which the car was to pass.

"It is possible," Capt. Greer said, "that she had a fainting spell while stepping from the car to open the door."

Relatives and friends refused to consider a suicide theory, declaring the couple was happy and that there could have been nothing to prompt such an action on Mrs. Dazey's part.

Funeral services for Mrs. Dazey were to be conducted at 11 a.m. Monday at the Gates, Mendenhall & Gates Mortuary, Santa Monica. Other arrangements at the time were incomplete.

The victim, Doris Dazey, had starred in the lead role as "Ramona" in author Helen Hunt Jackson's romance novel of the same name.

> "*Ramona* is an 1884 American novel written by Helen Hunt Jackson. Set in Southern California after the Mexican-American War. It portrays the life of a mixed-race Scottish-Native American orphan girl who suffers racial discrimination and hardship. Originally serialized in the Christian Union on a weekly basis, the novel became immensely popular. It has had more than 300 printings and has been adapted five times as a film. A play adaptation has been performed annually outdoors since 1923.
>
> Wikipedia

The outdoor performances referred to above are known throughout California and the nation as "The Ramona Pageant" and has been staged annually in Hemet, California, since its premiere on April 13th, 1923.

Doris Schwuchow Dazey performed the lead role as Ramona in the outdoor theatre in Riverside County for the first ten years (1923-1933) and then married Dr.

George Dazey in November 1934 and bore him a son, Walter, who was four months old at the time of her death.

The Ramona Pageant will celebrate its centennial season in 2023.

Undated postcard (possibly 1950s?) showing large attendance at the Ramona Pageant, where Doris Schwuchow performed as the lead in "Ramona" for a full decade from 1923-1933.

(Reverse of postcard reads):

RAMONA PAGEANT — "Ramona," California's greatest outdoor play, is staged each April and May, by the people of Hemet and San Jacinto, in the hills at famed Ramona Bowl. This Pageant has traveled far since 1300 strong-legged patrons climbed the virgin hills in 1923 and sat on rocks to see the first "Ramona." Now thousands trek annually from all parts of the world to experience this dramatic and soul-stirring epic of early California and relive the tragic story of Ramona and her Indian lover, Alessandro.

At the time of Doris's death, her husband, Dr. George Dazey, placed the young infant in the hands of the boy's maternal grandparents, Mrs. Schwuchow and her physician husband—thinking they could better care for the child's needs.

In a remarkable twist of fate, some four years later, a Los Angeles Grand Jury indicted Dr. George Dazey for his wife's 1935 murder.

The prosecution headed by District Attorney Buron Fitts presented a reasonably strong case that included a witness (night watchman) who testified to seeing Dr. Dazey carry his unconscious wife's body from the residence to the garage. Several other witnesses testified to hearing the doctor brag about "committing the perfect crime," and the victim's parents testified to their daughter's claim of abusive behavior from her husband and his flying into rages over the question of paternity of their son, Walter.

All the Los Angeles papers headlined the trial, and Dr. Dazey (below left) obtained famed criminal attorney Jerry "Get Me" Giesler (on right) as his defense attorney.

Attorney Giesler examines kimono that Doris Dazey was wearing at the time body was found in the garage.

Daily News February 18th, 1940

Photos above show Dr. Dazey and his son, 4-1/2-year old Walter. Article claims the murder "case hinges on paternity."

The Gaffney Ledger July 18th, 1940

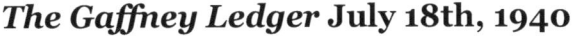

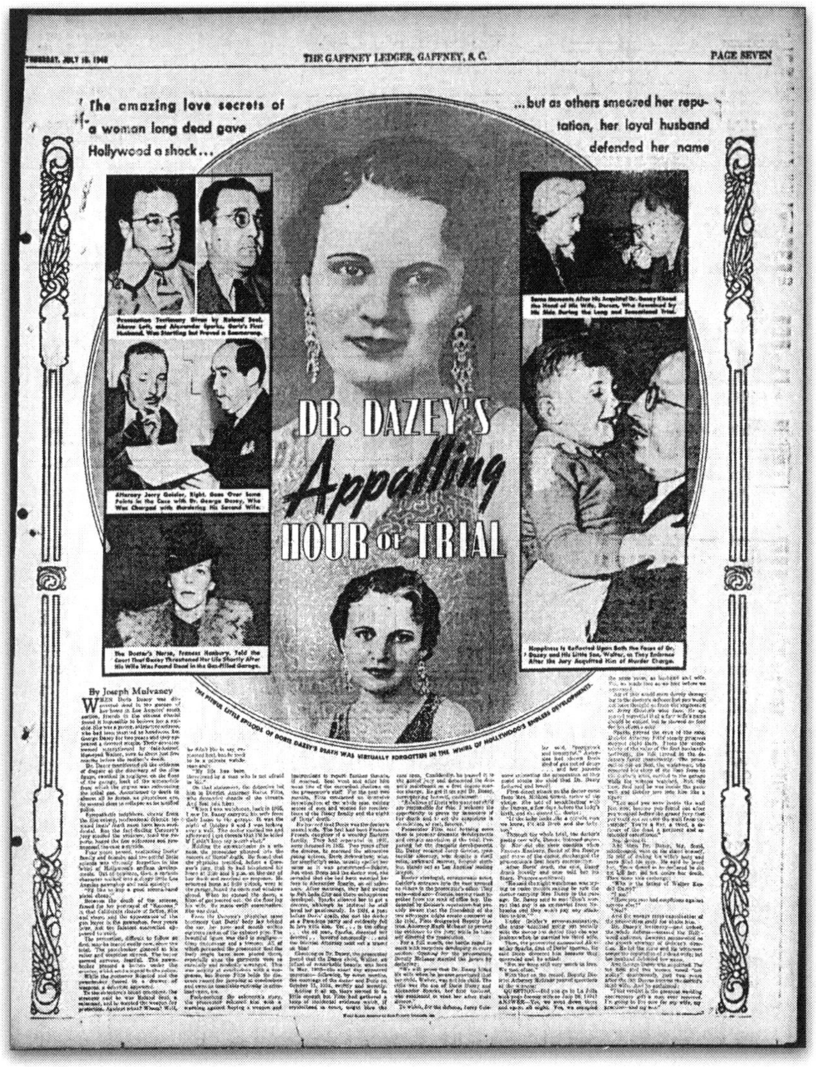

THURSDAY, JULY 18, 1940 THE GAFFNEY LEDGER, GAFFNEY, S. C. PAGE SEVEN

The amazing love secrets of a woman long dead gave Hollywood a shock...

...but as others smeared her reputation, her loyal husband defended her name

Prosecution Testimony Given by Roland Seal, Above Left, and Alexander Sparks, Doris's First Husband, Was Startling but Proved a Boomerang.

Attorney Jerry Geisler, Right, Goes Over Some Points in the Case with Dr. George Dazey, Who Was Charged with Murdering His Second Wife.

The Doctor's Nurse, Frances Hanbury, Told the Court That Dazey Threatened Her Life Shortly After His Wife Was Found Dead in the Gas-Filled Garage.

DR. DAZEY'S *Appalling* HOUR OF TRIAL

Some Moments After His Acquittal Dr. Dazey Kissed the Hand of His Wife, Dorothy, Who Remained by His Side During the Long and Sensational Trial.

Happiness Is Reflected Upon Both the Faces of Dr. Dazey and His Little Son, Walter, as They Embrace After the Jury Acquitted Him of Murder Charge.

THE PITIFUL LITTLE EPISODE OF DORIS DAZEY'S DEATH WAS VIRTUALLY FORGOTTEN IN THE WHIRL OF HOLLYWOOD'S ENDLESS DEVELOPMENTS.

By Joseph Mulvaney

Attorney Giesler, sometimes known as "The Magnificent Mouthpiece," once again worked his magic, claiming all the witnesses were lying and ultimately was able to convince the jury, which resulted in a "not guilty" verdict and freedom for Dr. Dazey.

SKH Note - Attorney Giesler, some eight years later, would represent and defend my father, Dr. George Hill Hodel, against charges of incest and child molestation with my then fourteen-year-old half-sister, Tamar Hodel.

Again, painting the witness/victim with a "pathological liar" brush, the jury after a three-week trial would acquit Dr. George Hill Hodel even though three adults were present during the sex acts and testified and confirmed Tamar's allegations. (We would later discover through secret DA files that a $15,000 payoff was likely involved in the acquittal.)

But I diverge from my original narrative.

None of the facts of the suspected murder by Dr. Dazey were known or voiced back in 1935. The witness accusations would not surface until 1939.

All that the public (including a young intern by the name of George Hodel, who was just six months away from receiving his MD) knew and read was that a beautiful young actress was found dead in her closed car garage.

The cause of her "accidental death" was the result of her becoming unconscious and breathing in toxic carbon monoxide.

For all intents and purposes, that was the end of her story.

Was Doris Dazey's death, in fact, an accident? Or was she murdered? We will likely never know.

But for now, let us reserve judgment and continue our narrative.

Death Investigation No. 2

Just ten weeks after the actress Doris Dazey's "accidental" death, Los Angeles newspapers reported a second carbon monoxide-related death.

On the morning of December 16th, 1935, at approximately 10:00 a.m., Ms. May Whitehead, as part of her routine duties as a maid, proceeded to her employer's two-car residence garage at 17531 Posetano Road, Pacific Palisades.

As was her custom, Ms. Whitehead routinely removed and drove her employer's 1934 Lincoln Phaeton convertible from the hillside garage down the hill (some 300 feet) and parked it in front of the owner's seaside restaurant on the Pacific Coast Highway (then named Roosevelt Hwy).

Ms. Whitehead opened the sliding garage door, and as she approached the automobile, much to her surprise, she observed her employer, slumped and asleep behind the driver's wheel.

She called out and gently touched, what she presumed was, the sleeping body of her employer to awaken her, then recoiled in horror.

She was not asleep; her mistress WAS DEAD. The first call went out to the Los Angeles Police Department's West Los Angeles Division, who responded to the "Death Investigation" call arriving at approximately 11 a.m. on the morning of December 16th.

The home known as "Castillo del Mar" was built in 1927 for Hollywood filmmaker Roland West.

Within an hour of the maid's discovery, the word was out on the street, and the local press responded *en masse*, and by evening the six-inch headlines proclaimed the tragedy:

THELMA TODD FOUND DEAD - Found Lifeless in Garage.

What usually would have been a single paragraph mention "Woman Found Dead in Car-Probable Accidental Death" on a back page of the local newspaper instantly became a national story.

Why?

Because the victim was none other than THELMA TODD.

Who Was Thelma Todd?

Thelma Todd was considered one, if not THE leading film actress/comediennes of her day.

Known as "The Ice Cream Blonde" and "Hot Toddy," millions of movie goers loved her.

Here is a brief biography:

Born in Lawrence, Massachusetts, on July 29th, 1906. (Ironically, she shared the same birthday as Elizabeth "Black Dahlia" Short, who was also born in Massachusetts, in Medford, just a short nineteen miles from Lawrence.)

College-educated, she was initially a schoolteacher and then entered several beauty contests and, in 1925 at the age of nineteen, won "Miss Massachusetts."

Talent scouts grabbed her, and she signed a contract with Paramount Pictures.

Her beauty and brains, along with a natural ability for romantic comedy, combined to make her a huge box office hit.

Thelma Todd

At the time of her death in 1935, at the young age of twenty-nine, Thelma Todd had already been credited with making 119 films, three of which would be released after her death in 1936.

To name just a few of her top film credits:

The Maltese Falcon (1931), *Monkey Business* (1931), *Horse Feathers* with the Marx Brothers (1932), *The Bohemian Girl* (1936, released after her death).

A year before her death the actress opened her restaurant, **Thelma Todd Sidewalk Café**, at 17575 Pacific Coast Highway, which quickly became a popular dining/drinking hangout for top celebrities as well as tourists and her film fans.

Thelma's private residence was located above the restaurant.

Farther up the hill was the large estate of her close friend and business partner, film director Roland West, and his former wife, Jewel Carmen.

Roland West's residence was adjacent to Thelma Todd's apartment.

Jewel Carmen, West's ex-wife, also a close friend of Thelma's, maintained a residence in the large home on the street above **Thelma Todd Sidewalk Café**.

(The home of the ex-Mrs. Roland West, Jewel Carmen, at 17531 Posetano Road, is where Thelma was allowed to garage her Lincoln Phaeton and where Thelma Todd's body was found.)

The Investigation

The first question asked by most readers was the same:

WAS ACTRESS THELMA TODD'S DEATH A SUICIDE, ACCIDENTAL, OR A MURDER?

Photo above showing the doors of the Roland West garage at Castellamare where, inside, maid May Whitehead found the body of Thelma Todd. *LAT* 12/17/35

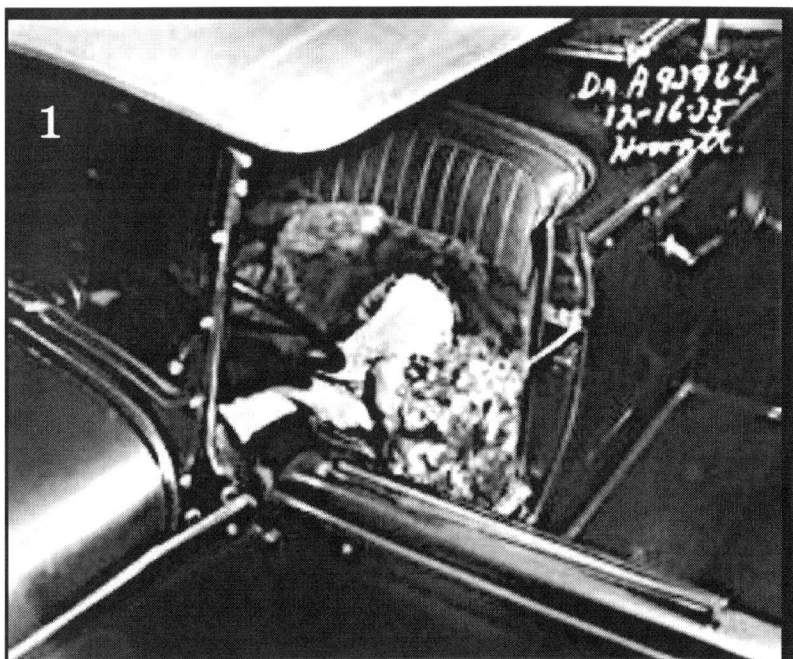

Photos: 1 & 2 show position of Thelma Todd's body as examined inside her Lincoln Phaeton (door open, top up) by LAPD Captain Bert Wallis. Photo 3 shows Wallis looking in at Todd's body with the vehicle's door closed.

SKH Note - Photos 1,2, & 3 may not represent the actual position of Thelma Todd's body when discovered.

Film Director Roland West, (below) owner of the estate and a close friend of Todd's seen grieving while seated on the running board of Todd's Lincoln Phaeton (top up) after the Coroner removed the body (above).

Thelma Todd's Sidewalk Café entrance from Roosevelt Highway (later renamed Pacific Coast Highway) bottom of photo.

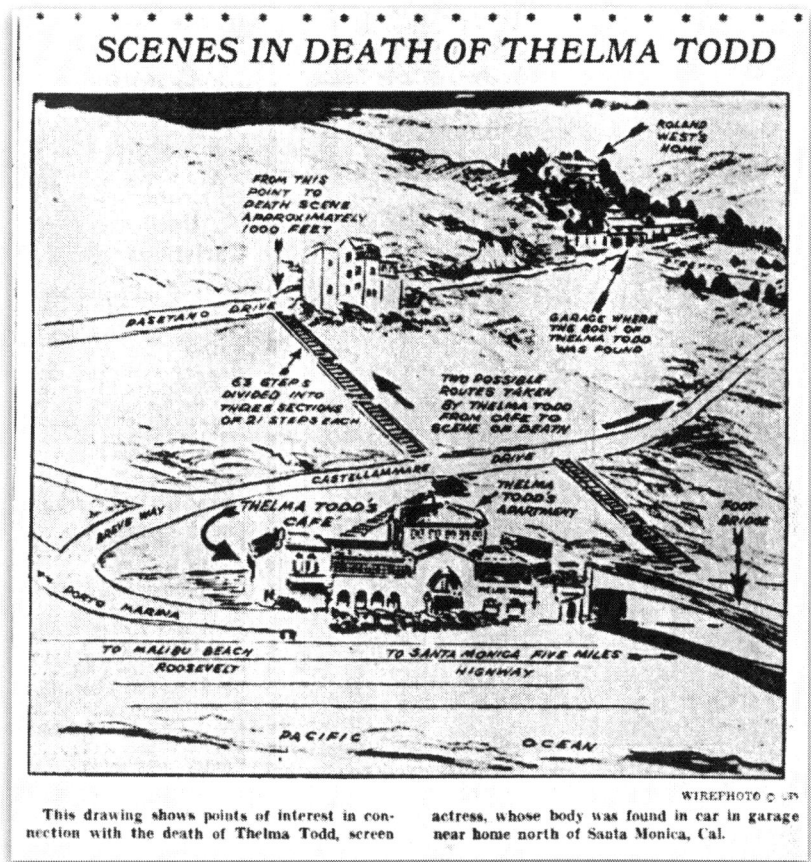

SCENES IN DEATH OF THELMA TODD

This drawing shows points of interest in connection with the death of Thelma Todd, screen actress, whose body was found in car in garage near home north of Santa Monica, Cal.

The preliminary on-scene investigation by LAPD detectives provided little information.

Trauma and a small amount of blood were observed on the victim's mouth and on the front seat. Additional blood droplets were found outside the vehicle on its running board.

The ignition switch to the automobile was in the "on" position indicating to detectives she had likely started the engine and fell asleep and was overcome by toxic fumes.

The engine stopped running and naturally drained the battery with the key in the on position.

Miss Todd was wearing a formal blue gown which was later determined to be the same as worn by her at a dinner party she attended on the previous Saturday evening, December 14th, where she had met and dined with friends at the famous "Trocadero" restaurant in Hollywood on the Sunset Strip.

Detectives ruled out "robbery" as a motive. The victim was still wearing her expensive jewelry valued at over $20,000, and her body was covered with her valuable mink coat, as seen in the previous photographs.

Pending further investigation and the interview of all pertinent witnesses, on-scene detectives initially voiced their suspicions that it was either a "suicide" or "accidental" death, probably caused by lethal fumes, which resulted in "monoxide poisoning."

No "suicide" note was found in or near the vehicle, and initially, no neighborhood eyewitnesses were found who could pinpoint the exact date and time of the victim's return and entrance to the garage.

On Day Two, December 17th, 1935, as was typical in most "high profile" death investigations, LAPD's Homicide Detail and Captain B.R. Steed and **Detective Thad Brown** [emphasis mine] were assigned to conduct the follow-up.

1934 photo of **LAPD Detective Thad Brown** (on right) arresting suspected abortionist Walter G. Brown (no relation)

THE AUTOPSY

A great deal of conflict and controversy surrounds the reportage of the conditions of the victim's body when examined initially at a Santa Monica mortuary and then some hours later at the Coroner's Office, in the basement of the DTLA Hall of Justice.

Without attempting to detail all of the trauma-related contradictions reported through the decades in books and magazine articles, I will here simply bullet point some of what I consider to be the most factual findings.

- A small amount of blood was found on her nose and mouth, and blood droplets were found inside on the front seat and outside on the car's running board.

- Crown of a tooth dislodged and found inside her mouth.

- Mortuary attendants at private mortuary claimed to observe trauma inside her throat as if someone had tried to force an object down her mouth. (This was denied by LA County Autopsy Surgeon Wagner, who performed the later autopsy and denied seeing any such injuries.)

- A blood alcohol reading of .13 (point-one-three).

- Partially undigested peas and beans were found in her stomach.

- Coroner initially listed the estimated time of death as occurring on Sunday morning, December 15th, 1935, at approximately six a.m. This time estimate was then later revised to Sunday afternoon December 15th, 1935, at about four p.m.

- The cause of death was Monoxide Poisoning due to a lethal dose. (75-80% blood saturation.)

Thelma Todd Reconstructed Timeline

As occurs in any high-profile death investigation, myth usually replaces truth. Fiction trumps fact as in the game of "Pass It On," where you start with a simple fact, whisper it in the players' ear, and they whisper it to the next player, and after six or seven whispered truths, what was fact becomes unrecognizable.

So, too, in the Thelma Todd death investigation.

There have been hundreds of newspaper and magazine articles written and dozens of books, numerous documentaries as well as several feature films made, each presenting their spin, their take on "whodunit."

As I did in the William Desmond Taylor review, I am here just going to stick to the facts as presented by eyewitnesses who testified under oath regarding their knowledge of the last few days and hours preceding her death. Percipient witnesses all.

The following timeline is a reconstruction based on witness statements presented at the Coroner's Inquest and Grand Jury investigation into the death of Thelma Todd. (All times are an approximation.)

Saturday, December 14th, 1935

8:00 p.m. Chauffeur Ernest Peters picked up Thelma at her beachside café along with her mother, Mrs. Alice Todd, and drove them to Hollywood. He left Thelma there and took her mother Christmas shopping, but was told to return to Hollywood later to drive Thelma home.

Thelma attended the dinner party with Stanley and Ida Lupino and guests at the **Trocadero Restaurant**, 8610 Sunset Blvd. As reported by guests, Thelma was in good spirits, had just a few drinks, and danced.

A vacant chair had been left next to Thelma's believed to be for her ex-husband, Pat DiCicco. However, while he was present at the restaurant with his date, the beautiful actress Margaret Lindsay, DiCicco, did not interact with any of the Lupino's dinner party members, including his ex-wife, Thelma Todd.

MIDNIGHT Thelma makes a telephone call to an unknown person from the Trocadero restaurant's ladies' restroom.

Sunday, December 15th, 1935

2:15 a.m. Robert John Anderson, bartender at Thelma Todd's Café, testified that he drove Miss Todd's 1932 Lincoln Phaeton from where it was parked in front of the café and parked it in the garage at 17531 Posetano Road as was his custom. He backed the car into the garage (difficult due to the confined space), parked it next to Roland West's vehicle, closed the door, and left the location.

3:00 a.m. Thelma calls for her chauffeur, Ernest Peters. He is waiting outside the Trocadero Restaurant when she leaves the dinner party. She instructs him to take her home to the beach house and mentions, "she has an appointment and is late, so please drive fast."

3:45 a.m. Thelma arrives at the front of her café on Roosevelt Highway (later renamed Pacific Coast Highway), and chauffeur Peters offers to walk her to her door. She declines, saying "I'm fine," and Peters leaves the location. (Peters in later Grand Jury testimony indicated "this was unusual and the first time that she didn't have me escort her to her door.")

9:00 a.m. Mr. W.F. Persson, owner of a cigar stand at Eighth and Figueroa Streets in DTLA says a woman he identified as Thelma Todd entered his store, appeared intoxicated and under the influence of alcohol or drugs. She asked Persson to dial a telephone number for her at the public pay phone. He complied and testified to the Grand Jury that he recalled the numbers he dialed for her as "7771," but he did not remember the prefix. Witness Persson testified that a second man in the store, Mr. Robert E. Fisher, also watched her leave the store and join a man holding a woman's fur coat. Mr. Fisher saw the couple go and sit on the steps of the First Methodist Church at 8th and Hope Streets.

4:00 p.m. Mrs. Martha Ford, the wife of actor Wallace Ford, received a call from her good friend Thelma Todd who informed her she would be a few minutes late to the cocktail party at Mrs. Ford's home on Laurel Canyon in Studio City. Thelma asked if it was all right to come in an evening gown, which she was still wearing—since at least 8 p.m. on Saturday December 14th—from the Trocadero Party, and also if she "could bring a friend." Mrs. Ford informed her yes on both counts, and Thelma said to expect her in about "a half-hour" and ended the conversation with, "You'll probably drop dead when you see who I am with".

4:10 p.m. Witness Sara A. Kane Carter testified to seeing Thelma Todd making a telephone call from a pay phone inside the drugstore at Laurel Canyon and Sunset Boulevard. She indicated she thought it strange that Miss Todd was wearing an evening dress and added she did not overhear any conversation. Mrs. Carter gave her home address as 8481 Utica Drive, in Laurel Canyon.

(Bizarrely, this address was the home immediately next to a large estate that my then wife, Kiyo, and I would purchase in 1963. Our house in Laurel Canyon, at 8451 Utica Drive, was built in the 1920s by the famed film director, Tay Garnett, whose screen credits include: *Mrs. Parkington, Wild Harvest, The Valley of Decision, The Postman Always Rings Twice, A Connecticut Yankee in*

King Arthur's Court and many more. We paid the outlandish price of $34,000 for the home back then, and I see it is listed on Zillow today appraised at $2.4 million.)

11:00 p.m. Witness Jewel Carmen was a close friend of Thelma Todd's and the wife of Roland West (they were separated but living in separate quarters on the estate). Jewel, who owned the estate at 17531 Posetano Road, Pacific Palisades, observed Thelma in her Phaeton convertible passenger seat in Hollywood. Miss Carmen testified that the driver appeared to be "a sleek, handsome man of foreign appearance as he was dark complected." Miss Carmen followed the couple south on Vine Street to Santa Monica Boulevard, where they turned and drove out of sight.

Monday, December 16th, 1935

3:00 a.m. Mr. J.E. Cummings, an employee at a Christmas tree lot located at Euclid and Wilshire Avenue in Santa Monica, testified and identified Miss Todd as a woman who came to his lot accompanied by a young man at approximately 3:00 a.m. on Monday, December 16th. She purchased a tree and requested he have it flocked, and she would pick it up later.

On December 23rd, five days after Cummings testified before the Grand Jury, two men came to his lot, and one of the men approached him and said, "Is your name Cummings?" He responded, "Yes." The man then threatened him, saying, "Well, you've got a good memory on the Todd case, but don't stretch it too far. There's been too much talking about it, and if I were you, I wouldn't have much more to do with it."

Later that same evening, two men approached the lot and accosted a friend of Cummings, a Mr. Arthur San Juan. One of the men confronted Arthur and asked, "Are you, Cummings?" Arthur denied he was, and the man yelled, "You're a damn liar" and punched him in the face. The man then said, "Forget all you know about the Todd case." The two men sped away from the Christmas tree lot in a car with covered license plates.

Monday, December 16, 1935

10:15 a.m. Miss Mae Whitehead, a longtime maid of Thelma Todd, went to the garage, as part of her regular duties, at 17531 Posetano Road to remove and drive Miss Todd's Lincoln Phaeton down to the front of the café. Upon opening the closed garage door, she finds the driver's door open with Miss Todd inside the car. Initially thinking Miss Todd was sleeping she attempted to wake her, but discovered Miss Todd was dead. Miss Whitehead immediately returned to the café and reported her discovery to R.H.W. Schafer, brother-in-law of Roland West and the manager of Thelma Todd's Sidewalk Café. Schafer accompanies Mae Whitehead back to the garage and verifies that Miss Todd is dead.

A Monoxide Murder?

LAPD police chemist Ray Pinker was called to the scene and recovered numerous blood samples that included samples from the car seat and the door and exterior running board of the Lincoln Phaeton. His analysis indicated these samples "contained positive traces of monoxide."

I queried my old friend, forensic scientist Dr. Doug Lyle. We exchanged several emails relating specifically to the Thelma Todd investigation.

However, first, let me present some extracted quotes from an article he wrote in the *3rd Degree*, a monthly magazine for members of Mystery Writers of America.

I quote from his essay of May 2009 entitled D.P. Lyle, MD Forensicfiles *"Can Carbon Monoxide Cartridges be Used as a Method of Murder?*

...

Carbon Monoxide (CO) is stealthy, treacherous, and deadly. It's also common. You've seen it in the papers or on the news. A family is found dead, and the cause is a faulty heater or fireplace. A suicide victim is found in his garage with the car engine running. Campers are found dead in a tent, a kerosene lantern burning in one corner. Each of these is due to carbon monoxide.

...

Carbon Monoxide's treachery lies in its great affinity for hemoglobin, the oxygen (O_2) carrying molecule within our red blood cells (RBCs). When inhaled, CO binds to hemoglobin, producing carboxyhemoglobin. It does so 300 times more readily than does oxygen and thus displaces oxygen.

...

The normal level is 1 to 3%, but may be as high as 7 to 10% in smokers. At levels of 10 to 20%, headache and a poor ability to concentrate on complex tasks occur. Between 30 and 40%, headaches become severe and throbbing and nausea, vomiting, faintness, and lethargy appear. Pulse and breathing rates will increase noticeably.

Between 40 and 60%, the victim will become confused, disoriented, weak, and will display extremely poor coordination. Above 60%, coma and death are likely.

Visit D.P. Lyle, MD at www.dplylemd.com, or read his book *Howdunnit Forensics: A Guide For Writers from Writers Digest.*

Here are excerpts from my Email exchange with Dr. Doug Lyle, where I presented him with individual facts without actually naming the specific crime.

Email to Dr. Lyle, October 14th, 2020

Hi Doug:

Can you tell me how long it might take a person to be overcome and die from monoxide poisoning in a situation where they are in a closed garage inside a vehicle windows down?

The scenario would go something like this:

Suspect drugs victim either using chloroform or injection of an unknown drug. Carries body and places it inside the vehicle in the garage and starts the engine of a large car: two-car garage but a small enclosed space with a second car parked next to the larger one.

The suspect places the unconscious victim in the car, starts the engine, and exits after closing the garage door.

Estimate how long it would take to kill the victim?

Any idea how long the engine might run before shutting down?

(I'm guessing the eventual lack of oxygen in the enclosed space would also affect the engine's ability to keep running?)

Thoughts?

p.s.

The victim was a small female. Blood alcohol around .13

If she were chloroformed just before placing in the car, would that keep her unconscious long enough for the CO to keep her unconscious and kill her? I've read where cops at scenes have said five to ten minutes would be long enough, but? The garage is maybe 12' deep by 24' wide with no ventilation.

Thanks, and stay safe.

Steve Hodel

Dr. Lyle's reply came the same day. Here is his response:

The danger of CO is that hemoglobin in the red cells will attach to it 300 times more readily than it will oxygen—O2. The net effect is that the amount of O2 available to the body's cells declines rapidly as it is replaced by CO. Folks have even died from loitering near the rear deck of a ski boat while the engine was idling and while sleeping too close to a smoldering campfire. An enclosed space is not always required— though most deaths do occur in closed spaces.

The variables in your scenario are many—the size of the garage, the ventilation inside the garage, the amount of CO produced by that particular car, the size, weight, and overall health of the victim, the meds or drugs the victim takes, and other variables. So there is no way to calculate the exact time. But, anywhere from 10 minutes to an hour should do it.

The addition of alcohol or any narcotics or sedatives, as you mentioned, would shorten the time considerably.

With two sedatives onboard, 10 minutes could easily do it. And yes, the combo of alcohol and chloroform could easily render her unconscious or at least so sedated she couldn't respond to or notice what was happening.

Doug

After discovering a newspaper article where the LAPD police chemist, Ray Pinker, stated publicly that "they found **traces** of carbon monoxide (emphasis mine) in the blood samples from the car seat and the exterior running board" I queried Dr. Lyle again.

October 25th, 2020

Doug:

One more query:

If the analyzing criminalist (this was a 1930s case) made a public statement that the blood found on the seat and running board of the car in the garage "contained positive traces of carbon monoxide," as I understand it from what you have said, that would be consistent with either scenario, but possibly more indicative of a bleed-out before the poisoning? I read his "traces" as a small amount rather than a lethal dosage. They did measure her blood level as 80% monoxide in the autopsy.

Doug's response:

He could say that and then clarify it by adding that it was near the normal range found in almost everyone, particularly those who smoke.

Doug

SKH Note - Thelma Todd did smoke cigarettes, so she would have shown "a trace" of carbon monoxide, which could well have been "the trace" that registered in her postmortem blood test.

The Missing Evidence

Twenty years ago, when I first looked at the Thelma Todd crime scene photographs, several items jumped out at me related to physical evidence.

Those were a man's handkerchief and a note left in plain sight for all to see but were never mentioned?

Through the years and most recently, in the past year, when I began to focus my research on the case, I could find no reference to either of these two items.

Why not?

It is as basic a crime scene investigation as you can get. Even back in 1935, every patrol cop and first responder to a crime scene knew that you DON'T TOUCH ANYTHING.

Nothing is to be removed, and nothing added to a crime scene until overall photographs have been obtained.

We can be almost positive that both the man's handkerchief and the full page note were there on the seat at the time of the detectives' arrival and, consequently, were photographed as they lay.

Why no mention in any police statements or in any testimony at either the Coroner's Inquest or the follow-up Grand Jury Investigation?

I could not find any mention of either item in the hundreds of articles and documents I had reviewed.

My first thought and absent any contradictions to it was that George Hodel had left the man's handkerchief at the scene after chloroforming Thelma Todd just as he had done in a half dozen of his other serial crimes.

Also, he likely left "the note" as some kind of taunt or "catch me if you can" type message as he had done on so many of his other murders.

Finally literally, four days ago, I found one possible answer.

On a back page of one of the newspaper's reportage, it said that "LAPD chemist Ray Pinker was processing a man's handkerchief found at the scene that had been left there by a witness.

It turns out that the handkerchief most likely belonged to R.H.W. Schafer, brother-in-law of Roland West, and manager of the café. Schafer had accompanied Mae Whitehead, Thelma's maid, back to the garage and claimed he used his handkerchief to dab blood off Miss Todd's mouth and left his handkerchief on the seat.

While rumors exist about a supposed "missing note" and a "police coverup," I have found no documentation or reportage anywhere that mentions "the note."

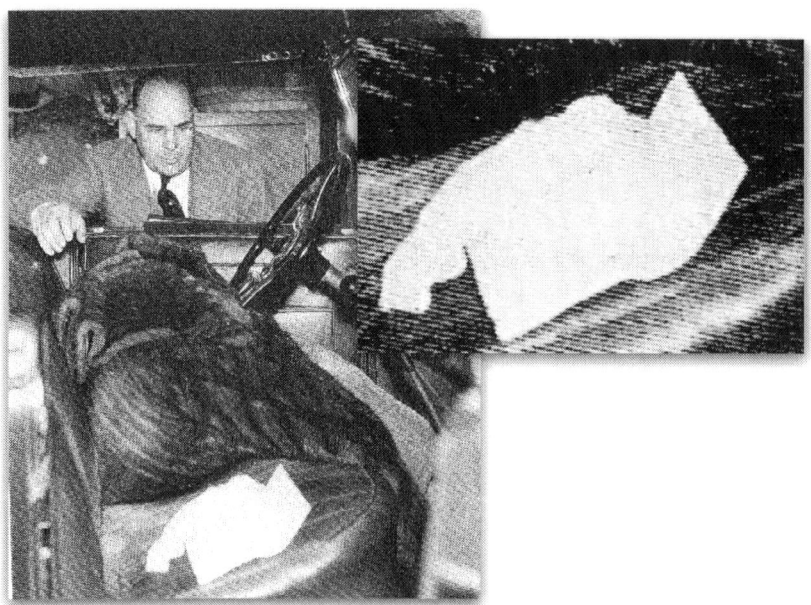

In the photo above, LAPD Captain Bert Wallis (left) is seen in the background looking inside the vehicle with the men's handkerchief and note in plain sight in the foreground. (The handkerchief and note shown enlarged, inset on right).

ACCIDENTAL DEATH or MURDER?

That question still remains unanswered some eighty-five years later.

My opinion based on witness statements and in reading the 125-page transcript of the Coroner's Inquest and the findings from the Grand Jury investigation combined with the minimal amount of forensic information available is that Thelma Todd was more than likely MURDERED.

But, by whom and why?

Dr. George Hill Hodel – The Linkage

1. Physical Description

A physical description was based on the separate witness statements and the obvious suspect was the man seen with her at multiple locations in DTLA, Hollywood, and Santa Monica just seven hours before her body was found.

The combined descriptions of this man were consistent, and the separate witnesses described him as, "A dark-complexioned dark-haired young male, foreign-looking with a sleek appearance and well dressed."

George Hodel, on December 16th, 1935, fit that description. He had just turned twenty-eight years of age on October 10th, 1935. He had black hair, was dark-complected, and was always a dapper dresser.

Dr. George Hill Hodel circa 1936

2. "The Mystery Man"

"The Mystery Man" and Thelma Todd's current love interest was never identified other than being "a businessman from San Francisco."

George Hodel lived in San Francisco for the previous eight years and was currently working as an intern at San Francisco General Hospital. He was just months away from receiving his MD degree from the University of California San Francisco, graduating in June 1936.

3. "The Death Car"

Witness Carmen Jewel testified to seeing her good friend Thelma riding as a passenger in her Lincoln Phaeton convertible in Hollywood with the "handsome dark-complected man driving" at 11 p.m. on Sunday night. She followed them for six blocks, but then they turned and drove off.

Actress Jewel Carmen photo by noted Hollywood photographer, WITZEL. See various references in *The GHH-Murders, The Early Years, Part 1.*

I submit that while I believe she did see them together, it was not in Thelma's car, but it was in George Hodel's vehicle.

How? Why?

After my father's return from Asia and relocation to San Francisco in 1990, I became quite close to him and his wife, June.

I would regularly "come down" from my home in Bellingham, Washington, and spend a weekend with them.

They both loved to "get out" and take day trips.

On one particular weekend sometime in the summer of 1996 or 1997, Dad wanted to visit the Blackhawk Museum in Danville, California. It was an easy thirty-mile drive from their penthouse apartment in DTSF, so acting as chauffeur, off we went in my 1991 Audi 200 Quatro.

The museum had opened some eight years prior and displayed beautifully restored "classic cars," both foreign and domestic, from the bygone years.

During the tour, we came across a 1930 black Packard Phaeton convertible, and Dad smiled broadly and said:

"This is the exact make and model car I owned and drove back in my early doctoring days. It has 12 cylinders, and my friend, Chief Tom Dodge, and I would race up and down the highways in it. A wonderful car."

I was impressed. It was, in fact, a beautiful machine.

Just a little piece of Dad's personal "history" that came and went. Until now.

Twenty-five years later, I believe this can now be considered a "thoughtprint."

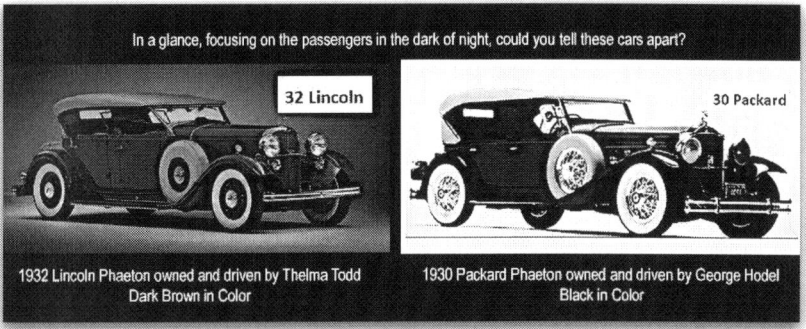

In a glance, focusing on the passengers in the dark of night, could you tell these cars apart?

32 Lincoln

30 Packard

1932 Lincoln Phaeton owned and driven by Thelma Todd
Dark Brown in Color

1930 Packard Phaeton owned and driven by George Hodel
Black in Color

In a glance, focusing on the passengers in the dark of night, could you tell these cars apart? *Unknown if top up or down.*

I do not believe Thelma Todd's car ever left the garage after being moved from the restaurant parking area on Roosevelt Highway and backed into position inside the garage as testified to by her café bartender Robert Anderson who moved the car at 2:15 a.m. on Sunday, December 15th.

Numerous articles mentioned that Thelma Todd always chose not to back her car into the garage but parked it down below in front of the café.

This was her choice when sober, and certainly, she would not have been able to do it in the dark of night with a blood alcohol of .13, which indicated she was intoxicated.

I believe that witness Jewel Carmen did see and recognize her good friend Thelma seated as a passenger next to the handsome young man driving. It is very likely that she simply mistook the dark-colored Phaeton as being Thelma's. It was dark on Hollywood's streets, and a black Packard Phaeton could easily be mistaken for Thelma's dark brown Lincoln Phaeton, as the above photographs demonstrate.

MO and Crime Signature

Notes and Threats

In the months before Thelma Todd's death, she had received, by mail, numerous threats to kidnap and or kill her.

I believe there were a total of five threatening letters, several postmarked from San Francisco. Not all were published in the newspapers.

A possible suspect was arrested in New York on some of the earlier notes; however, several more were received in the week before her death. Those threats were handed over to her personal friend and attorney, **Kent Kane Parrot.** [Emphasis mine]

Some of my readers may readily recognize this name as referenced in my first book, *Black Dahlia Avenger: A Genius for Murder.*

Here is an excerpt from that 2003 publication from Chapter 26, *"George Hodel: Underworld Roots-"The Hinkies"* (Updated in Skyhorse/Arcade 2015 ed.) Keep in mind that I wrote this early on in my investigation some twenty-years ago.

...

Among these personal effects to be destroyed were his [George Hodel's] early photographs, which June had showed me on a visit to San Francisco some months after Father's death. The photographs, which had been taken in the mid-1920s, had been shown in a Pasadena art gallery as part of Dad's one-man show.

...

There was also a group of savvy, street-smart faces from the 1920s. Who were these men? Friends? Were they people he knew when he was driving a cab in LA? His wife didn't know. Perhaps they were nobodies, forgotten people from a distant past. June kept the originals but allowed me to make copies for myself.

Among these photographs were six men I was curious about and wanted to identify. Cops have a term for men with faces like these; we call them *hinkies*. "Hinky" is a combination of "suspicious," "evasive," "dirty," or just plain up to no good. And these faces were hinky; they had too much experience with what cops normally see—the dark side of life. They had eyes that said, this guy has seen and known hard anger and brutality. These were criminal eyes, gangster eyes, part shifty, part confrontational, mostly desensitized—thoroughly tough. I wanted to know who they were and why they were part of his past.

To date, I have not been able to obtain positive identification on all of these men, but in exhibit 60, I do have tentative identification for three of them.

Based on the fact that three of the six photograph subjects (see page 86) were connected with LA's underworld, there is a strong probability the remaining three have gangster connections as well.

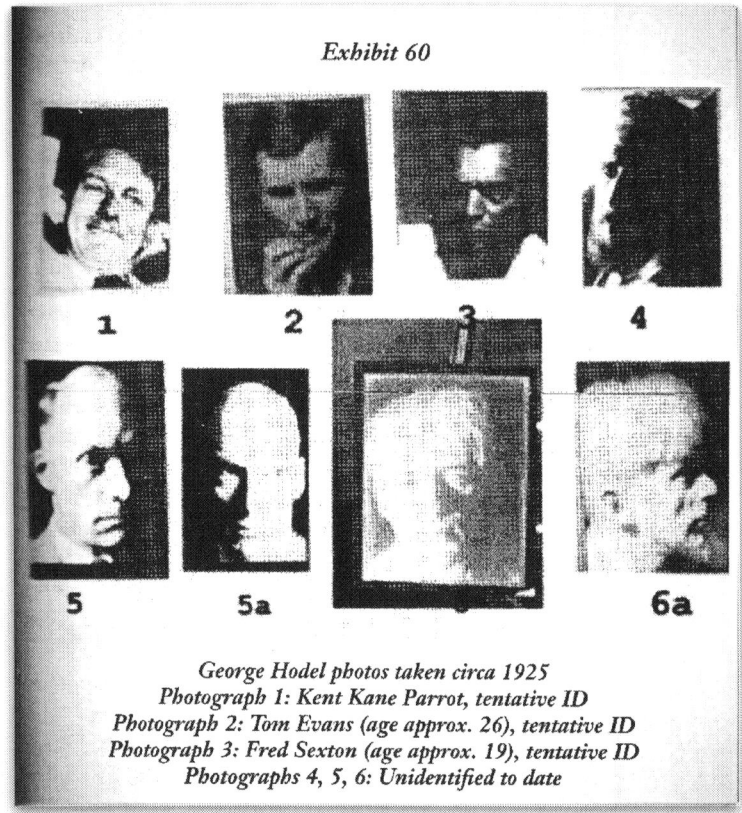

Exhibit 60

George Hodel photos taken circa 1925
Photograph 1: Kent Kane Parrot, tentative ID
Photograph 2: Tom Evans (age approx. 26), tentative ID
Photograph 3: Fred Sexton (age approx. 19), tentative ID
Photographs 4, 5, 6: Unidentified to date

I believe that George Hodel and Fred Sexton were either full-fledged henchmen of an early crime gang or remained close friends and associates for the next twenty-five years. To me, these photographs are more dark shadows from George Hodel's past, which might well connect him to notorious gangsters and killers of the time.

Photo 2 is especially compelling: it's of Tom Evans at age twenty-six, the convicted rum-running, drug-smuggling conman we have earlier identified as Tony Cornero's bodyguard, the same man who in his words, was "rousted" by LAPD in 1949 under suspicion of the kidnappings and murders of both Mimi Boomhower and Jean Spangler. These photographs show that Evans was linked to George Hodel as far back as 1925. What was my father, who prided himself on his intelligence, erudition, and culture, doing hanging around with a thug like Tom Evans? Perhaps the answer lies in photograph 1, which I suspect is a much younger picture of early LA's least familiar but most powerful syndicate boss, the notorious Kent Kane Parrot.

Kent Kane Parrot arrived in Los Angeles to attend law school at the University of Southern California in 1907, the same year Father was born. He was a big man, six foot two, and possessed a magnetic personality. He obtained his law degree and was admitted to the state bar.

Parrot was a deal-maker with phenomenal "people skills," whose real talent lay in his ability to bring together people of diametrically opposed beliefs and lifestyles (such as conservatives and liberals, prohibitionists and rum-runners), to establish some common cause that would allow them to unite. He didn't do this out of the goodness of his heart. A consummate broker, he pocketed handsome commissions either in hard cash or by somehow making his clients beholden to him in exchange for future payment in the coin of power or influence. Through his ability to forge relationships, Parrot got himself into politics, which he once defined very simply as "people in motion." And that's exactly how he played the game.

By 1924, Kent Parrot had become the power behind the throne in Los Angeles municipal politics. In the 1921 race for mayor, he successfully selected and got elected George Cryer, who became known as "Parrot's Puppet," at which point Parrot quickly aligned himself with Los Angeles's vice lords, including the young bootlegging czar Tony Cornero. Parrot, while publicly discreet in his dealings with the underworld, would entertain its members and broker relationships among them at his private apartment at the city's newest and finest downtown hotel, the Biltmore, about which he once boasted, "Everyone in the state of California has possibly been there in the official line."

As Parrot's influence and power grew, he placed more and more importance in the Los Angeles Police Department. Wielding payoffs, bagmen, and vice-supervisors, Parrot wound up with most of LAPD in his pocket and, though out of the public eye, became the most powerful man in Los Angeles politics from the 1920s through the 1940s. Citizen Kent Kane Parrot's word was law because he owned the law.

In researching Parrot's early days in Los Angeles, hoping to find an early photograph to compare to the one my father had taken, I contacted his old alma mater. They didn't have one, but they were able to provide me with his classmates' prophetic reference to him in his 1909 law school yearbook, *Stare Decisis*:

Not all the pumice of our college town can smooth the roughness of this New York clown.

SKH NOTE - As a personal note, I have only seen my father stumble, falter, and find himself at a loss for words on two occasions.

The first was in 1965, when he met my wife, his ex-mistress, Kiyo, in the lobby of the Biltmore. The second occurred some three years before his death, during a weekend visit in San Francisco, at Sunday brunch.

Knowing Father always had a reason for choosing specific names, and knowing that my older brother Michael Paul's namesake was chosen from Mother's close friendship with renowned bacteriologist and "microbe hunter" Paul De Kruif, and my younger brother, Kelvin George, was named after Father, I asked him what was the source of my own middle name, Kent. Who had I been named after?

It seemed as if he was caught off guard as he hemmed and hawed nervously and finally came out with a most implausible, "Oh, no reason. It's just a nice-sounding name, that's all."

Though surprised, I took his statement at face value. Armed with today's biographical knowledge, the photograph, their twenty-year friendship, and Father's admiration for the man and his influence and power, I submit that Father chose to honor his old friend, Kent Parrot, by making me his namesake.

With this much fuller backgrounding on Kent Kane, let us return to 1935 and the Thelma Todd investigation.

Kent Kane Parrot was a personal friend of Thelma Todd's, and in the weeks before her death, she went to him with several death threat notes she had received in the mail.

At least one of the extortion notes was mailed and postmarked from San Francisco and signed, "**a Friend**."

George Hodel, both as the "Black Dahlia Avenger" in 1947 and later as "Zodiac" in 1969, sent taunting notes to the press signed, "**a friend**."

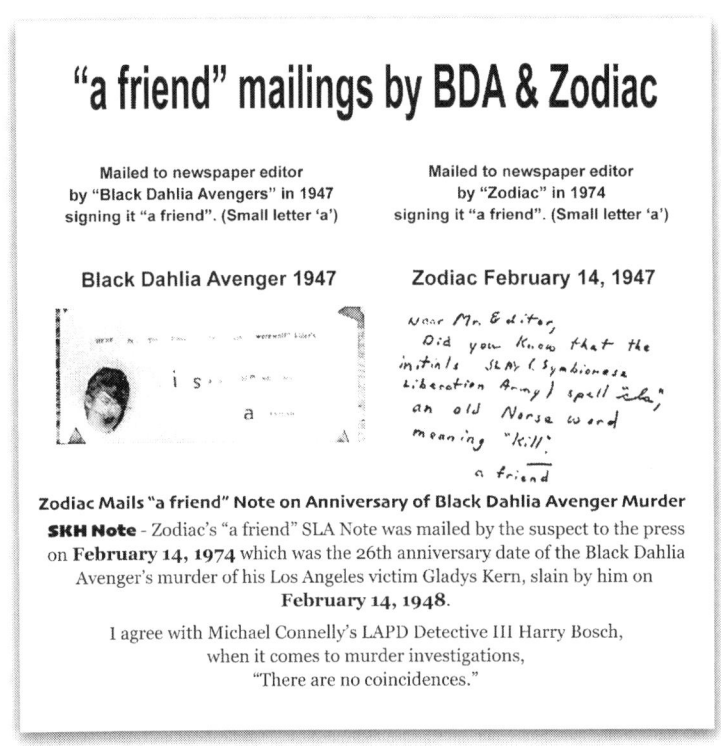

"a friend" mailings by BDA & Zodiac

| Mailed to newspaper editor by "Black Dahlia Avengers" in 1947 signing it "a friend". (Small letter 'a') | Mailed to newspaper editor by "Zodiac" in 1974 signing it "a friend". (Small letter 'a') |

Black Dahlia Avenger 1947   **Zodiac February 14, 1947**

Zodiac Mails "a friend" Note on Anniversary of Black Dahlia Avenger Murder

SKH Note - Zodiac's "a friend" SLA Note was mailed by the suspect to the press on **February 14, 1974** which was the 26th anniversary date of the Black Dahlia Avenger's murder of his Los Angeles victim Gladys Kern, slain by him on **February 14, 1948**.

I agree with Michael Connelly's LAPD Detective III Harry Bosch, when it comes to murder investigations, "There are no coincidences."

Dr. George Hill Hodel "a friend" notes sent to press

In December 1935, Kent Parrot was called and testified before the Grand Jury regarding his connection to Thelma Todd but could not provide any hard information other than that Miss Todd had come to him, expressing her concern over the written threats.

Parrot attended her funeral and then married his third wife in January 1936 and was off on his honeymoon.

George Hodel photo of Parrot taken in 1925

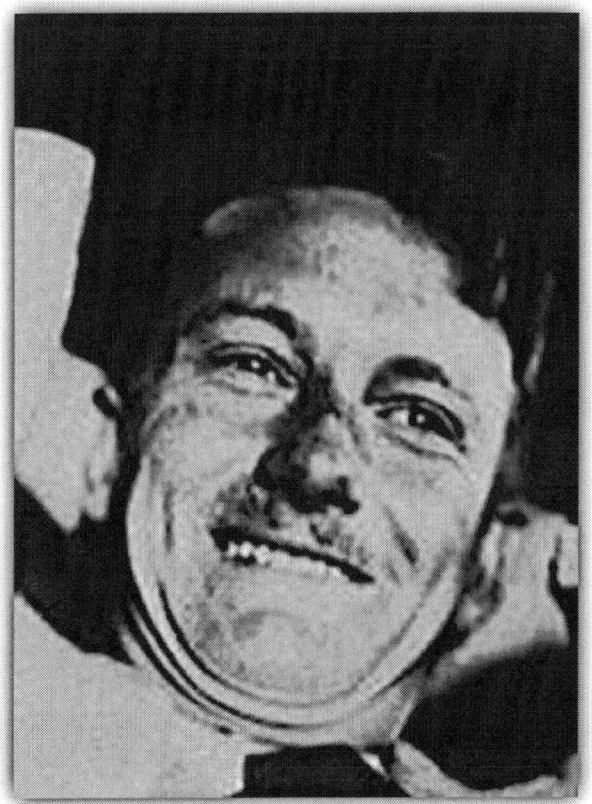

Untitled

(SKH Note-A possible early photo of LA Politico and Crime Boss Kent Kane Parrot. See details in *Black Dahlia Avenger* (Arcade 2003), *Chapter 26, George Hodel: Underworld Roots, The "Hinkies"*)

Kent Parrott

Newspaper photo 1936

Kent Parrot Marries; Leaves on Honeymoon

Already married, Kent Parrot, Los Angeles political figure, and his bride, the former Mrs. Lucille Rosa 'n Santa Barbara over the week end and embarked on the Santa few hours later.

Mrs. Lucille Parrot   Kent Parrott

Los Angeles Times January 28th, 1936

Witness Alex Hounie

Alex Hounie was the head waiter at the Trocadero Restaurant (see page 67) on Saturday night, December 14th, 1935. Mr. Hounie supervised service at the Lupinos' dinner party.

Mr. Hounie felt terrorized from two separate threats that he received shortly after he testified at the inquest.

The first threat was a postcard mailed to him at the restaurant, and the second occurred later the same day, Thursday, December 19th, 1935, as he was driving home when two men forced his car to the side of the road and in a menacing voice said, "You got your warning."

He was again threatened with being kidnapped "if he talks about the Todd case."

Alex Hounie was placed under police guard, and his response was printed in the dailies:

"I don't know who would want to play a cruel joke like that on me, and the men who threatened me Thursday night were total strangers."

Below is the front and back of the pasted threat on a postcard mailed to Alex Hounie at the Trocadero restaurant and printed in *The Times*.

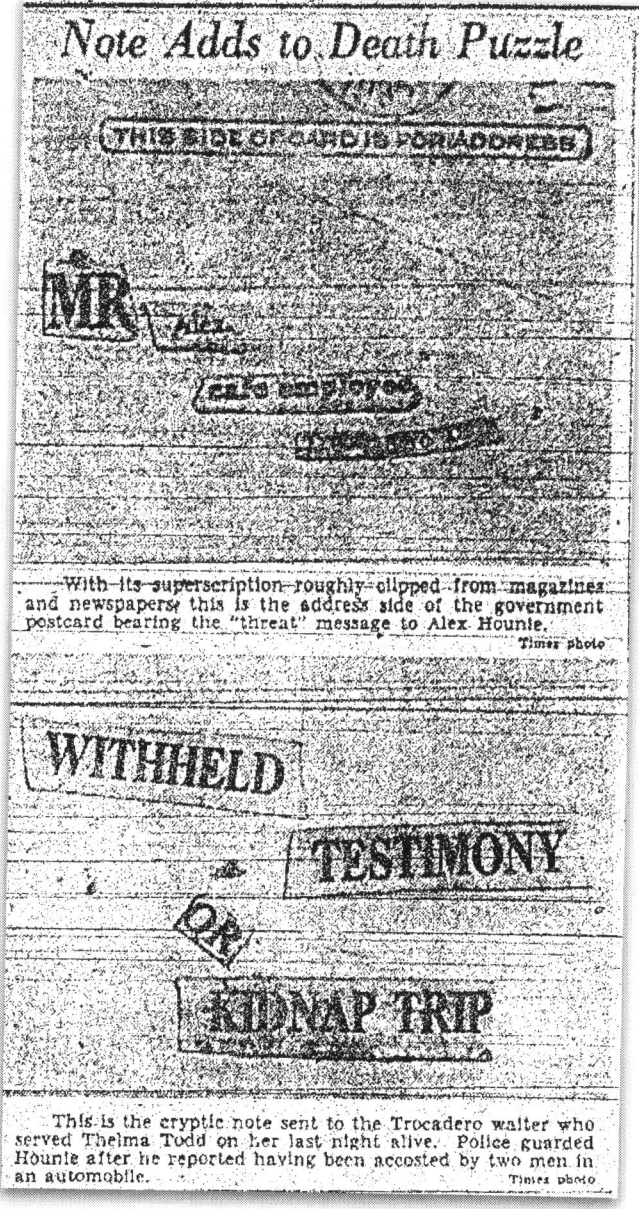

With its superscription roughly clipped from magazines and newspapers, this is the address side of the government postcard bearing the "threat" message to Alex Hounie.

Times photo

This is the cryptic note sent to the Trocadero waiter who served Thelma Todd on her last night alive. Police guarded Hounie after he reported having been accosted by two men in an automobile.

Times photo

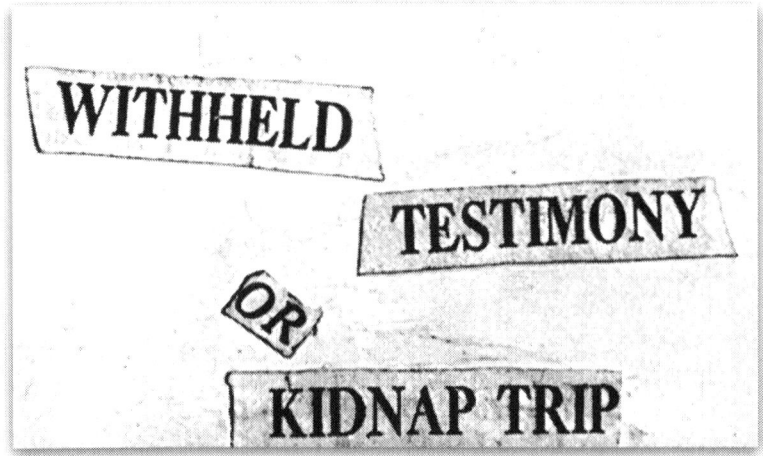

Alex Hounie kidnap threat 1935

Cut and pasted note mailed by George Hodel to press in 1947 as "Black Dahlia Avenger," asking for a deal if he surrenders.

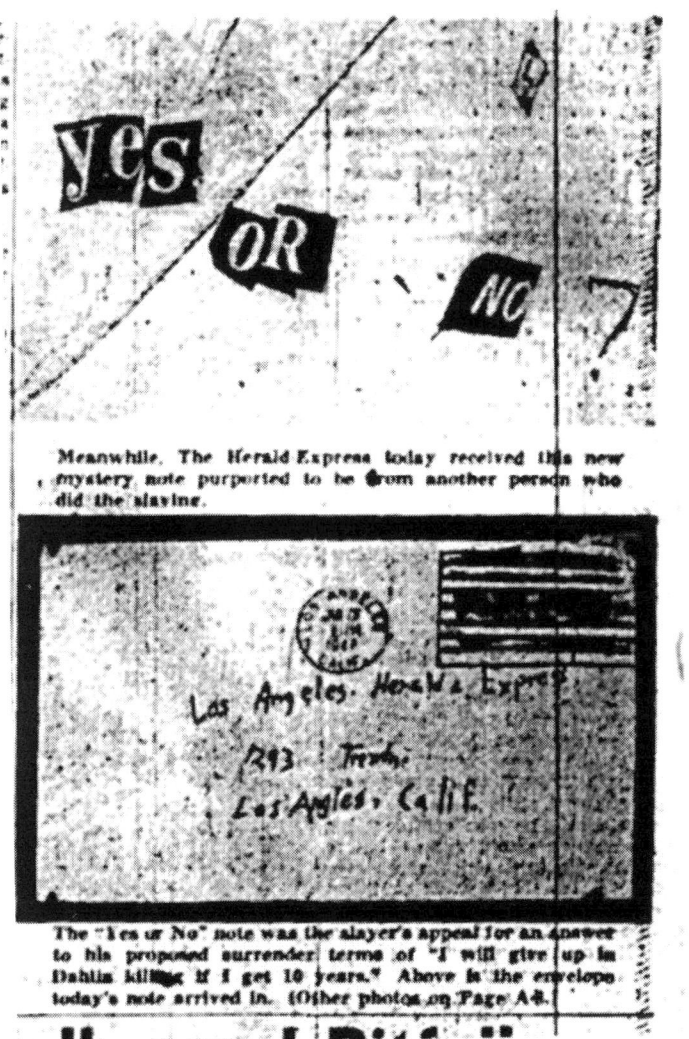

Caption reads:
"The "Yes or No" note was the slayer's appeal for an answer to his proposed surrender terms of "I will give up in Dahlia killing if I get 10 years." Above is the envelope today's note arrived in.

Below are two additional notes sent to the press by George Hodel as the "Black Dahlia Avenger" in 1947 shortly after Elizabeth Short's body was found posed naked on a vacant lot and surgically bisected in the Leimert Park district, some four miles south of Hollywood.

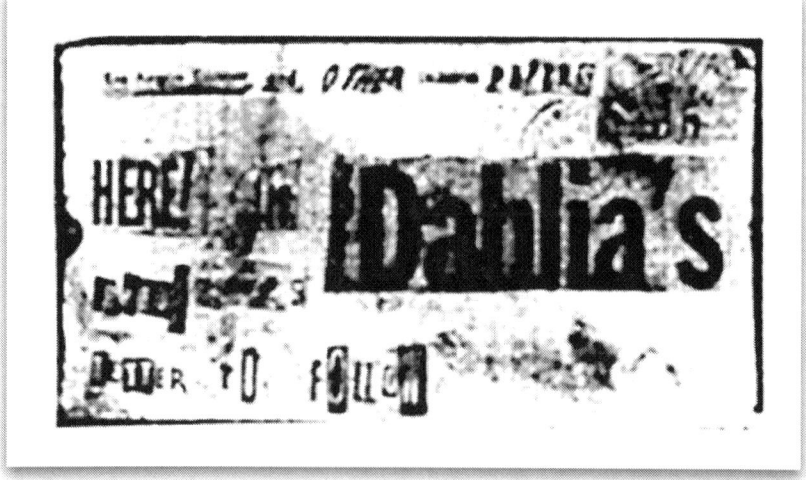

"BORDERTOWN" – The Movie

Bordertown, the movie,was released for viewing in the US on January 23rd, 1935, less than a year before the death of Thelma Todd.

It starred Bette Davis, Paul Muni, Margaret Lindsay, and Eugene Pallette. The promo advertisement below reads:

Son of a Mexican labourer, Johnny Ramirez studies for the law and becomes an attorney. But is disbarred over his very first case, and full of bitterness, drifts south to Bordertown, where he makes money out of a desert "Monte Carlo"—but is falsely accused of murder. An intensely dramatic story of thwarted ambition, starring Paul Muni.

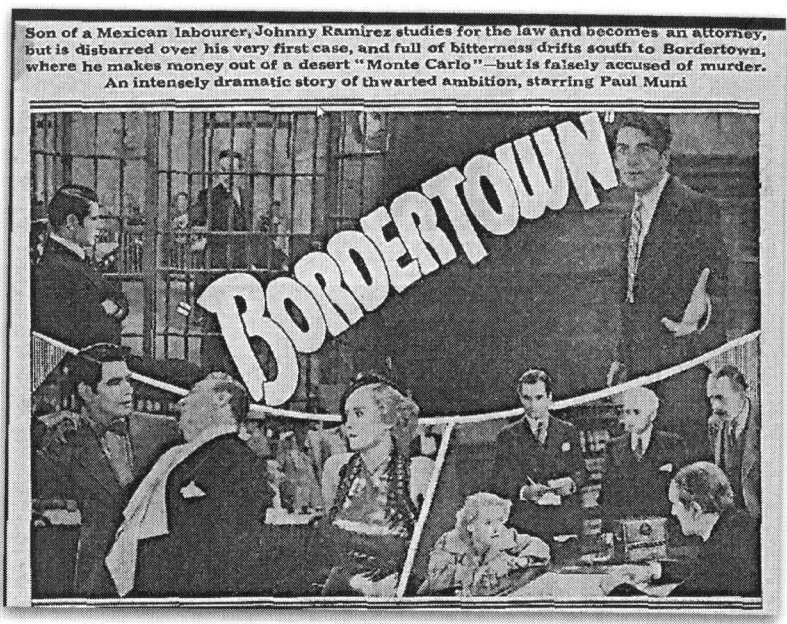

Son of a Mexican labourer, Johnny Ramirez studies for the law and becomes an attorney, but is disbarred over his very first case, and full of bitterness drifts south to Bordertown, where he makes money out of a desert "Monte Carlo"—but is falsely accused of murder. An intensely dramatic story of thwarted ambition, starring Paul Muni

Paul Muni and Margaret Lindsay in *Bordertown*

Archie Mayo
Director

Paul Muni
Johnny [Juanito] Ramirez

Bette Davis
Marie Roark

Margaret Lindsay
Dale Elwell

Eugene Pallette
Charlie Roark

Robert Barrat
Padre

Coincidentally, Actress Margaret Lindsay, who co-starred with Bette Davis and Paul Muni in the film, was the date of Thelma Todd's ex-husband, Pat DiCicco, at the **Trocadero Restaurant** (see page 67) on the night of December 14th, 1935. However, she and DiCicco reportedly had no contact with Thelma Todd or the other Lupino guests at their private party.

After Thelma Todd's death, there was speculation that her killer's "MO" may have been inspired by this movie.

In the scenes below, we see Bette Davis, who is in love with Johnny Ramirez (Muni), driving her drunken husband "Charlie Roark," played by character actor Eugene Pallette, home to their residence. She then attempts to get her intoxicated husband out of their open convertible back seat, but he is too drunk and too heavy to be moved. She then decides to murder him by monoxide poisoning, turns the car engine on, leaves the driver's door open, and exits the garage and closes it by way of a newly installed "electric eye."

In later scenes, we see her informing the police of his drunken condition and finding him in the garage. The case is initially ruled "accidental," but then as the investigation continues, her love interest, attorney Johnny Ramirez, gets blamed for intentionally killing the husband by monoxide poisoning and is put on trial. I'll leave the ending for you to discover yourselves.

Scenes from the movie *BORDERTOWN*. Johnny Ramirez is having drinks with Mr. and Mrs. Roark. Mr. Roark becomes drunk at the party. His wife drives him home, leaves him in the back seat, **turns on the car engine, and closes the garage door, resulting in his death by monoxide gas**.

The film was adapted from the novel, *Border Town*, by author Carroll Graham, published by The Vanguard Press, New York, in 1934.

I suspect that George Hodel may well have used the "MO" for murder after reading the book or, more likely, from seeing the film which aired in Los Angeles just a year before Thelma Todd's death.

The possibility of the film *Bordertown* being an inspiration for the Todd murder is not original to me. It was presented as a possibility back during the investigation in 1935.

I quote from the *Los Angeles Examiner* of December 17th, 1935:

...

Detectives recalled and wondered if some ingenious slayer might also have recalled, the successful film play of last spring, *Bordertown,* in which Bette Davis starred, and which dealt with a mysterious "garage murder" in which the feminine principal tricked her husband into his garage, seated him at the wheel, stupid with whiskey, and then started the motor running and closed the garage doors.

SKH Note - (In the film the husband, is actually left passed out in the rear seat, not behind the driver's seat, but no harm, no foul. Results are the same.)

What is of particular interest to me and those of you who have read my other series of books that detail my father's serial crimes are aware that this was a unique and specific crime signature/MO for George Hodel.

Copying a particular action from a film and including the act as his inspiration and part of his new crime was an essential MO for George Hodel.

To date, in examining his crime signatures from the 1940s and 1960s in the series of my already published books, I have documented his use of a portion of a scene from each of the below films as part of his crime signature:

The Most Dangerous Game (1932)
Red Dust (1932)
Charlie Chan at Treasure Island (1939)
The Mikado (1939)
Spellbound (1945)
The Sniper (1952)

Considering this, I think it is quite reasonable to include *Bordertown* (1935) as an additional source to that "list."

SKH Note - I was able to locate a rare copy of the original *Border Town* book written by Carrol Graham and published by Dell Books in 1934.

In reading the original story, which was adapted for the film the following year, I found an additional potential link, suggesting that George Hodel (in addition to seeing the movie) may well have read this dime novel (actually, it was 25 cents) the year before the film *Bordertown's* release.

BORDER TOWN – The Book

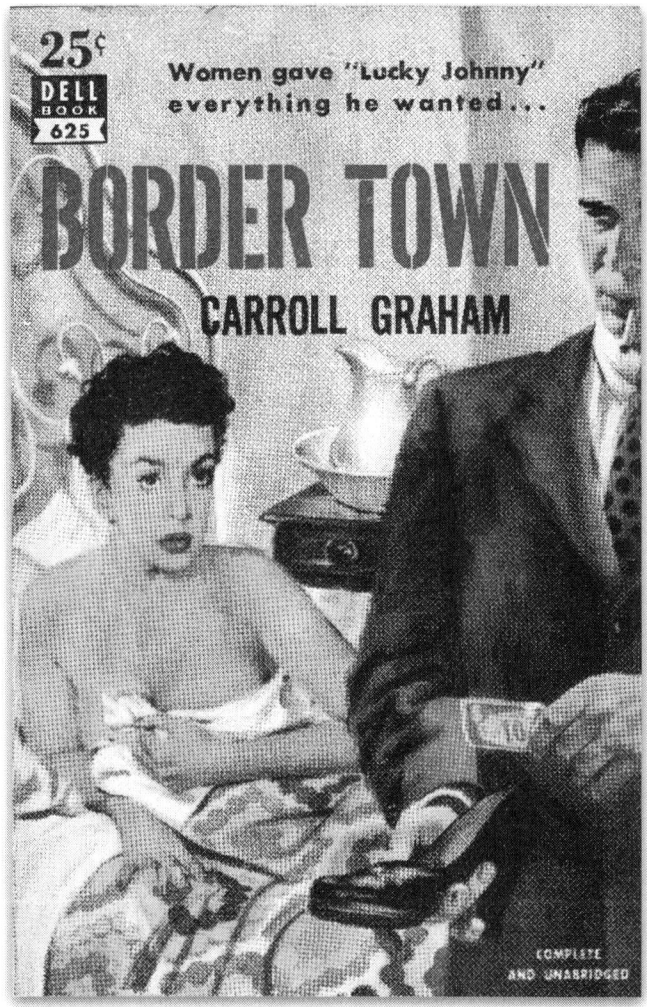

BORDER TOWN (Dell Publishing Co. NY, 1934)

In reading the original story, I found this familiar signage in an "anonymous letter written in a disguised, shaky handwriting on a page of cheap, ruled paper." Also, note the author's intentional misspelling of the word "**hous**."

Border Town page 91:

not created the effect he had hoped for, finished his beer, paid for it, and departed.

Having finished the sporting pages, Harris walked around the end of the bar to pour himself a drink. As he reached for a glass his eye fell upon an envelope propped up on the cash register, as are all envelopes delivered to all bars.

His name was on it in a crude, penciled scrawl. Harris was not a man who received much mail, and he took the envelope in some surprise.

"What's this?" he asked.

"Oh, that come for you this morning," the bartender said. "I forgot to give it to you."

Harris noted, as he tore it open, that the envelope was postmarked Calexico.

On a sheet of cheap ruled paper he read, in shaky handwriting:

Dear Buck Harris:

I am a friend of yours, and I think you ought to know your wife is playing around with Benny Kaplan. Kaplan says he is a friend of yours, but he ain't, because he has been playing around with Mrs. Harris for one two month now. He hangs around your hous in Calex when you are over at your business and they were out last night and the night before when you was in San Diego. This ain't none of my business but you are a square guy and I think you ought to know it.

A Friend.

Buck Harris read the bad, disguised handwriting slowly and without change of expression. He read the letter again, still without facial reaction, then folded the sheet

As mentioned earlier in this chapter, (page 90), the extortion notes sent to Thelma Todd from San Francisco were also signed, "**a friend**".

And, as referenced here, George Hodel used the "**A Friend**" as signage in his Avenger and Zodiac mailings. Also, note in the *Border Town* letter (page 104) the writer's intentional misspelling of the word "**hous**".

Could this have been the original source for George Hodel's later taunting letters to the press?

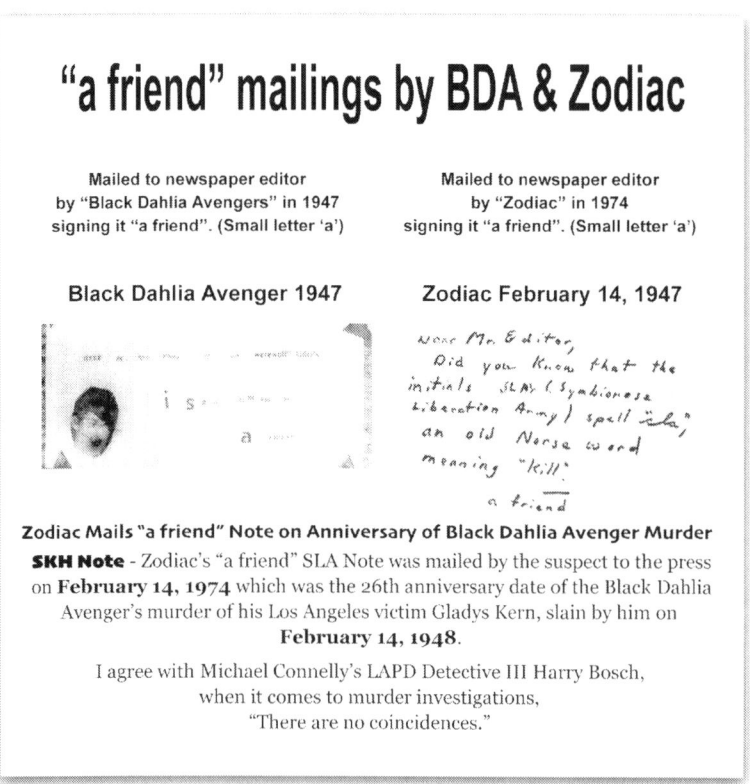

"a friend" mailings by BDA & Zodiac

Mailed to newspaper editor
by "Black Dahlia Avengers" in 1947
signing it "a friend". (Small letter 'a')

Mailed to newspaper editor
by "Zodiac" in 1974
signing it "a friend". (Small letter 'a')

Black Dahlia Avenger 1947

Zodiac February 14, 1947

Zodiac Mails "a friend" Note on Anniversary of Black Dahlia Avenger Murder

SKH Note - Zodiac's "a friend" SLA Note was mailed by the suspect to the press on **February 14, 1974** which was the 26th anniversary date of the Black Dahlia Avenger's murder of his Los Angeles victim Gladys Kern, slain by him on **February 14, 1948**.

I agree with Michael Connelly's LAPD Detective III Harry Bosch, when it comes to murder investigations, "There are no coincidences."

And, yes, as we move through the 1930s, "there will be more."

SKH Note - I also find the Monoxide Murder of Doris Dazey, which occurred just ten weeks before the death of Thelma Todd, highly suspicious and believe it could well have been committed, not by George Dazey, but rather by George Hodel.

Several factors figure into my suspicions, which include:

- A witness seeing a man carrying Doris Dazey's body in the dark from the house to the garage and who may have assumed it was the husband, Dr. Dazey, and made the "ID."

- The victim's confession to her parents that George Dazey was not the father of their child, Walter Dazey, but she did not name the true father.

- LAPD's follow-up investigation to San Francisco to attempt to discover the actual paternity and additional information surrounding a "mysterious possible lover."

Absent any additional information, the Dazey case is not solvable, with one possible exception.

That would be a DNA comparison to my father's or my DNA with the son Walter Dazey's DNA, or if he is no longer alive, then perhaps with one of his offspring or relatives?

If the analysis showed us to be half-brothers then that would be enough to confirm the crime. Absent that, the case of whether Doris Dazey's death was a murder or an accidental death will forever remain a mystery.

**Doris Schwuchow who plays Ramona in the
annual Ramona Pageant in the 1920s** (see pg 47)
later marries Dr. George Dazey

I came across the below excerpt on the *Bay City Press*
website found in the article "Bay City Doctor," which
summarizes the Dr. George Dazey investigation.

Excerpt from Website baycitypress.com

http://www.baycitypress.com/?page_id=40

Bay City Doctor

> After almost fifty years, it may be unfair to speculate,
> but a few items in historical records are intriguing. The
> *Santa Monica Evening Outlook* noted at the time of
> Doris' death that Dr. Dazey, who claimed to be an expert
> in narcotics abuse, had an "extensive practice, including
> many prominent movie folk." This specialization is
> intriguing in light of a lawsuit Dazey filed in 1931 against
> the estate of actress Mabel Normand. The doctor
> claimed that in 1927 and 1928, he made thirty-six visits

to Normand's home. We know now—and many knew then—that the actress was addicted to narcotics. What we don't know is the nature of Dazey's treatment—and whether it was the cure or the cause of Normand's condition.

This, of course, is of incidental interest to us as it connects Dr. George Dazey to another one of George Hodel's suspected crimes, the murder of William Desmond Taylor, as summarized in *The Early Years - Part I*. Apparently Dr. Dazey may well have been "Dr. Feelgood" for Mabel Normand, who, as we know, was one of the prime witnesses in the murder of William Desmond Taylor.

Who knew?

Thelma Todd Summary

In considering Dr. George Hill Hodel as the potential killer of actress Thelma Todd, I have done my best to try to stick to the known facts without involving myself or you, the reader, in the thousands of pages of mythology that exist.

Much like the William Desmond Taylor and Elizabeth Short, "Black Dahlia," murders the fictionalized version of Todd's death far exceeds the facts and blurs the truth with each passing decade.

As we have discovered, there is much that potentially links GHH to her crime.

In the here and now, some eighty-five years later, I see no possible way of making a definite determination as to his guilt or innocence.

Any potential suspect DNA does not appear to exist.

The only possibility would be if, as was done in the Dahlia investigation, we discovered some long-hidden police report that showed or named him as the "San Francisco Mystery Man" or as an actual named suspect in the original investigation.

With that, let's move on to our next crime, which followed hard upon the death of Hollywood's "Ice Cream Blonde."

Chapter 3

District Attorney Buron Fitts

Let me begin with a condensed and excerpted biography of Buron Fitts as provided in Wikipedia:

> Born in Belcherville, Texas, Fitts received his law degree in 1916 from the University of Southern California, and while a student there worked as a clerk for the prominent attorney Earl Rogers.
>
> > (**Author's Note**: Rogers was one of Los Angeles's most noted criminal defense lawyers. During his distinguished career, he had seventy-seven murder trials and only lost three. Author Erle Stanley Gardner created "Perry Mason" based on Earl Rogers's career.)
>
> Fitts was a severely injured veteran of World War I whose base of political support lay in the American Legion organization of war veterans. He had been shot in the knee in the Battle of Argonne and limped for the rest of his life.
>
> Fitts was appointed deputy district attorney for Los Angeles County in 1920 during the term of Thomas Lee Woolwine and chief deputy in 1924 under Asa Keyes.

In 1928 Fitts was elected Los Angeles District Attorney and would serve three terms until his defeat by a reform candidate in 1940.

During his career, Fitts was indicted twice for bribery, the first being connected with the Julian Petroleum Company scandal in 1928 and the second in 1934 for allegedly receiving a payoff from a wealthy real estate promoter for dropping a statutory rape case against the man. Fitts was acquitted on both charges.

In January 1936, Fitts was charged with perjury and was represented by Los Angeles attorney Jerry "Get Me" Giesler, who, some thirteen years later, would also defend Dr. George Hill Hodel from his 1949 incest and child molestation charges. Fitts and Hodel would both be acquitted thanks to the efforts of their attorney, "The Magnificent Mouthpiece."

Los Angeles Times January 16, 1936

The caption reads: "Courtroom scene yesterday as Buron Fitts, District Attorney, went on trial on charges of perjury. Left to right. W.E. Simpson, Joseph Scott, Fitts (standing), Jerry Giesler, then W.O. Gordon, L.H. Lashbrook, and Clyde C. Shoemaker. Giesler, Scott and Simpson are defense attorneys. Shoemaker is special prosecutor; Lashbrook is his chief investigator and Gordon, his legal adviser. Fitts is accused of giving perjured testimony before the 1931 grand jury."

In May 1937, DA Fitts made headlines with the "breaking news" that he had reopened the fifteen-year-old, cold-case murder investigation of William Desmond Taylor.

The Crime

On March 8, 1937, Angelenos awakened to the shocking news that an attempted assassination had occurred the previous night in which their District Attorney had been shot and wounded.

ASSASSIN WOUNDS BURON FITTS

BULLET HITS ATTORNEY IN ARM WHILE DRIVING ALONE NEAR MONROVIA

Suspects Lying in Wait

Here is a first report from the morning edition of the *Pasadena Post* of March 8, 1937:

District Prosecutor Taken To Hospital
In Hysterical Condition After Attack:
Doctor Fears Infection In Wound

District Attorney Buron Fitts' habit of propping his left arm over the top of his automobile steering wheel unquestionably saved his life last night when would-be assassins "gunning" for him shot a copper-jacketed bullet through his arm as he drove from his Duarte estate.

Early this morning, a hastily drawn cordon of deputy sheriffs and district attorney's investigators had failed to find a trace of the three or more who raced away in a small dark sedan after one of their members had fired a single well-aimed shot at Mr. Fitts.

The bullet, piercing the windshield of the district attorney's car, went through Mr. Fitts' forearm and dropped to the floor-board.

Mr. Fitts was rushed by ambulance to the Good Samaritan Hospital, Los Angeles where his condition was described as not serious. He was reported in hysterics, and doctors refused to permit interviews by the press.

Early deductions of investigators laid the attempted killing at the feet of the district attorney's recent drastic moves in helping break the Douglas Aircraft sit-down strike by indicting 345 strikers.

GUESTS AT DINNER

Last night Mr. and Mrs. Fitts had as dinner guests Jerry Geisler [sic] well-known Los Angeles trial lawyer; Eddie Meyers, member of the district attorney's staff, Dave Cushman, and the wives of the three men.

Mr. Fitts had been playing tennis. He was clad in sports clothes, coatless and hatless.

Arising from the dinner table, he said, "I'm going down and see Dad for a minute." Apparently, he wanted to talk about something concerning the estate as his father, Buff Fitts, takes care of the property.

Going to his county-owned car, he drove, alone, down the quarter-mile-long driveway through an orange and lemon grove fronting his 18-acre estate at 1433 Royal Oaks Place.

The 20-foot roadway was dark. Mr. Fitts' first thought he later told his mother was that "some nut" was merely driving about without lights. It was then a few minutes after 8 o'clock.

THREE MEN IN CAR

As the unlighted car came in range of Mr. Fitts' headlights, he saw at least three men, but in the dim light and fleeting moment could make out nothing more.

Without warning, a shot rang out that was said to[2] sound like a revolver.

Carefully aimed for his head, it zinged through the windshield and spent its remaining force in his arm.

Then the dark, small, "nondescript" sedan sped away in the night.

Stunned and bleeding, the district attorney swung his car around the corner and pulled in front of his parents' home.

...

Reeling from shock and dripping blood, he made his way to his father's[3] front door.

---

[2] Ed.: Original (a shot rang out, sound like a revolver.) changed for clarity.

[3] Ed.: Original (he made his way to the front door) changed for clarity.

Steve Hodel

TAKEN TO HOSPITAL

Renaker's ambulance brought Dr. Kelly from Monrovia, and after emergency treatment of Mr. Fitts' wound, he was placed in the ambulance and taken to[4] the Good Samaritan Hospital.

**Buron Fitts in the hospital
with his wife, Marian, by his side**

**Photographic depiction of Fitts' direction of travel and position of
his and the shooter's vehicle when Fitts was fired upon -
Law enforcement recreation of the shooting scene.**

---

[4] Ed.: Original (started for the Good Samaritan Hospital) changed for clarity.

Los Angeles Times March 9, 1937

Above is shown the position of Dist.-Atty. Fitts's sedan and that of his assassins when the first pistol shot was fired, striking his left elbow and tearing an ugly wound through the muscles of his forearm. When this shot struck him, Fitts jammed on his brakes and the bandit car rolled forward. The line and arrow show the course of the second shot which shattered the windshield, glanced off the steering wheel and buried itself in the roof of the Fitts car, as the gunmen sped their machine west on Foothill Boulevard.

Times photo

**Bottom photo on page 117 shows a bullet hole
in the windshield of DA's vehicle
& passenger side sun visor.**

**Below, at the end of pencil points, are the metal
jacketed spent slugs recovered from the floorboard
& sun visor of DA Fitts' vehicle.**

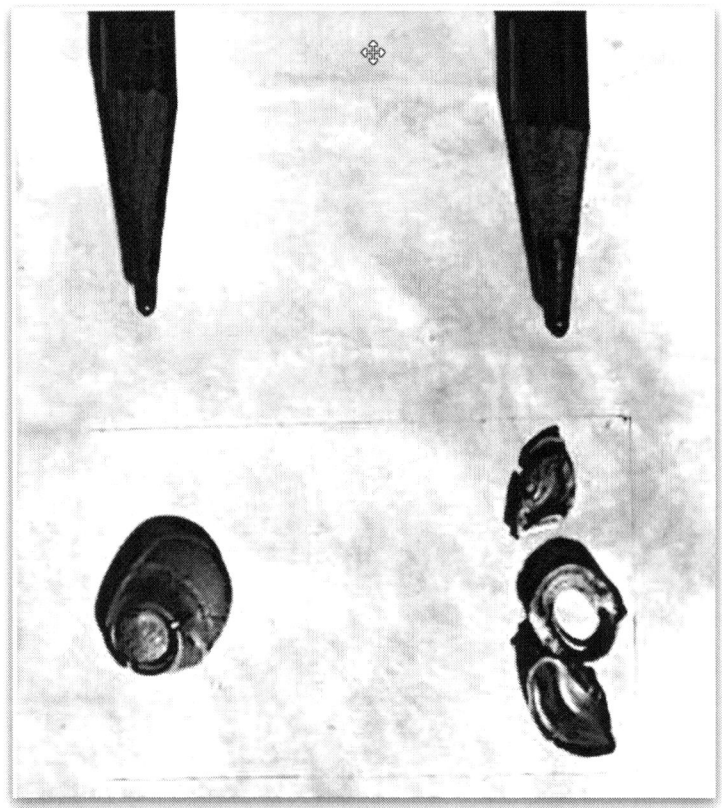

**Ballistics analysis revealed them to have been fired
from a .32 caliber handgun.**

SUSPECT'S VEHICLE

District Attorney Fitts was unable to provide investigators with the actual make and model of the suspect's vehicle as it was nighttime, and the driver of the other car was driving in the dark with the car's lights turned off.

Fitts could only say, "It was a dark-colored sedan," and could provide no further details.

"Two Men and a Woman"

The follow-up description of the shooting suspects changed from "three men" to more likely "two men and a woman."

The *Pasadena Post* on March 9, 1937, reported the following:

Numerous Threats Against District Attorney Traced As All Forces Join Probe

Possibility Of Woman Being Involved Seen
As Feminine Footprint Is Discovered
Near Scene Of Monrovia Attack

Out of a swirl of conflicting rumors and theories surrounding the attempted slaying of District Attorney Buron Fitts near his Duarte estate Sunday evening, several developments had definitely emerged early today.

A woman's shoeprints were found leading toward the road where the prosecutor was ambushed and wounded, indicating a woman may have participated.

Instead of one shot, two were fired by the gunmen, probably simultaneously, both hitting the prosecutor's car, but only one taking effect.

The woman theory was strengthened by Kurt Seiffert, a chauffeur living near the Fitts' home, who remembered "it was last Thursday that I saw a car cruising about the neighborhood with two men and a woman. Yesterday a car I am sure was the same one returned with the same three persons, cruised about a while and then left."

...

FINGERPRINTS TRACED

Fingerprints on the notes mailed Chief Dice and Mr. Fitts several hours before the shooting definitely proved the same person sent them. Also, the wording was similar:

The one to the prosecutor Fitts said: "Keep your eyes on the road to liberty."

To Chief Dice: "The road to liberty is coming, and it's some road to watch." The word "watch" was underlined. Neither note was signed.

More and more, the finger of suspicion pointed to "imported labor agitators."

ACCUSES AGITATORS

Donald W. Douglas, president of the aircraft corporation at Santa Monica, where more than 300 strikers were indicted by the district attorney recently, accused "the lawless group of invading Communist agitators brought here to create labor unrest."

NOTE THREATS

"Mr. DA" Buron Fitts had received dozens of written threats in the years and months preceding the shooting. Consequently, it was impossible to determine the motive, the why, of this attempted assassination.

Early speculation focused on the two notes received just hours before the crime. Two separate notes: one to Fitts "Keep Your Eyes On The Road To Liberty" and a second note sent to Santa Monica Police Chief Charles Dice, as described in the previous *Pasadena Post* article.

However, to my knowledge, no individual was ever identified to match *the fingerprints obtained from the two letters*, and no real proof ever was established that the writer was a "Communist agitator."

Dr. George Hill Hodel—A Suspect?

The actual linkage of George Hodel to this crime is thin, but relevant.

The shooter(s) most certainly will forever remain unknown and unidentified. But what about *the fingerprints obtained from the two letters*? Could they belong to GHH or one of his associates?

That said, to my mind, there is just enough Motive, Opportunity, and Means to include GHH as a possible suspect.

Why?

✓ Physical description was insufficient to identify any individual, but it does include a familiar GHH MO— "Two Men and a Woman."

This threesome fits many of George Hodel's crimes, including the staged Sister Aimee kidnapping in May 1926.

The description also matches the 1938 kidnap double homicide of Nancy and Hazel Frome just one year after Fitts was shot, where "two men and a woman" were seen driving their dark-colored sedan.

That crime was followed by the 1946 Chicago Lipstick Killer kidnap/murder of little Suzanne Degnan, which also included a description of "two men and a woman."

Again, in the Elizabeth Short "Black Dahlia" murder, we learned that "two men and a woman pursued Ms. Short to her hiding residence in San Diego, and fled when a neighbor saw them. The trio then turned up a week later when LAPD uniformed beat officer Myrl McBride saw "two men and a woman" escorting Ms. Short from a DTLA bar and asked Elizabeth, "Are you OK?"

✓ The handgun used was a .32 caliber, which GHH was also known to use in several of his later crimes. **Note** - In the 1938 double homicide of the Fromes, a .32cal handgun and a .38cal handgun were used to execute each victim.

✓ The vehicle fits the description, make, and model that GHH later owned (1936 black Packard), which he used in multiple kidnaps and crimes in his "Lone Woman Murders." It also was identical to the description of the 1936 model black sedan that was observed driving away from the vacant lot where Elizabeth Short's body was posed in the Leimert Park district of Los Angeles.

✓ The handwriting on the suspected Fitts Note appears similar to the known writing of George Hodel, and comparison by Questioned Document

Expert Hannah McFarland resulted in a finding*
of "probably written by George Hodel."

SKH Note - * A HW expert's finding of "probable" is defined as: "The
evidence contained in the handwriting points rather strongly toward the
questioned and known writings having been written by the same individual;
however, it falls short of the virtually certain degree of confidence."

CRYPTIC NOTES SEEN AS CLEW TO SHOOTING

LOS ANGELES, March 8. (AP)—
Sheriff's investigators began checking fingerprints on two cryptic un-
signed letters tonight as a possible
clew in the mysterious shooting
and slight wounding of District Attorney Buron Fitts in his automobile last night.

The letters were addressed to
Fitts and to Police Chief Charles
Dice of Santa Monica. A crayon-
printed letter which was mailed
last night before Fitts was shot
and came to his office this morning merely said "Keep your eyes
on the road to liberty." Chief Dice
said he had warned Fitts to be
careful because of a telephoned
threat.

**Above: Note and envelope sent to DA Fitts's office,
received just two hours before the shooting.**

Criminalist fingerprints & examines threatening note

In *Black Dahlia Avenger II* (Thoughtprint Press 2014), I referenced a note sent to the Los Angeles Sheriff's Office, Hall of Justice in 1950, almost four years after the kidnap murder of Elizabeth Short.

It appeared to be written in George Hodel's block printing with the usually misspelled words ("Elizabed Short"; "Philadelfia St"; "Whitier"), and in my opinion, the date it was mailed and postmarked was no coincidence.

Postmarked in Los Angeles on *October 10, 1950*, the very day of Dr. George Hodel's forty-third birthday. (To my mind, a "catch me if you can" taunt.)

Also, the addressing of both letters was identical. Neither contained any actual numbered physical address.

Though written and mailed over a span of thirteen years, the words were also identical and addressed as:

Hall of Justice
Los Angeles, Cal
(or) **California**

Page 385: *Black Dahlia Avenger II*
(Thoughtprint Press 2014)
1950 Avenger Letter

Letter No. 2 [LAPDHS Exhibit 3] was mailed to sheriff's office at the downtown Hall of Justice. It reads:

Sheriff

The party that killed Elizabed Short is Manuel L. Merino.
512 South Philadelfia St.
Whitier

M.S.

It is written in the customary block printing with what I believe are deliberately misspelled words (Elizabed, Philadelfia, Whitier) that, as we know, are consistent with previous known and identified Avenger mailings.

However, what really caught my attention was that this letter was postmarked in 1950, some three-plus years after the murder. Why would anyone, be they a "crank" or the legitimate killer, send in information on the Black Dahlia murder long after it had fallen from the front pages and was no longer in the public eye?

1937 Buron Fitts Threat Envelope:

"Distict [sic]Attorney Fitts

Hall of Justice

Los Angeles, Cal"

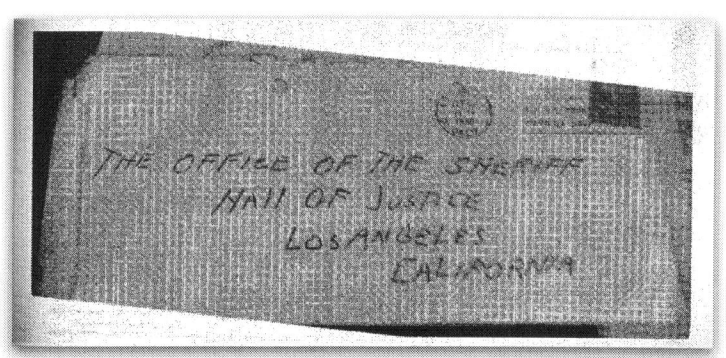

1950 Black Dahlia Avenger Note

**"The Office of The Sheriff
Hall of Justice
Los Angeles
California"**

OUT OF THE PAST - THE MARTIN LETTER

It began with an Email received on July 21, 2018, from a woman in Indianapolis, Indiana.

It read:

Dear Steve:

I am closing my parent's Estate, and yesterday I came across a hand-written statement (buried in a box for the past 69+ years), drafted in October 1949 by my Grandfather, who was a resident of Los Angeles and affiliated with the Los Angeles Police Department. The statement concerns the Elizabeth Short murder and possibly offers some insightful discernment as to the case investigation during the time up to and surrounding the date of the statement.

So now that I've found this statement.... What do I do with it? I started researching Black Dahlia files on the web and ran across an article and a YouTube video of yourself and your connection to this case. While most of America has heard of and/or watched documentaries of this case, not all of us find a hand-written statement composed by their Grandfather regarding it.

I would like for you to read this letter. It may (or may not) be of interest to you.

    Sincerely,

    Sandi Nichols

Here was my immediate response to Sandi:

Hi Sandi:

Thanks for the email information. I would be happy to take a look at your Grandfather's letter.

Can you scan and email it to me? Or, if you don't have a scanner, maybe make a copy and snail mail it to me at the below address.

> *Steve Hodel*
> *12400 Ventura Blvd Box 378*
> *Studio City, California 91604*

You say your Grandfather was "affiliated with LAPD." What was his affiliation?

Best Regards,
Steve Hodel
Los Angeles, California

SKH Note - Five days later, on July 27, 2018, I received the scanned copies of the letter, which had been handwritten by her Grandfather on October 23, 1949. He had sealed it in an envelope with instructions that it should be opened in case of the death of either one of his two daughters. (Margaret Ellen or Glenna Jeans). The envelope read:

> "In case of Margaret Ellen's or Glenna Jeans Death"
>
> "WGM"

Immediately upon receiving Sandi Nichols's grandfather's 1949 handwritten letter, I made telephone contact with Sandi and conducted a ninety-minute taped interview.

In our talk, Sandi backgrounded me on what she knew about her grandfather, William Glenn Martin, and his life in Los Angeles from the 1920s forward.

I also had her read her grandfather's three-page letter in full.

My complete investigation and linkage of William Glenn Martin to Dr. George Hill Hodel and the Los Angeles Police Department were documented and published in *Black Dahlia Avenger III* (Rare Bird Books 2018) in the final chapter, *The Afterword: Out of The Past-1949 "In Case of Death Letter" Identifies Black Dahlia Killer.*

I am tempted to reproduce the complete "Afterword" chapter here.

However, since much of it relates also to the 1949 Louise Springer Lone Woman Murder, I have decided instead, to include excerpts (scanned pages of *BDA III*) of some of the more essential links that relate to District Attorney Buron Fitts and the Los Angeles District Attorney's Office from the 1930s.

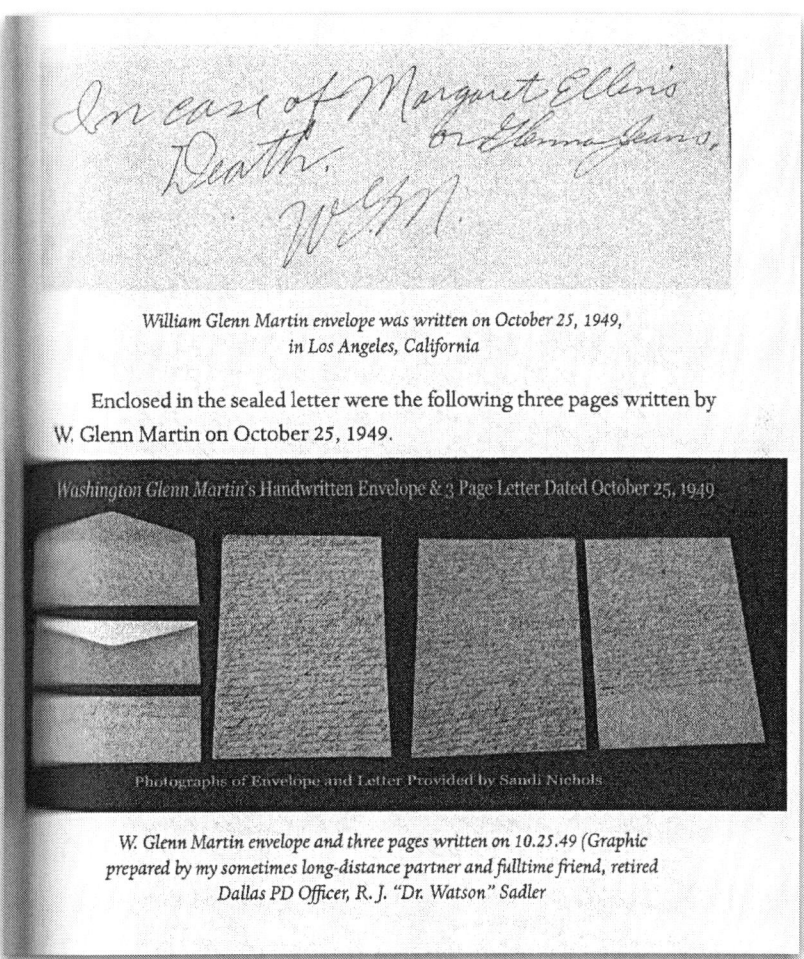

William Glenn Martin envelope was written on October 25, 1949,
in Los Angeles, California

Enclosed in the sealed letter were the following three pages written by
W. Glenn Martin on October 25, 1949.

Washington Glenn Martin's Handwritten Envelope & 3 Page Letter Dated October 25, 1949

Photographs of Envelope and Letter Provided by Sandi Nichols

W. Glenn Martin envelope and three pages written on 10.25.49 (Graphic
prepared by my sometimes long-distance partner and fulltime friend, retired
Dallas PD Officer, R. J. "Dr. Watson" Sadler

Scan of page 243, *Black Dahlia Avenger III*
(Rare Bird Books 2018)

To WHOM IT MAY CONCERN:

I, SANDi NICHOLS, AM THE GRANDDAUGHTER OF THE LETTER WRITER, W. GLENN MARTIN AND DO HEREBY CERTIFY THAT THIS LETTER WAS FOUND IN MY MOTHER'S PERSONAL EFFECTS AND HAS REMAINED IN THE CUSTODY OF OUR FAMILY SINCE MY GRANDFATHER WROTE IT BACK IN 1949. I HAVE PERSONALLY PLACED MY INITIALS ON EACH PAGE OF THE ORIGINAL LETTER FOR IDENTIFICATION PURPOSES.

SIGNED: *Sandi Nichols*
DATE : AUGUST 30, 2018
LOCATION: ███████████
INDIANAPOLIS, INDIANA

INITIALS ███

Signed Declaration of Sandi Nichols identifying handwriting and establishing the provenance of her grandfather W. Glenn Martin's letter as being in the family possession since 1949

Typed SKH transcription of Washington Glenn Martin Letter (Verbatim)

Oct 25, 1949

Page 1

I believe Choate framed this with McCawley to let G.H. get out of it or (as?) Black dalia killer.

This is what happened. I or we Mother, G.H. & me were eating supper.

ST. McCawley [Sgt. McCauley?] of LA Police Dept called me & said I have another one night job for you, like before. Will you take it? I said "I'll be down in AM and talk to you about it." (I had worked on 2 different nights for him. I knew not what job was to be till I was with him & other officers those nights. Then it was to try to see if other officers could be inveigled into crime.) So after supper G.H. got a call in which he answered OK Ray, I'll be down. Next A.M. I called McCawley & told him I would not take the job so he said, "OK, the job was over anyway." I saw in paper where a girl had been murdered at 116 E 3rd St. an unidentified body, plus other conditions mentioned in paper. I had sent a telegram to my daughter, 18, Margaret Ellen who is very large reading, "I love you & will always stand by you," her birthday greeting I believe it sent back here & received by someone who grabbed a chance to misinterpret the card. Recently,

Page 2

G.H. was grilled by police on Louise Springer death; he
and I both knew her: The investigation officers became
G.H. friend so matter dropped. He threatened to get
even with me. I had nothing to do with it. He bragged
while drunk in a salloon [sic] (the charge). I believe Joe
Choate who Margaret Ellen feared took her to the hotel
where the police especially McCawley tried to make
her admit that I, her father had committed the much
famous Black Dalia. [sic] Of course she would not do
that, as God & she knows I did not; her [assume Dahlia
or possibly Springer?] face was beaten so badly, hardly
recognizable. I have friends in Coroners Office who in
talking next AM let me see the body, as do a lot of those
known on jury [?] there see. I near came sick at sight. It
now developes G.H. got credit at "Starr" 949 S. Brdway
[Broadway]. On it he says his wife's name is Ellen. The
papers in Coroner's Office name police officers present
in case. Of course people from Okl. [Oklahoma?
Oakland?] were sent word of a Lucille Bowen (Hodges)
death I believe that a phoney made by G.H. as he knew
all Okla City neighborhood. They would think it Lucille
but where is Margaret Ellen Martin & Glenna Jean.
G.H. was with Joe when he took her to hotel & knew he
would get out of it.

Signed W. Glenn Martin

Page 3

I believe Choate Framed this with McCawley to make M.E. (Margaret Ellen?) mistake (misstate?) or accuse another, so the real killer would continue free. Choate always knew and was paid off as att. (attorney?) first and then blackmail.

Now $$ have stopped & Grand Jury is pressing, not Grand Jury bribe, but Choate to a police officer, either Jack Donahue or McCawley. Remember the other murdered girls at time of Dalia (sic) were all (2 or 3) dumped near City Hall. They were all friends. Perhaps knew too much. Why just Mirror call on M.E. murder?

All friends of "Nell Vaughn" alias, 519 S. GRANDVIEW who I believe is very anxious also, with Joe to convict someone else on all these including Oakes; and man found in Mts. San Ber. (mountains, San Bernardino?) & others. Same as Eva Krone Guilty arson & murder in Crestline this by newspaper. These crowd knew I worked for Law and did not have me in there (sic) crowd.

END Of TRANSCRIPTION

Excerpts from *BDA III* pages 257-259

Examining the W. Glenn Martin Letter's Contents

GLENN MARTIN HANDWROTE HIS letter just three weeks after my father's arrest for the Incest and Child Molestation (October 6) and prior to his actual trial.

Clearly, Martin is terrified that "GH," who knows and is associated with one or both of his daughters, will harm one or both of them.

He writes and seals the letter "In Case of Their Deaths." While Martin only refers to him as "GH," it is clear he knows LAPD knows who he is referring to and claims they are working to protect "GH" from being connected to both the Black Dahlia and Louise Springer murders.

Here are some bullet points on the contents of the letter:

- Glenn Martin is personally acquainted with, and he and his mother are having dinner with "GH" when LAPD calls his home.
- On the call, LAPD detective McCawley asks Martin if he wants to work a job for them? Probably undercover as a CI (Confidential Informant).

- An individual calls back the same night and asks to speak with "GH" who indicates he will meet with him, "Ray" the following morning. [I believe this is a separate caller and probably totally unrelated to the earlier Martin call from "McCawley."]
- Martin writes that his daughter, Margaret Ellen was taken to a hotel and met with an attorney Joe Choate and Sgt. McCawley who try to get her to fabricate a lie that her father killed "The Black Dahlia." He writes, "GH was with Joe when he took her to hotel & knew he would get out of it."
- Martin goes on to write that these officers are friendly with GH and that GH was the actual killer of the Dahlia.
- Martin acknowledges in the letter that both he and GH knew the victim Louise Springer and that GH "was grilled by detectives who believe GH killed Springer," but because he was friends with LAPD, they covered it up."
- Martin claims GH was upset with Martin because he believed he (Martin) turned the police onto him on the Springer Murder and speculates that GH may seek "revenge" on him by harming one or both of Martin's daughters, which is the reason he writes the letter, "In Case of their Death."
- Martin goes on to implicate attorney Joe Choate in the corruption and cover-up by LAPD detectives who were attempting to transfer the guilt from GH to Martin and or? [In 1949 Choate was a private attorney and had been a former LA Deputy DA for six years in the late twenties and early thirties, a very corrupt time in LA which continued through the early Fifties. In 1948 Choate was Gen. MacArthur's California for America campaign manager.]
- It is obvious that the "GH" referenced by Martin is known to law enforcement (LAPD) and is friends with attorney Joe Choate.
- Knowing this, Martin did not need to provide GH's full name, since GH was directly involved with Choate and McCawley and was in effect an "accomplice."
- On page two of the Martin letter he writes, "It now develops G.H. got credit at "Starr" 949 S. Brdway. On it he says his wife's name is Ellen." At the time this letter was written by Glenn Martin, George Hodel was known to be actively engaged in a relationship with his housemaid,

"Ellen," and numerous sexual encounters between them ("Sounds like George got another blowjob from Ellen") were tape-recorded and later documented by the stakeout detectives in the Hodel DA transcripts., just three months after Martin made his "Ellen" mention in this letter.

Absent additional information, we may never be able to prove that the "GH" mentioned in the Martin letter was in fact, George Hodel.

However, what are the odds that another "GH" was also known and was actively being investigated by LAPD and the DA?

George Hodel was named not only in confidential LAPD reports but also as the top suspect identified and *named by Lt. Jemison in his report to the Grand Jury just three days after this letter was written.(* None of these written police reports would have been known or accessible to Glenn Martin.)

Martin in this letter in real time, just months after the Springer murder, confirms what LAPD homicide detectives Harry Hansen and Finis Brown suspected back in 1949, that the Dahlia and Springer murders were likely committed by the same suspect.

Further, he states boldly that both he and GH knew the Springer victim and that GH "was grilled by LAPD detectives for that reason." (*To this day, to my knowledge, current Cold Case LAPD detectives have never even looked at the Springer case, as being serially related, though as previously stated, the original detectives believed it and other "Lone Woman Murders" were connected to the Dahlia murder.)*

Attorney W. Joseph Choate

Walter Joseph Choate was born on January 14, 1900 [ironically, the same month/day that Elizabeth "Black Dahlia" Short was abducted and murdered]. He was seven years older than George Hodel, who was born in 1907.

Choate died on October 14, 1997. [Ironically, the same day in 1949, that Dr. George Hodel was "held to answer" in Superior Court on two felony counts: Incest and Child Molestation.]

After obtaining his law degree, Choate joined the Los Angeles County District Attorney's Office and worked directly under DA Fitts from the late twenties to the mid-thirties.

The newspapers of that time show DDA Choate handled numerous high-profile criminal cases, including being assigned by his boss, Buron Fitts, to assist in the reinvestigation of the then fifteen-year-old cold case unsolved murder of William Desmond Taylor.

Attorney Choate, after leaving the DA's Office, began a private law practice in DTLA, located at 530 West 6th Street, just two blocks away from Dr. George Hill Hodel's medical practice in the Roosevelt Building at 7th and Flower Streets.

Los Angeles Evening Express **August 11, 1930**

SEEKS FAME IN PATH OF NOTED FORBEARS

Knocking at the door of fame through which have passed two of his distinguished relatives, W. Joseph Choate, youthful deputy in the district attorney's office (lower), today is well started on a legal career which, he trusts, will ultimately reflect to the glory of his famous kin, Joseph H. Choate (upper left), noted barrister of New York and ambassador to the Court of St. James, and Rufus Choate (upper right), brilliant contemporary of Daniel Webster, both of whom have played important parts in fashioning the legal history of the United States.

Deputy DA W. Joseph Choate 1930

Washington Glenn Martin

W. Glenn Martin was born in Indianapolis, Indiana, on August 4, 1893, which made him seven years older than Joseph Choate and fourteen years older than George Hodel.

Martin married Mary M. Taylor (date of birth, April 8, 1906) in Marion, Indiana, in 1925. Daughter, Glenna Jean Martin, was born in Indianapolis, Indiana, in 1926.

In advance of the family's relocation to Los Angeles, California, Glenn Martin went west to look for employment. In a letter home dated June 12, 1931, he wrote that he was attempting to obtain employment with the Los Angeles District Attorney's Office. I quote from a section of that letter provided me by his granddaughter, Sandi Nichols.

...

You cannot imagine the vastness of this place. Beautiful, and otherwise, I was out to Long Beach. It is the same way. Have not seen Venice & Ocean Park. Went thro (sic) the boulevard. *Have been trying to get a Good Job, first with Fitts office District Attorney. Don't know yet.* (**Italics - SKH**)

A scan of W. Glenn Martin's 1931 letter indicating he is seeking employment with LADA.

Excerpted scan from *BDA III* pages 275-281:

This information is of interest for the following reasons.

While Glenn Martin did not get the job with the LADA's Office then headed by legendary DA Buron Fitts, we know that, as mentioned previously, Joe Choate in 1931 was employed as a deputy district attorney working for Fitts on active criminal prosecutions.

Also of interest is the fact that in 1934, LADA Buron Fitts would be indicted for perjury and hired top criminal defense attorneys Jerry Giesler and William E. Simpson to defend him.

Fifteen years later, in 1949, at the same time Glenn Martin wrote his "In Case of Death" letter, Giesler would be hired by my father, Dr. George Hill Hodel to defend him in trial for the incest and child molestation charges. (October to December 1949)

Giesler's ex-defense partner, William Simpson had by then become Los Angeles's district attorney and would have been aware that Dr. Hodel was his investigator, Lt. Frank Jemison's "prime Black Dahlia suspect."

Four months later, William Simpson still in charge of the DA's Office, would also have been the one to order the return of all the evidence, witness statements and taped confessions made by Dr. Hodel to the custody of the LAPD, and give the order to Lt. Jemison to "back off and shut it down."

November 1934 Buron Fitts indicted in LA for perjury

Attorney Jerry Giesler (lt) DA Buron Fitts (middle) and William Simpson (rt) in court in 1934 preparing Fitts defense on perjury charges.

A second daughter, Margaret Ellen was born to Glenn and Mary Martin in Los Angeles on November 12, 1931.

Glenn and Mary divorced in 1944, and his wife and two daughters moved back to Indianapolis, Indiana.

According to Martin's letter, his younger daughter, Margaret Ellen, returned to Los Angeles [possibly only for a short visit?] and became involved with LAPD who interrogated her at a hotel. It is believed this occurred in 1949, but Glenn Martin provided no exact date of the police contact, so could have been earlier?

In my interview with Martin's granddaughter, Sandi, though she had minimal information on her grandfather, she did state that during his time in Los Angeles "he was employed as an insurance agent with the Prudential Insurance Company."

W. Glenn Martin died in North Hollywood, California, on July 3, 1976, at age eighty-three.

In early September, Sandi Nichols mailed me a second packet containing some of her grandfather's additional personal effects. Included were some family photographs along with a hardbound "Desk Private" book for the year 1947.

Inside the book, Glenn Martin had written:

"This Belongs to W. Glenn Martin, 1806 5th AVE, Los Angeles 6, California."

Within the pages of this book, Martin had secreted an original newspaper article from the *Los Angeles Herald-Express* dated Wednesday, March 17, 1948, headlined, "Missing- Have You Seen Any of These Girls?

The article displayed the names and photographs of four Missing Girls and requested the public's help in locating them. (See below photograph).

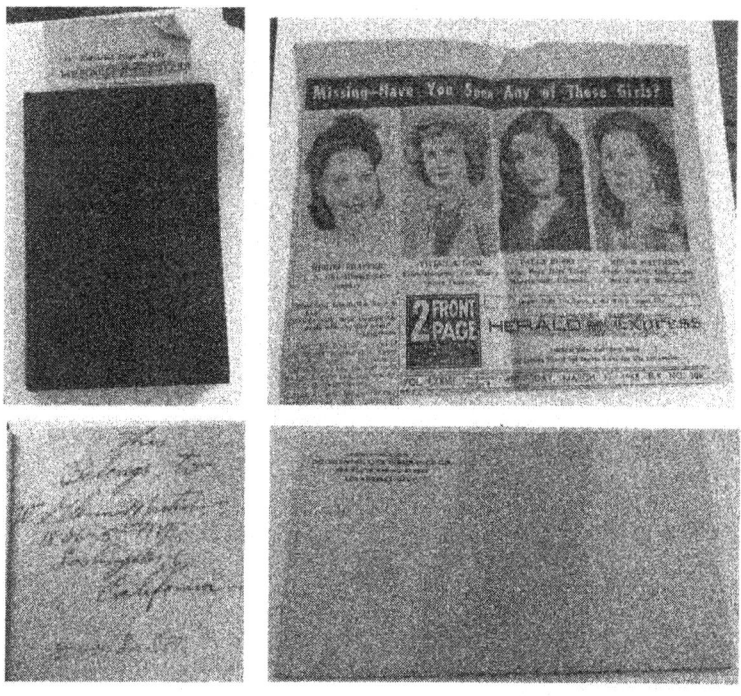

1948 LA "Missing Girls" Muriel Shaffer, Vivian A. Lash, Paula Rubio, Mrs. R. Matthews

Also found inside Martin's "1947 Private Desk Calendar" was an unaddressed blank envelope with a return address that read, "Return in five days to OCCIDENTAL LIFE INSURANCE CO. 756 South Spring Street Los Angeles." (This may have been a second employer of Glenn Martin.)

W. Glenn Martin in 1928(top left), 1953 (top right), and 1954 (bottom).

Margaret Ellen Martin

THE YOUNGEST DAUGHTER OF W. Glenn Martin. Born in Los Angeles in 1931.

After her mother, Mary M. Martin (Taylor) divorced her father in 1944; she returned with her mother and older sister, Glenna Jean, to Indianapolis, Indiana.

Margaret Ellen married in 1951 in Indianapolis, had a daughter in 1958, and passed away on October 4, 2015.

Margaret Ellen Martin 1949

Glenna Jean Martin

ELDEST DAUGHTER OF W. Glenn Martin. Born in Indianapolis, Indiana, in 1926. Lived with parents in Los Angeles until their divorce in 1944, when she returned to Indianapolis, with her mother and sister, Margaret Ellen.

Glenna Jean died in Tempe, Arizona, in 1997.

Glenna Jean Martin, 1943, age seventeen (Los Angeles)

Aurilla Bland Polen Martin

BORN ON APRIL 15, 1870, in Indiana. Mother of Washington Glenn Martin.

According to her son's letter, she was acquainted with "GH" and had dinner with him and her son at their residence, sometime in 1949.

The 1940 US Federal Census shows that Aurilla (age seventy), Glenn (age forty-seven), Mary (age thirty-four), Glenna Jean (age thirteen), and Margaret Ellen (age nine) were all living together in the same residence in Los Angeles, California.

Aurilla Martin died in Los Angeles on October 19, 1956.

Aurilla and Glenn Martin 1920 (Tijuana, Mexico)

Thanks to Sandi Nichols's "Out of the Past" purloined letter, we can connect some of the long-lost dots and make real and direct connections from Buron Fitts to Joseph Choate, to Glenn Martin to George Hodel.

Additionally, thanks to Glenn Martin, LAPD's paid underworld informant, we have identified and connected six additional individuals, (some of them actual legal accomplices); let's call them "the supporting cast." Identified by Martin as: Attorney Jerry Giesler, LAPD detectives Captain Jack Donahoe, Sgt. Ken McCauley (later promoted to Inspector McCauley in 1955) and William Parker (later LAPD Police Chief in 1950), and the newly appointed DA William Simpson (Giesler's former co-defense attorney for Buron Fitts in his 1930s bribery trial.)

Based on Martin's Letter—(which was intended to be opened under special circumstance) written and sealed by him in December 1949, as his "In Case of Death" of either of his daughters, and penned just three days from the beginning of the "GH" trial for incest and child molestation—we can genuinely conclude, "Hail, Hail, The Gang's All Here."

MOTIVE

✓ In his brief biography we discovered that DA Buron Fitts, just eight weeks after he had been wounded while driving his car, "reopened the investigation into the fifteen-year-old, Cold Case of William Desmond Taylor due to "New Evidence."

On May 6, 1937, it was headline news.

Could there have been a connection? Could George Hodel have obtained advance warning from his "inside connections" that District Attorney Fitts was about to go "full speed ahead" and take a deep dive back into that old unsolved whodunit?

History records that Fitts did take a new look at the Taylor murder. Still, it seemed to focus on information that Taylor's friend and actress Mary Miles Minter had or did not have and appears, while they may have considered her a possible suspect, it went nowhere.

Once again, the 1922 murder case went cold and has remained in deep freeze (as far as any actual suspect) for the past ninety-nine years.

Likewise, the identity of the three attempted assassins of DA Buron Fitts, the "two men, and a woman," was never learned.

Buron Fitts committed "suicide" (gunshot to the head) at his home in Tulare County in Central California in 1973, at the age of seventy-eight.

~

In closing this chapter, I am fully aware that we are nowhere near what would be required to make a case against Dr. George Hill Hodel from an investigative legal perspective.

I seriously doubt, based on the little that is known regarding the Buron Fitts attempt murder that a case could ever be "made" then or now.

Even if the fingerprints were a "make" on George Hodel, it would still be insufficient for a felony filing. All that would prove is that George Hodel sent in the note, which may or may not connect to the attempted murder.

I'd say the chances of identifying the three persons—my father with another male (Fred Sexton?) and a "woman"—that keep showing up at GHH crime scenes absent the weapon would, without a confession and corroboration of that confession, be impossible to prove.

Full stop.

I have included it here because the MO and crime signatures fit in with everything we know about GHH past, present, and yet to come.

Here now is more of the "yet to come."

Chapter 4

The Inglewood Babes

June 26, 1937

In presenting this crime, as I have in previous chapters, I will only provide a broad overview of the facts surrounding the abduction, triple murder, and investigation that led to the arrest of the *alleged killer*.

Several books have been written that detail the crime, arrest, and trial. At the end of this chapter, I will refer you to those books should you be interested in a fuller account of what many consider (including myself) to be one of California's most horrific crimes of the Twentieth Century.

On Sunday morning, June 27, 1937, Angelenos opened their morning papers and were shocked by the headlines which read:

And on Monday

Los Angeles Times
June 28, 1937

ING, JUNE 28, 1937.   **DAILY, FIVE CENTS**

Three Children Feared Kidnaped; Hundreds of Police Join Hunt

Girls Believed Lured Away by Stranger

In the most intensive manhunt in Southern California in the past twelve years, more than 500 police, Legionnaires and private citizens last night were searching for three small Inglewood girls who vanished from Centinela Park in the heart of the suburban city shortly before noon Saturday.

Convinced that the children are in the hands of a degenerate, Chief of Police Oscar D. Campbell said that he feared now the results of the hunt. Each added hour, police felt, spelled doom for the little girls.

VANISHED TRIO

The missing children:

Madeline Everett, 7 years of age, daughter of Mr. and Mrs. Merle D. Everett of 571 East Hazel street, Inglewood.

Melba Marie Everett, her 9-year-old sister.

Jeanette Marjorie Stephens, 8, daughter of Mr. and Mrs. Floyd Stephens of 517 East Hazel street, Inglewood.

VAST TERRITORY HUNTED

Every vacant house, weeded lot and the vast stretches of the rolling Baldwin Hills, where the two Martin sisters met their horrible fate in 1924, were being thoroughly combed by grim and determined men.

Among the searchers were forty members of the Santa Monica Mounted Police, under the direction of Capt. William J. Steinbrink. On foot and in automobiles last night they planned to

Working against a tragic race to work on, police, Sheriff's deputies and volunteers are searching for these girls who disappeared mysteriously Saturday from Centinela Park, Inglewood. Left to right, Jeanette Marjorie Stephens, Madeline Everett and Melba Everett.

The Crime

Preliminary investigation into the three missing girls revealed the following.

Madeline Everett, age 7, her sister, Melba, age 9, and their friend Jeanette Stephens, age 8, were playing together in Centinela Park, just a few blocks from their homes on Saturday, June 26, 1937.

Witnesses at the park informed police that they had seen the three girls talking with a man at approximately noon, just before their disappearance.

According to the missing Everett girls' older sister, Olive Everett, age 12, who had been with them at the park on Saturday, the suspect had shown the girls some rope tricks tying different kinds of knots.

Olive informed police that the man "Eddie the Sailor" had sent her to the store to purchase some clothesline and then showed the girls and entertained them with sleight of hand tricks both on the preceding Friday and again Saturday, the day the three girls went missing.

Based on hers and other witness statements, the suspect who had been seen on prior occasions loitering in the park and speaking with the victims on the day of their disappearance was:

"Eddie the Sailor"

"Eddie the Sailor"

Was described in a *Los Angeles Examiner* article dated June 27, 1937 as being:

**Male, 5-10, 150-60
blue eyes, brown hair, small mustache,
light brown shirt, blue jeans**

INGLEWOOD, June 29, (U.P)— Police today issued a composite description of the man who committed the triple "babes of Inglewood" slayings.

After talking to witnesses, they described him as:

Five feet 10 inches tall; weight 150 to 160 pounds.

Blue eyes; brown hair.

Small moustache (but by this time he may have shaved it off).

When seen in the park, the suspect was wearing a light brown shirt and a pair of blue overalls.

Los Angeles Examiner June 1937

"The suspect's car is a Model A Ford roadster, 1929 or 1930, color not known, but dark in appearance, no running boards, fenders, or top. Also had written or painted slogans on the side."

Ventura County Star Free Press
June 29, 1937

Once again, a dragnet was thrown out in Los Angeles, and numerous of the "usual suspects" were rounded up and brought in for questioning.

Twelve-year-old Olive Everett repeatedly made multiple "positive identifications" when shown photographs by police officers, "Yes, that's the man," and as the falsely accused individuals would present their alibis, the preteen's unreliability as a witness should have effectively voided her as far as being able to identify the actual suspect.

By "Day 2," the press made the connection and voiced their opinion that the children's "disappearance" was an identical MO to the Martin Sisters murder in 1924. Here's the *LA Herald Express* article printed on June 28.

Los Angeles Herald Express
June 28, 1937

Inglewood Mystery Close Parallel to Martin Sisters Case

The strange disappearance of three tots from Centinella Park parallels in many respects the tragic saga of the Martin sisters—May and Nina—whose vanishing from the Glen Airy section in 1924 stirred the city. The bodies of the girls were found many months later in a dry wash in the Baldwin hills, and a 60-year-old night watchman, Scott C. Stone, was arrested, convicted and sentenced to hang for their murder. Governor C. C. Young commuted Stone's sentence to life imprisonment. He is still in San Quentin. Here in brief is the story of the Martin sisters:

On the evening of Aug. 23, 1924, 12-year-old May Martin, garbed in a gingham dress and a Little Red Ridinghood cape, took her smaller sister, Nina, 8, by the hand and started from her parents' home at 2854 South Mansfield avenue for the home of her grandmother a few blocks away.

Hours later the parents learned that May and Nina had stopped but briefly at the grandmother's place, then supposedly had started back to their own home. They never arrived.

Because the children's own father was divorced from his wife and had several time threatened to take his daughters, police, supposed the sisters had been taken to the father's home in the state of Washington. The search lagged and not until Glen Airy district residents became incensed and demanded action was an organized hunt for the tots began. A reward was offered for the children—dead or alive. Hundreds of Boy Scouts, deputy sheriffs and citizens trugged through the Baldwin hills for days looking for bodies.

But the effort was fruitless until Feb. 15, 1925, when a Mexican, hunting for rabbits in a wash, came upon the dried remains of a human foot, clad in a patent leather slipper, in a clump of brush. Beneath the brush were found the remains of the Martin sisters.

STONE IDENTIFIED

Scott Stone, aged, lame, already under arrest on a morals charge brought by a 16-year-old Glen Airy girl, was identified by several persons as having been seen in an automobile with the Martin girls the night they disappeared.

Stone denied knowing the girls, but under the bed in his shack house on the outskirts of Glen Airy was found a tiny vanity case that had belonged to May Martin.

This and other evidence led a jury to return a quick verdict of guilty in the murder trial that followed. Stone was twice sentenced to hang—once for either murder, but a prolonged battle by his lawyer resulted in the commutation by Governor Young, a commutation that came largely because all of the evidence against Stone was purely circumstantial.

The Crime Scene

A massive search of the hilly area some five miles northwest of Centinela Park began the day after the "Inglewood babes" disappeared.

This was based on information that the suspect had taken them "rabbit hunting," and the nearby Baldwin Hills were specifically known and popular for precisely that purpose.

Hundreds of police officers, concerned citizens, and a Boy Scout Troop all focused their foot search efforts in and through this rugged terrain.

A low flying airplane also aided in the search and radioed, seeing what appeared to be clothing in the heavy brush in a Baldwin Hills ravine.

Boy Scouts following the pilot's directions were the first to arrive at the scene and confirmed all three of the children's bodies were there in the underbrush.

June 28, 1937

Crime Scene photos from the
Los Angeles Evening Herald and Express

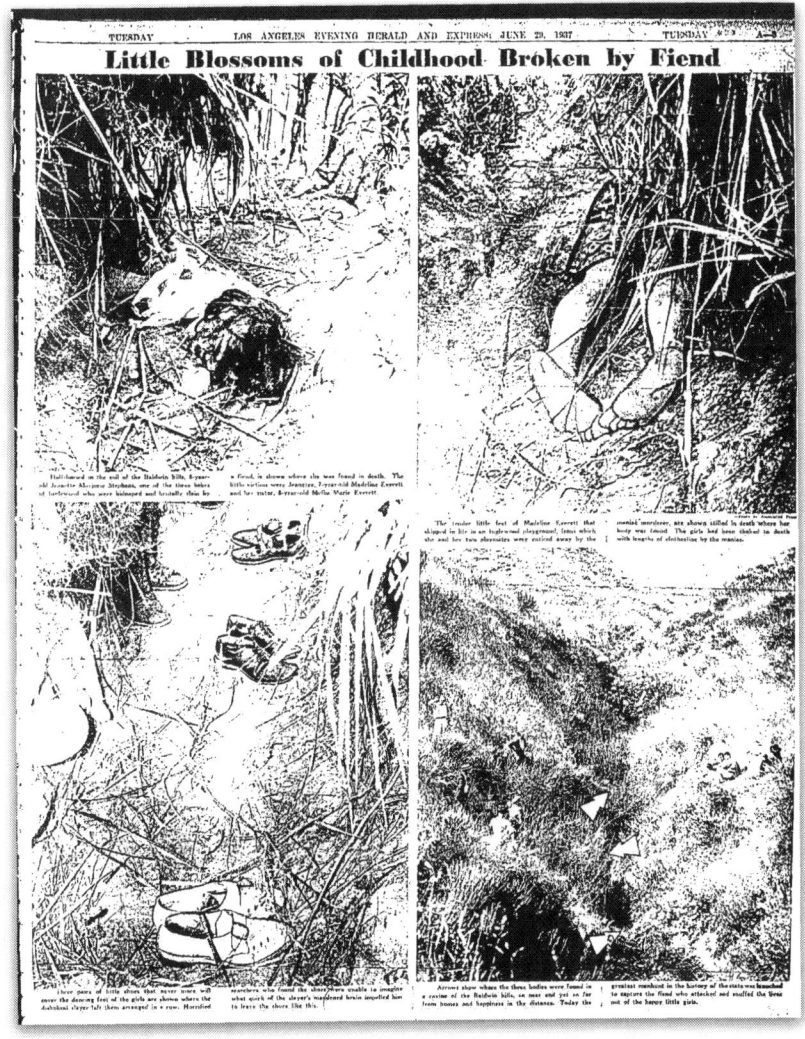

Los Angeles Evening Herald and Express
June 29, 1937

Captions read: (from newspaper crime scene images page 161)

(Upper Left)

"Half-buried in the soil of the Baldwin Hills, 8-year-old Jeanette Marjorie Stephens, one of the three babes of Inglewood who were kidnaped and brutally slain by a fiend, is shown where she was found in death. The little victims were Jeanette, 7-year-old Madeline Everett, and her sister, 8-year-old Melba Marie Everett."

(Upper Right)

"The tender little feet of Madeline Everett that skipped in life in an Inglewood playground, from which she and her two playmates were enticed away by the maniac murderer, are shown stilled in death where her body was found. The girls had been choked to death with lengths of clothesline by the maniac."

(Lower Left)

"Three pairs of little shoes that never more will cover the dancing feet of the girls are shown where the diabolical slayer left them arranged in a row. Horrified searchers who found the shoes were unable to imagine what quirk of the slayer's maddened brain impelled him to leave the shoes like this."

(Lower Right)

"Arrows show where the three bodies were found in a ravine of the Baldwin Hills, so near and yet so far from homes and happiness in the distance. Today the greatest manhunt in the history of the state was launched to capture the fiend who attacked and snuffed the lives out of the happy little girls."

Physical Evidence

Fingerprints

Appeal-Democrat **June 29, 1937**

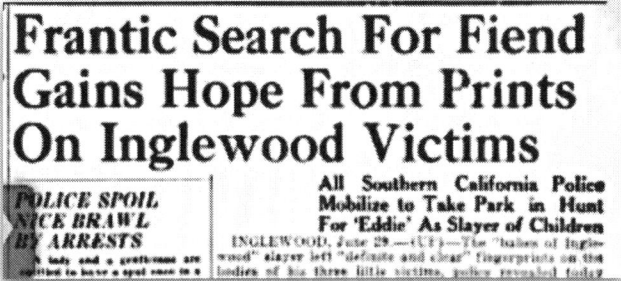

INGLEWOOD, JUNE 29. (UP)

The "babes of Inglewood" slayer left "definite and clear" fingerprints on the bodies of his three little victims, police revealed today as they held 12 known degenerates as possible suspects.

Don J. Oliver, police fingerprint expert and uncle of Madeline, 7, and Melba Everett, 8, two of the victims of the kidnap-slaying, said fingerprints found on the bodies were "very definite."

"It is only a matter of checking these fingerprints with police records," he said.

"A man with a previous record of sex crimes could only have done this terrible thing."

Author's Note: While the newspaper statements made by the LAPD criminalist/fingerprint expert did not indicate exactly where the "definite and clear fingerprints" were obtained, I would assume the most likely source would have been the children's shoes, but this is only an educated guess.

Ligatures

Separate lengths of clothesline (apparently cut from the same rope) were used to strangle each of the victims.

According to twelve-year-old Olive Everett (the surviving sister of Madeline and Melba), on Saturday, June 26, while with her sisters at the park, she was ordered by the suspect to go buy the clothesline from a nearby store, which she did and then returned and gave it to him to "perform tricks."

Fingernail Scrapings

LAPD Criminalist Ray Pinker responded to the scene and obtained scrapings from under each of the victim's fingernails to aid in identifying a possible suspect.

Author's Note - The science of DNA was still fifty years into the future, but should those scrapings still exist (doubtful in my mind), they could potentially reveal the identity of the actual killer.

Clothing

Based on police photographs that I have viewed taken at the Coroner's Office, all three girls were partially clad, and it appears that their clothing was torn and likely ripped open. (Again, if the clothing remains in police custody, it could be processed and analyzed using "Touch DNA" and potentially provide suspect DNA.)

Los Angeles Evening Herald and Express
June 29, 1937

Caption Reads:

"Carrying the tiny, bruised body in a small stretcher, members of a searching party are shown removing the body of one of the three slain Inglewood girls from the Baldwin hills gully. where the bodies were discovered by four Boy Scouts after an airplane had located the girls' dresses from the air. The boys who searched for the bodies are aiding in the hunt for the suspect."

Autopsies

Los Angeles County Coroner Dr. A.F. Wagner performed the autopsies on all three victims and estimated the time of death to have been late Saturday afternoon or in the dark of night on Saturday evening, June 26, 1937.

Dr. Wagner performed the autopsies on all three victims beginning in the afternoon/evening hours of June 28, 1937, and into the early morning hours of June 29.

The cause of death on each victim was by ligature strangulation. Each victim had been strangled with a piece of clothesline that had been "tied in the back with a double hitch knot."

Police photographs taken at the time of the three autopsies have been published and circulated in other book publications. While I have copies, out of respect for the children and their families, I am not publishing those photographs.

The photographs confirm that the children were beaten and bruised about the face and body and, according to the coroner, were sexually attacked. Spermatozoa were found in each of the three victims' vaginas. Slides were obtained. Additionally, an act of sodomy (anal rape) was inflicted on each separate victim.

Author's Note - If these slides exist, an analysis could lead to a positive ID of the rape/murder suspect. Even in 1937, testing could have revealed the blood type and RH factor, which could have been used in court to include or potentially exclude the killer. I am unaware of any report that anyone's blood type and RH were obtained and or compared to the evidence slides.

Caption reads:

"This map of the Baldwin Hills area shows, by dotted line, the path probably traced by the degenerate slayer of the three Inglewood babes as he lured them from Centinela Playground to their deaths. The girls' bodies were found ravished and strangled in a lonely ravine of the hills. Today a great statewide manhunt was on to bring the killer to justice."

Author's Note - Observe arrow at the top of hill indicating where a witness observed "a parked car." Additionally, some witnesses at the playground believed there were "two men and the victims were seen near or inside their vehicle at Centinela Park."

LA Times artist rendition of a larger map showing the 5.5-mile route to Baldwin Hills

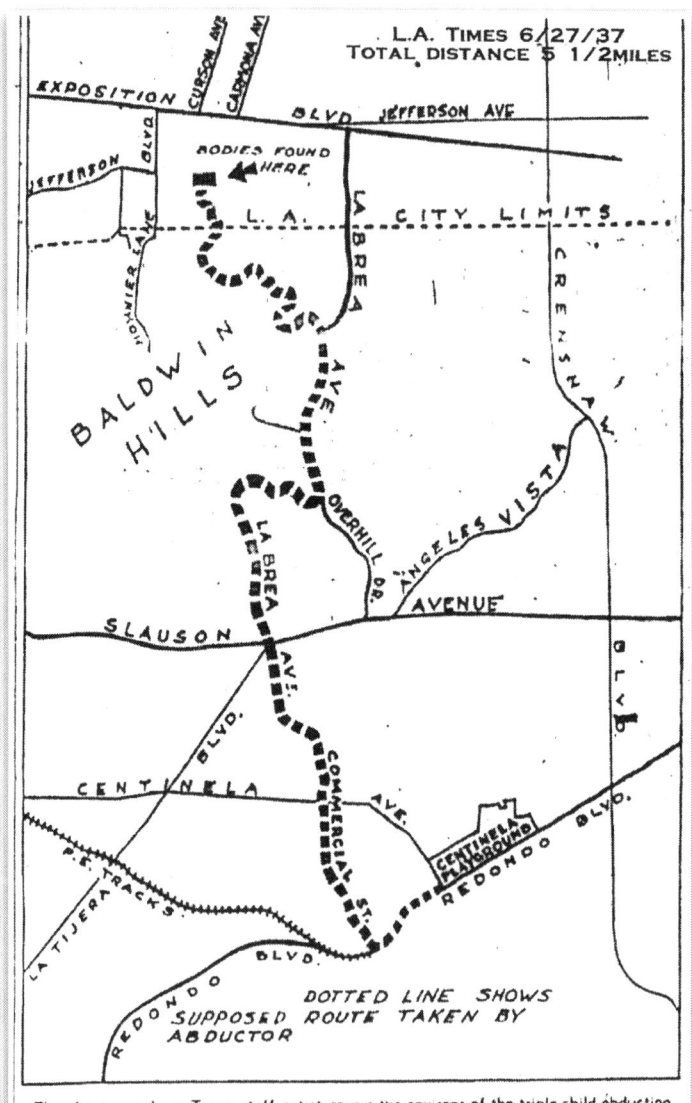

The above map by a Times staff artist covers the environs of the triple child abduction and murder. The dotted line shows supposed route taken by man and three girls from scene of abduction to spot where the children were slain.

The Suspects
Othel Leroy Strong, Fred Godsey, Albert Dyer

Los Angeles Times June 29, 1937

Othel Leroy Strong

Description of Youth Broadcast

Triple-Murder Suspect Wears Overalls and Drives Dark Roadster

A description of the previously convicted youth being sought for questioning in connection with the murder of the two little Inglewood sisters and their 8-year-old girl playmate was broadcast yesterday through the Sheriff's communication system.

The description, also broadcast on short wave radio, was as follows:

"Wanted on suspicion of kidnaping and murders which occurred near Inglewood on the afternoon of June 26, 1937, Othel LeRoy Strong, 22, 135 pounds, 5ft. 9in. tall, medium brown hair, fingerprint classification 21 L-S 1-1 R10-Ua 22-18.

WORE OVERALLS

"When last seen, needed a shave; dressed in light brown shirt, blue overall pants; wearing a small black mustache. This man is probably driving a Model A Ford roadster, 1929 or 1930, color unknown, but dark in appearance. Has box body on rear. Also has writing painted slogans on side of car. He is a truck driver by occupation."

On July 29, 1936, according to Sheriff's records, Strong was arrested on suspicion of attacking 14-year-old June Arthur of 8923 Fifth avenue, Inglewood. The girl's mother, Mrs. Ethel Arthur, complained to officers that Strong had attacked the little girl while she was standing at a street corner waiting to go home.

SOUGHT FOR QUESTIONING

Othel Strong, convicted of a morals offense but released on probation, who last night was the object of a manhunt by authorities who wish to question him in connection with the murder of three Inglewood schoolgirls.

Othel Leroy Strong

OTHEL LEROY STRONG

Wanted on suspicion of Kidnaping and Murder

Description:
Male White, 22, 5-9, 132, med brown hair small mustache

Possible Vehicle:
1929 or 1930 Model A Ford roadster, dark color, box body on rear, writing or printed slogans on side of the car

As previously indicated, more than a dozen "suspects" were rounded up and arrested on suspicion of committing the horrific kidnap/murders; however, all were released based on solid alibis.

Within days of the triple murder, an APB (All Points Bulletin) was issued to arrest, Othel Leroy Strong, (pictured on page 169), who had been identified as the probable killer.

However, within a day of the issuance of the wanted information, Washington State authorities contacted Los Angeles. They informed them that Othel Strong was in their state and could not have committed the crimes.

Fred Godsey

A week later, on July 3, 1937, a new nationwide APB was issued for the arrest of Fred Godsey, who had been identified as "Eddie the Sailor," the wanted killer of the three "Inglewood babes."

Fred Godsey

Los Angeles Times, July 3, 1937

Author's Note - Fred Godsey Wanted Killer shares headline with Aviatrix Amelia Earhart's disappearance

Los Angeles Times
July 4, 1937

NEW CLEW LINKS GODSEY
WITH MURDER OF GIRLS

Fixing of Sewing Machines in Inglewood
Told as Dozen Identify Suspect's Photo

Fred Godsey's knack for repairing sewing machines last night supplied the link connecting him definitely with Inglewood and intensifying the hunt for this Cherokee quarter-blood for questioning in connection with the attack on and murder of Madeline and Melba Everett and Jeanette Stephens.

While a dozen townspeople of the suburban city identified pictures of Godsey, obtained exclusively by *The Times*, as the man they had seen playing with the triple killing victims in Centinela Park, Burt Sorrenson of 435 East Redondo Boulevard, proprietor of the awning company, was the first to identify him under his real name.

MACHINES REPAIRED

Godsey pursued his trade of repairing sewing machines in Los Angeles and Inglewood during last December and January, according to information given last night by Sorrenson.

When shown a picture of Godsey, Sorrenson adjusted his spectacles and exclaimed: "Great Scott, that's Godsey!" Sorrenson said Godsey, driving a 1929 Ford roadster with a box on the rear, came to his shop just before Christmas and asked for work.

"I'm an expert sewing machine repair man," Godsey is said to have told Sorrenson.

...

Among the dozen or more Inglewood citizens who identified Godsey's picture as the man they had seen in Centinela Park playing with the children were G.W. Cawthon of 1032 South Fir Street, a gardener employed in the park, and W.D. Frantz, superintendent of the park.

Others who had seen "Eddie the Sailor" entertaining the murder victims with rope tricks include Haskell Wright, W.P.A. recreational director in the park; J.M. Rouard, who saw the three girls sitting in the car; Mrs. Martha Rigby, who saw the man running down the road late Saturday afternoon from the Baldwin Hills, and John Reynolds and John Veltrie, who purchased a goat from the suspect.

...

First to identify the suspect yesterday were Jack Reynolds of 2661 ½ North Johnson street and John Veltrie of 15614 Hawthorne Boulevard. The latter has a half-brother, James Bender, at the latter address who runs a feed and livestock store.

Carrying the exclusive picture of the suspect published in yesterday's *Times*, they arrived at search headquarters in

Inglewood and sought Eugene Williams, chief of the District Attorney's Bureau of Investigation.

"He sold us a goat Saturday morning," the men told Williams.

ARRIVES IN FORD

"He arrived at the store in a dilapidated 1928 or 1929 Ford roadster with a box on the back. It had no top or fenders.

"He had this goat tied in the back with a piece of clothesline. We argued about the price of the goat. He wanted $3, and we offered him $1.50. Finally, we tested the goat to see the quality of milk it gave and found out it hadn't been milked for a couple of days so we compromised on $2."

"THAT'S THE GUY."

"That's the guy we bought the goat from." This was considered important, Williams said, because animal hairs were found by Police Chemist Pinker while checking the ropes with which the three little girls, Madeline and Melba Everett and Jeannette Stephens, were throttled a week ago yesterday.

Officers immediately ordered hair clipped from the goat for comparison with that found near the bodies.

Next to select the pictures obtained by *The Times* and given to authorities to aid in the search was Mrs. Margaret Rigby, 530 N. Commercial Avenue—on the direct route from the park to the Baldwin Hills where the murders occurred.

MAN SEEN RUNNING

She had told officers that she saw a man running past her home, blood on his clothes, about 5:30 p.m. on the afternoon of the murders.

According to Capt. Penprase of the Sheriff's Bureau of Investigation, she was handed the pictures by Deputy Sheriff Carroll and said:

"Yes, that's him."

This, with the positive identification by Al Blythe, 6107 Long Street, a recreational worker in Centinela Park, who declared the pictures of Godsey are those of the man who turned his wrist back against his arm and entertained children with other tricks and the declaration of park workers that the pictures "look exactly like Eddie the Sailor," led the police investigators to seek Godsey at all points.

Los Angeles Times
July 4, 1937

1] Al Blythe, an Inglewood recreation department employee, identified pictures of Fred Godsey, kidnap suspect, as having been seen with the slain children.

2] From her Inglewood home last Saturday, Mrs. Margaret Rigby, above, saw a man with blood on his clothes passing. She identified pictures of Fred Godsey.

3] Jack Reynolds of Inglewood is shown holding the goat, which a man he and others identified as Fred Godsey sold him last Saturday morning, shortly before the triple slaying.

Albert Dyer

Albert Dyer

Albert Dyer, age 32, resided in Inglewood at 518 Commercial St. He was married, no children, and was employed by the Work Projects Administration as a school crossing guard at the cross streets of Prairie and Redondo Boulevard.

(The WPA was a federal agency that hired the unemployed and mostly unskilled during the Great Depression to perform labor in support of the infrastructure such as the maintenance of public parks, buildings, and roads.)

Albert Dyer was acquainted with the three victims (on sight only) in his work capacity as a crossing guard, escorting them and the other school children safely across the streets.

Albert Dyer was formally tested and found to be mentally deficient, having an *IQ of 60, and **possessed the mental age of an eight-year-old***. In 1937 the word used to describe his mental capacity was the term of a "Moron."

Based on newspaper accounts and police statements, here is a reconstruction of the investigation and arrest of Albert Dyer.

Albert Dyer Chronology of Arrest

Monday, July 28, 1937

Albert Dyer, as a local resident, was one of the many "volunteer citizens" who aided in the search for the missing girls.

When word went out that "the girls' bodies had been found," Dyer, like many other locals, responded to where the Boy Scouts had been directed to search in the ravine by the pilot, after seeing what appeared to be children's clothing from his flyover in a small aircraft.

Tuesday, July 29, 1937

Michael Huerta, age fourteen, also a local resident, went to the office of Inglewood Police Department and spoke to Police Chief Oscar Campbell, stating to the chief, "I've got an idea who the murderer is."

The teenager then named Albert Dyer as a person "that I saw acting suspiciously around little boys and girls."

As Huerta was relating his information, LAPD detective lieutenants Leroy Sanderson and *Thad Brown* (emphasis mine) walked into the Inglewood PD office. They advised the chief they were assigned to "assist his officers in the investigation."

Chief Campbell introduced the two men to Huerta, saying, "Well, here's something you can start with."

Lieutenants Brown and Sanderson listened to the boy's story and "on a hunch" decided to have him show them where Dyer lived.

The boy directed the two detectives to the Dyer residence, and they door-knocked it and discovered that Albert Dyer was not home. However, his wife Isabel was, and they spoke briefly with her and informed her to tell her husband to come down to the Inglewood Police Headquarters as they wanted to "speak with him."

Here is the rest of the story, as reported in the *Los Angeles Examiner* of July 5, 1937 (see page 179), crediting LAPD Lieutenants Thad Brown and Leroy Sanderson for "*Playing a Hunch Wins for Officers— Might Have Ignored Boy's Clew, but Didn't.*"

Playing a Hunch Wins for Officers

Might Have Ignored Boy's Clew--but Didn't

They played a hunch and it worked out as they thought it might.

That's how the investigators brought about the confession last night of Albert Dyer that he murdered the three little Inglewood girls.

Chronologically the story is:

On Tuesday morning, July 29, the day after the bodies were found, 14-year-old Mike Huerta of 500 Meadowbrook Lane, Inglewood, went to the office of Police Chief Oscar Campbell.

"I got an idea who the murderer is," Mike said to the chief.

The boy then said he suspected Dyer because he had seen Dyer acting suspiciously around little boys and girls and thought him "strange."

SOMETHING TO START ON

Mike had no sooner told his story than Detective Lieuts. Leroy Sanderson and Thad Brown walked into the chief's office to introduce themselves and arrange to work with him on the crime.

"Well, here's something to start with," said Campbell, and he turned Mike over to the two Los Angeles detectives, who listened to his story and, instead of tossing it aside because of Mike's youth, played a hunch.

They took Mike in their automobile and he pointed out Dyer's home at 518 Commercial street. Sanderson and Brown went inside and met Mrs. Dyer. Her husband wasn't home.

"We asked her a few simple questions and she mumbled her replies," said Sanderson last night. "There was nothing really to hang a suspicion on but somehow Brown and I had a hunch that Dyer would be worth watching. It wasn't very strong but strong enough for us to tell Mrs. Dyer to tell her husband we wanted to see him and to come down to headquarters."

PRESENTS ALIBI

Later in the day Dyer appeared and told his story. He said he had been home working around the house on Saturday, the day of the murders. His story sounded reasonable but Sanderson, Brown, Chief Investigator Eugene Williams, of the District Attorney's office, and Captain William Penprase of the sheriff's office all felt the hunch again and decided to have a "shadow" watch Dyer day and night.

Last Friday night Dyer walked into the investigator's headquarters at the Inglewood city hall.

"I want you to tell me why I'm being suspected," he demanded angrily.

"Sit down over there and we'll talk to you later," said Williams.

Later they again took Dyer's statement, this time in more detail.

About nine o'clock yesterday morning, on orders of Sanderson and Williams, two Los Angeles detectives, Williams and Chandler from Los Angeles, took Dyer into the Baldwin Hills.

BEGINS TO BREAK

"Get this man to talk. We believe he's lying," was their command.

At 2:30 yesterday afternoon,

(Continued on Page 4, Col. 4.)

Los Angeles Examiner
July 5, 1937

Hunch Wins

Police Credit Story of Youngster

(Continued From Page 3.)

still in the hills with the two detectives, Dyer began to break. He admitted he had lied in his statement to Williams. He admitted for the first time that he had known the girls and had talked to them in the park.

But when the detectives accused him of the murder all he would do was cry.

That was enough. They took Dyer to the constable's office in Inglewood and sent for Sanderson, Williams and Penprase.

It soon became obvious to the officers that Dyer was "cracking," in police parlance. Their hunch was wroking out.

'I KILLED THEM'

They took him to the District Attorney's office at 5:15 p. m.

Five minutes later Sanderson looked Dyer in the eye and said:

"Now listen, Albert, I know you killed them and if you would rather talk in Inglewood we'll take you down there and you can talk from the City Hall steps."

"I killed them . . . I killed them . . . I killed them," Dyer cried.

DYER PRESENTS ALIBI

Later in the day, Dyer appeared and told his story. He said he had been home working around the house on Saturday, the day of the murders. His story sounded reasonable, but Sanderson, Brown, Chief Investigator Eugene Williams of the District Attorney's office, and Captain William Penprase of the sheriff's office all felt the hunch again and decided to have a "shadow" watch Dyer day and night.

Last Friday night Dyer walked into the investigator's headquarters at the Inglewood city hall.

"I want you to tell me why I'm being suspected," he demanded angrily.

"Sit down over there, and we'll talk to you later," said Williams.

Later, they again took Dyer's statement, this time in more detail.

About nine o'clock yesterday morning, on orders of Sanderson and Williams, two Los Angeles detectives, Williams and Chandler from Los Angeles, took Dyer into the Baldwin Hills.

BEGINS TO BREAK

**"Get this man to talk. We believe he's lying,"
was their command.**

At 2:30 yesterday afternoon, still in the hills with the two detectives, Dyer began to break.

He admitted he had lied in his statement to Williams. He admitted for the first time that he had known the girls and had talked to them in the park.

But when the detectives accused him of the murder, all he would do was cry.

That was enough. They took Dyer to the constable's office in Inglewood and sent for Sanderson, Williams, and Penprase.

It soon became obvious to the officers that Dyer was "cracking" in police parlance. Their hunch was working out.

'I KILLED THEM'

They took him to the District Attorney's office at 5:15 p.m. Five minutes later, Sanderson looked Dyer in the eye and said:

"Now listen, Albert, I know you killed them, and if you would rather talk in Inglewood, we'll take you down there, and you can talk from the City Hall steps."

Author's Note - This was in effect a threat from the detective to "throw Dyer to the wolves" as over a hundred citizens, a "lynch mob," was outside city hall wanting to hang Dyer right then and there. (Keep in mind detectives Sanderson and Brown are attempting to force a confession out of a man with the mental age of an eight-year-old boy.)

**"I killed them...I killed them...I killed them,"
Dyer cried.**

The Confession

As a follow-up to the arrest, detectives in searching Dyer's residence found numerous newspaper articles.

These showed that Dyer had been following the daily accounts which reported witness statements of the girls meeting the suspect in the park and being offered the chance to go "rabbit hunting."

As indicated previously, Dyer knew the girls on sight from his job as a crossing guard and wanted to help in the search and was "following the case."

We are all familiar with the term "leading the witness." We have seen it done in dozens of courtroom dramas. "Objection, your Honor. The prosecutor is "leading the witness." Judges routinely sustain such objections as improper courtroom procedure.

Well, so, too, with police interrogations in attempts to get the suspect "to confess," "leading the witness" is sometimes employed as an interview technique however in police interrogations there are no such courtroom restrictions.

It is not particularly difficult when interrogating an intelligent and mature man or woman, so how much easier to "interrogate and obtain a confession" from a mentally disabled suspect with an eight-year-old mentality?

Daily News July 6, 1937

An anonymous telephone "tip" that Inglewood citizens were forming a "lynch party" to force Dyer's release from County Jail last night led Sheriff Biscailuz to double his guards and to block off his cell from all others. Orders were issued to hold him incommunicado and not to remove him from the cell except on a direct order from the sheriff.

Emotionless, the stark confession of Dyer was released in part last night.

Here is an excerpt from the transcript of the "confession," demonstrating how the interrogating detective is asking leading questions, where he provides the "what, where, when, and how" and, for the most part, allows Dyer to give a "Yes or No" response.

Also, keep in mind this comes after hours of duress and threats to let him explain it to the howling mob outside who want to hang him on the spot.

Judge for yourself.

The question and answer confession as released follows:

Q. It was after you saw the girl in the bathing suit that you saw Madeline, Jeanette, and Marie and talked with them, wasn't it?

A: Yes, sir.

Q. You do string tricks, don't you?

A. Yes, sir.

Q. Did you do any string tricks for those girls Saturday morning in the park?

A. Yes, sir.

Q. Are you sure about that?

A. Yes, sir.

Q. Where were you when you showed them the tricks?

A. Near the ball diamond.

Q. Did you see any book with the children? A Mickey Mouse book?

A. That was with the children.

Q: Which one had the book?

A: I judge it was Madeline.

Q. Just about when did you speak to them, Albert, about going rabbit hunting?

A. That was Saturday morning.

Q. What time was it, and how long had you been in the park?

A. I would judge about two or three hours.

Q. What did you say to them?

A. I asked them if they would go rabbit hunting.

Q. Whom did you ask?

A. Madeline, Jeanette, and Marie.

Q. What did they say?

A. They said they would.

Q. They knew you very well, didn't they?

A. Yes, sir.

Q. And when they said they would go, you left almost immediately, didn't you?

A. Yes, sir.

Q. Then the three children came out of the park and followed you?

A. Yes, sir.

Q. How far ahead of the children?

A. Not very far, a block, I guess.

Q. You kept walking ahead, and they were following you?

A. Yes.

Q. You didn't want anyone to see you with the children, isn't that so?

A. That's right.

Q. Now, when you started from the park, you weren't going home, were you?

A. No, sir.

Q. Then you were taking the children into the hills. What for?

A. To murder them and to have them.

Q. You walked across the bean field, didn't you?

A. Yes, sir.

And so it went.

You get the idea. The detective provided the details in his questions, and the eight-year-old mind of Albert Dyer was simply responding.

With police threats to take him outside and let Dyer "explain it to the citizens on the steps of City Hall," a little man with an eight-year-old mind, "confesses."

Albert's Wife, Isabel Dyer

Mrs. Isabel Dyer was taken into custody for "safekeeping" and detained at the LA County Jail, supposedly in "protective custody."

Authorities said, "she will be detained until the state of feeling in Inglewood, still considered dangerous, subsides. Her appearance as a material witness is not anticipated since she is the wife of the confessed slayer."

Here are excerpts from an article printed in *The Fresno Bee* on July 6, 1937, that helped us get a sense of what Albert Dyer's wife, Isabel, had been through and was experiencing.

...

In the twenty-four years she has lived Isabel has found little peace.

She quit school when she was in the seventh grade because her father had no money to send her further.

She went to work and hoped to marry the boy she cared for. She was sent to reform school instead.

At eighteen, she worked as a maid for a San Francisco family, finally left when the drudgery proved too much for her strength.

Then she met Al, in the romantic setting of a picture show on Market Street.

Two years ago, they were married in Santa Ana.

They hitchhiked to Inglewood, where Al had friends.

And here, they have lived quite contentedly for the past seven months since Al got a WPA job as a crossing guard.

On Easter Sunday, in the blinding rain, they moved into the little shack where they stayed until Dyer was arrested

...

LA County Jail Chief Matron Vada Sullivan said Mrs. Dyer told her that Dyer asked her shortly before the bodies were found to go with him into the hills to aid in the search.

Los Angeles Examiner
July 5, 1937

Mrs. Isabel Dyer, age 24

"No, I can't see how he was capable of this horrible crime. I still can't realize it. I still can't really believe it."

Mrs. Isabel Dyer detained for "safekeeping" in LA County Jail

***Los Angeles Times* July 5, 1937**

On page 2 of the *Los Angeles Times,* we see three separate articles. One was describing the "confession" of the crossing guard, Albert Dyer. The second showing the photograph of a young girl identifying a picture of Fred Godsey as the suspect seen at Centinela Park. The third, "FRIENDS BELIEVED SUSPECT CRAZY BUT HARMLESS," is an interview with Albert Dyer's neighbors and his barber saying Dyer is well known to them and "is crazy, but he's harmless."

FRIENDS BELIEVED SUSPECT CRAZY BUT HARMLESS

How Albert Dyer, confessed Inglewood slayer, "needed a little money" on the Sunday morning following the tragedy, was told last night by C. C. Coop, Inglewood barber.

"He lives around the corner from me in a two-part shack in an alley," Coop said at his home, 510 North Commercial street.

"He said he needed a little money that Sunday and asked if I had any job for him. I gave him $2 to clean the yard and some other work.

"I've known him for about a year. I've shaved him during that time whenever he had money.

"The men in the barber shop have always considered him crazy but harmless. He lies in the chair and rambles, sometimes incoherently. The men have said at times it wouldn't be bad if he were cooped up in a sanitarium."

The Alibi Witnesses

Daily News, July 14, 1937

HAVING ALREADY POINTED OUT several suspects as "the man" she saw playing with the three Inglewood children the Saturday of their murders, Olive Everett, 12, sister of two of the victims, told district attorney investigators yesterday that Haskell Wright, Centinela Park recreation director, had molested her. Wright, pictured above with the girl, told the Grand Jury that the girl's charges were ridiculous. He also testified that he believed Albert Dyer, accused killer, innocent of the crime.

Author's Note - Little Olive Everett's unreliability as a witness has been previously noted. During the trial and months that followed, she would continue to accuse six additional park attendees and employees of "molesting her," all of which were "unfounded."

While I am far from being considered a psychology expert, simply from a lay person's perspective, I would suggest that the murder of Olive Everett's two sisters and her friend, Jeanette Stephens, must have had a massive psychological impact and inflicted horrendous trauma to the twelve-year-old child's mind.

This would be doubly so if what she claimed about the suspect, "Eddie the Sailor," instructing her to go to the local store and bring him some clothesline rope, which she claimed she did in fact do—was true.

Now, imagine the effect, just days later, of discovering that her sisters and friend *were likely strangled to death with that rope. The rope she bought and brought to their killer.* That would cause any normal adult to totally "flip out." So how much more would that knowledge have on the psychology of a child?

Imagine yourself an twelve-year-old thinking, *"I gave the killer the rope that he used to kill my two sisters and friend."*

Little Olive Everett had to be suffering from massive psychological post-traumatic stress. Consequently she tried to do anything to help catch the killer. When shown a photograph from police authority figures, she assumed they had their man and responded to at least three different suspects at three separate times with a, "Yes, that's him. Yes, that's him. Yes, that's him."

The Record
(Hackensack, New Jersey, June 30, 1937)

Witnesses Offer New Evidence In Triple Crime

Two Girls Who Escaped Describe Him

Inglewood, Calif. June 30

A man identified only as Eddie the Sailor by police became Suspect No. 1 today in the search for the degenerate slayer of the three little Inglewood girls.

**Rewards totaling $25,000
spurred the hunt for his capture.**

Eddie the Sailor police learned, almost succeeded in luring two more girls into his automobile Saturday—the day Madeline Everett, 7, her sister Melba, 9, and Jeanette Marjorie Stephens, 8, were slain.

Lillian Popp, 11, told officers she and her cousin almost joined the three victims in what Eddie the Sailor represented was going to be a rabbit hunt in the hills.

"When we reached the car, I kicked my cousin and reminded her in whispers, what her mother had told her about going riding with a strange man," Lillian said. "So, we didn't go, but Melba and Jeanette and Madeline got into the car with the man."

...

Various children who play in the park know a man who has frequented it only as Eddie the Sailor.

Olive (Everett) recalled the man once told her he had helped build the park swimming pool last year. Police found it was built by seven men as a WPA project and sought the seven for questioning.

Author's Note - This article appeared in the newspapers on June 30, 1937, *some five days before Albert Dyer's arrest and alleged "confession."*

Lillian Popp became a critical defense witness in the later trial and testified to the same facts and also eliminated Albert Dyer as the man believed to be "Eddie the Sailor." Lillian Popp described the suspect's vehicle in detail and observed the victims enter it and leave with the suspect "to go rabbit hunting."

Additionally, to my knowledge, none of the names of the seven WPA workers on the list that supposedly were involved in building the park swimming pool were ever made public. I would be very interested in seeing those seven names, one of whom could have been the actual suspect.

The following witnesses were called by the Dyer defense lawyers and testified as alibi witnesses for Albert Dyer, and their statements/ affidavits were published in the local newspapers.

Here is a summary from that article:

WITNESS OFFER NEW EVIDENCE
IN TRIPLE CRIME

Four new witnesses in the Inglewood girls murder case came forward last night with statements tending to bear out the position taken yesterday by Public Defender Frederic H. Vercoe when after Albert Dyer pleaded not guilty to the three kidnappings, ravishings, and murders, said:

"There are persistent rumors that the wrong man has been arrested and charged with the crimes, and a considerable number of persons, more or less familiar with the facts of the case, have expressed a doubt as to whether Albert Dyer is the man who committed the ghastly and horrible crimes."

These witnesses are:

1] Emma A. Robinson, Dyer's landlady, who states she saw and talked with him between noon and 1 p.m. on June 26, the day of the kidnappings.

2] Margaret Rigby, 530 N. Commercial Street, Inglewood, who saw Dyer about 2 p.m. the same day, "picking up paper from in front of my house." Later on, about 5 p.m., she saw and closely observed a tall, very thin, foreign-looking man who came running toward her house, through a field. He was smeared with blood. He was not Dyer, nor did he resemble Dyer, Mrs. Rigby stated.

3] Charles H. Atkins, shoe repair man, 328 Commercial Street, Inglewood, who saw Dyer and his wife, Isabel, in front of his shop about 5 or 6 o'clock in the afternoon.

4] Haskell Wright, Centinela Park recreation director, who in a statement, which he will repeat to the Grand Jury at 2 p.m. today, says he is positive he can identify the "Eddie the Sailor" who was teaching the three girls rope tricks in the park the day before they disappeared.

(**Author's Note**- Wright would later testify and eliminate Albert Dyer as "Eddie the Sailor" and the man with the three victims on the day of their kidnapping.)

Affidavits sworn to by Mrs. Rigby, Mrs Robinson, and Atkins were obtained by an attorney who has been retained by a group of prominent Inglewood citizens to sift the conflicting facts in the case. They are printed in full elsewhere in this edition.

The principal point of the affidavits is to show that Dyer was seen downtown in Inglewood at the noon hour, again at 7 p.m., and again between 5 and 6 p.m. on the day of the kidnappings and murders.

These persons declared he (Dyer) **never had** an **automobile** and that he said **he could not drive one**.

...

In view of these facts, in order to have committed the crimes, Dyer would have had to walk from his home, near which he was seen at 3 p.m. by Mrs. Rigby, to Centinela Park, pick up the three little girls, walk five miles to the Baldwin Hills ravine, commit the murders and the abuses on the children's bodies returned home, changed his clothes.

Salt Lake City Tribune
August 12, 1937

Court Hears Sex-Slayer Called 'Moron'
Psychiatrist Laws Defense Basis For Albert Dyer

Los Angeles, August 19 (UP)

A psychiatrist, Dr. Glen Myers, Thursday described Albert Dyer as a low-grade moron with the "mentality of an illiterate nine or ten-year-old boy."

The defense thus made its principal bid to save Dyer from the gallows for the sex-slaying of three little Inglewood girls, Melba and Madeline Everett, sisters, and Jeannette Stephens.

The defense rested without placing Dyer on the stand, and after the court took under advisement a motion to take the jury to the scene of the slayings.

...

CAN COUNT TEN

"Dyer can count ten, but multiplication and subtraction are as Latin to him," Dr. Myers testified.

"He can neither spell nor remember anything for any length of time. Geography to him is as mysterious as scientific elements to laymen."

Dyer, during his examination, said he did not know how much he would have left if he spent seven cents out of a dollar, and he included "Texas" in his list of the country's largest cities, Dr. Myers said.

The defendant's attorneys read into the record the fifth confession he is alleged to have made, indicating discrepancies among them.

Claim Dyer Not Killer

Among witnesses, the accused man's counsel placed on the stand in an attempt to show that Dyer was not the man seen playing with the three victims in a park before they were lured into the hills, strangled and assaulted, was Lillian Popp, aged nine.

Lillian testified she was with the girls when a man accosted them, offered to buy them ice cream, and take them into the hills on a rabbit hunt. She did not go, but her playmates did and never returned, the child related.

The man was not Dyer, Lillian testified.

THE VERDICT

Oakland Tribune, June 26, 1937

Ventura Star Free Press
August 26, 1937

SLAYER CALM
AS JURY VERDICT SEALS HIS DOOM

Los Angeles, August 26. (U.P.)

Albert Dyer today was found guilty of the murder of three small Inglewood girls.

The jury made no mercy recommendation. It is mandatory under California law that Dyer die on the gallows.

A jury of seven men and five women returned the guilty verdict with no recommendation for mercy after 43 hours of argument. For many hours the count had stood 11 to 1 against Dyer, with one juror holding out against the death penalty.

...

Dyer made nine confessions but later repudiated them and said he confessed only because police officers threatened to throw him to a "lynch mob," which gathered outside the Inglewood jail.

The Dyer Case Investigating Committee

A month before Dyer's scheduled execution, a group of Inglewood citizens held a "mass meeting" at the Inglewood Bowl to assist in Dyer's defense and review all the contradictions in the investigation and subsequent trial.

Los Angeles Evening Citizen News
July 15, 1938

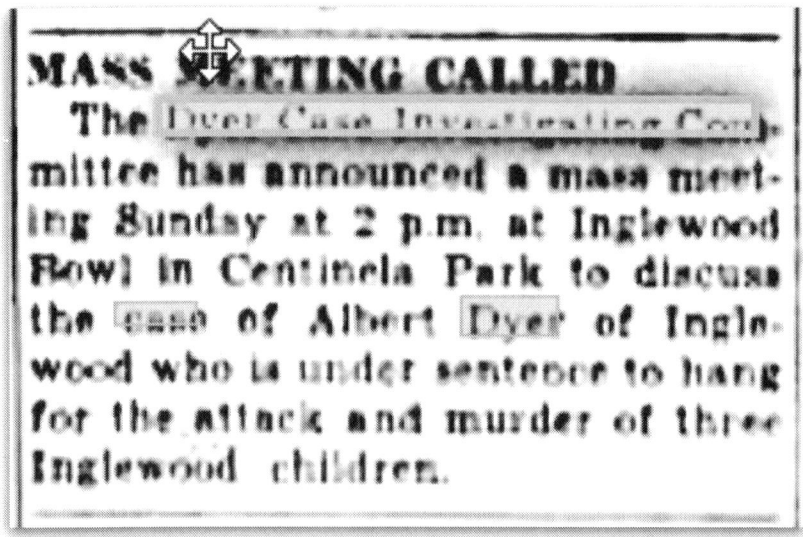

MASS MEETING CALLED

The Dyer Case Investigating Committee has announced a mass meeting Sunday at 2 p.m. at Inglewood Bowl in Centinela Park to discuss the case of Albert Dyer of Inglewood who is under sentence to hang for the attack and murder of three Inglewood children.

San Pedro News Pilot
July 14, 1938

Dyer Case Mass Meeting Sunday

A circular which states "Hanging an innocent moron will not protect our children from further attack" is being distributed by the Dyer Case investigating committee of Inglewood, under chairmanship of R. E. Perry of that city.

The leaflet announces a mass meeting at Inglewood Bowl at 2 p. m. Sunday, and states that "many people doubt the guilt of Albert Dyer," convicted of the fiend-killing of three Inglewood girls and sentenced to hang on September 16.

…"Hanging an innocent moron will not protect our children from further attack"…

But, it was all to no avail.

Los Angeles Examiner
September 12, 1938

In what can be one of the most unusual pleas for clemency that I've ever heard reported, on the day before Albert Dyer's execution, *one of the twelve jurors that convicted him makes a public plea to the governor of California to spare his life, claiming he is convinced* **"another man did it."**

Here is the article reported in the *Los Angeles Examiner*, the day before Dyer's scheduled execution.

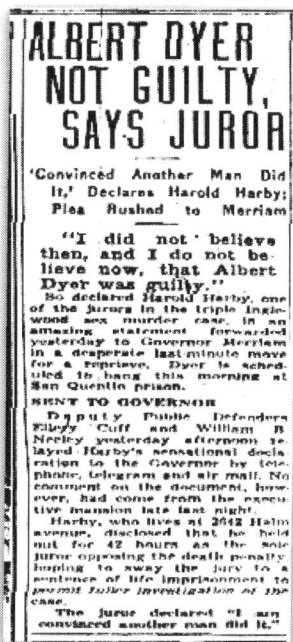

ALBERT DYER NOT GUILTY, SAYS JUROR

'Convinced Another Man Did It,' Declares Harold Harby; Plea Rushed to Merriam

NOT GUILTY, SAYS JUROR

'Convinced Another Man Did It,' Declares Harold Harby; Plea Rushed to Merriam

So declared Harold Harby, one of the jurors in the triple Inglewood sex murder case. In an amazing statement forwarded yesterday to Governor Merriam in a desperate last-minute move for a reprieve. Dyer is scheduled to hang this morning at San Quentin prison.

SENT TO GOVERNOR

Deputy Public Defenders Ellery Cuff and William B. Neeley yesterday afternoon relayed Harby's sensational declaration to the governor by telephone, telegram, and airmail. No comment on the document, however, had come from the executive mansion late last night.

Harby, who lives at 3642 Halm Avenue, disclosed that he held out for 42 hours as the sole juror opposing the death penalty, hoping to sway the jury to a sentence of life imprisonment to permit fuller investigation of the case.

The juror declared, "I am convinced another man did it."

SIX WOMEN AND SIX MEN SELECTED FOR SLAYING JURY

Albert Dyer jury was selected in August 1937.
Juror Harold Harby (arrow)

The Execution

San Quentin Prison

On September 16, 1938, just over one year after he was found guilty, with no appeals left, Albert Dyer walked up the thirteen steps at the prison gallows, a noose was placed around his neck, the trap door opened, and he dropped to a slow, torturous death.

Witnesses watched as he writhed in agony for thirteen long minutes until his heart finally stopped beating.

"No friends to claim his body, which was shunted off to the prison cemetery in a rough wood box."

The Press

The real judge, jury, and executioner in the Albert Dyer "Inglewood Babes Murder" was, in actuality—The Press. All six Los Angeles newspapers. Each was vying for the bigger headlines to sell their dailies.

On a local level, in Los Angeles, the sensationalized coverage of this 1937 murder investigation equaled or surpassed the infamous Leopold and Loeb Murder Trial.

From Day One of Albert Dyer's arrest, in their minds, the press had determined he was "guilty" and portrayed him to the public as such.

Dyer, the sex-crazed maniac. Dyer, a "Dr. Jekyll, and Mr. Hyde." "A Monster."

And sadly, Albert Dyer, "the Moron," performed and posed for them just like a trained seal would.

Here are just a few of the *free and fair press* photo depictions of the "innocent until proven guilty" young man with the eight-year-old mentality.

Daily News, Los Angeles

DAILY NEWS, LOS ANGELES, CALIF.

May Know Fate Today

Accused and Accuser as Artist Sees Them

Albert Dyer in Court

T. Costa

THROUGH THE UNDERSTANDING EYES and sensitive pencil and brush of P. Tino Costa, world-celebrated portrait painter, The Daily News today presents two sketches that point out contrasts in the trial of Albert Dyer, now swiftly running to its climax. Agony, protest, choking fear are engraved on the face of Madeline Everett (above) as she tugs at the rope about her neck. This sketch is from a photograph taken of the child lying in the Baldwin Hills murder gulch. The sketch of Dyer (left) was done by Costa in court last Friday at the close of the prosecution's rebuttal. "Dyer," the artist says, "is to me the victim of an oversensual temperament. His deep-set eyes, his full, curling upper lip and flaring nostrils show violent, uncontrollable passion."

Rev. Dr. Briegleb

"THROUGH THE UNDERSTANDING EYES and sensitive pencil and brush of P. Tino Costa, world celebrated portrait painter, *The Daily News* today presents two sketches that point out contrasts in the trial of Albert Dyer, now swiftly running to its climax. Agony, protest, choking fear are engraved on the face of Madeline Everett (above) as she tugs at the rope about her neck. This sketch is from a photograph taken of the child lying in the Baldwin Hills murder gulch. The sketch of Dyer (left) was done by Costa in court last Friday at the close of the prosecution's rebuttal. "Dyer," the artist says, "is to me the victim of an oversensual temperament. His deep-set eyes, his full, curling upper lip, and flaring nostrils show violent, uncontrollable passion."

Author's Note - How is that caption for "yellow journalism!" *The Daily News* outdid themselves. That copy is way beyond yellow; let's call it AMBER JOURNALISM.

John and Jane Q. Citizen open their morning paper not only to read **but to see the alleged child rape/ murderer strangling the life out of one of his three child victims**. Is there really any need for a trial?

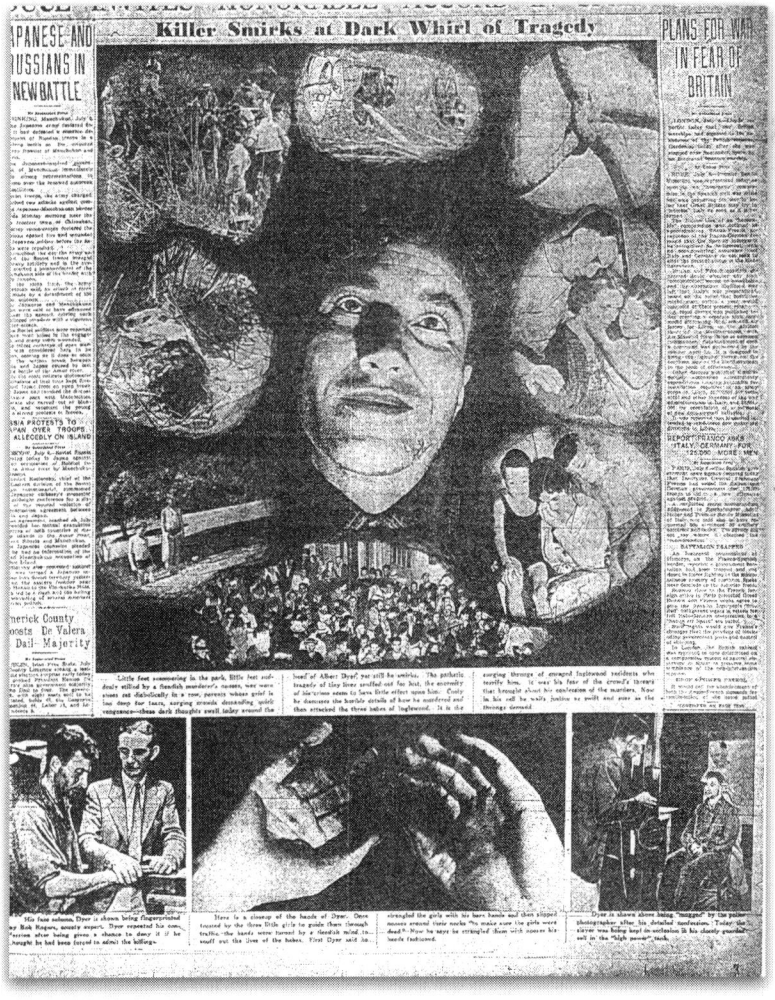

Caption (top page 207) - Little feet scampering in the park, little feet suddenly stilled by a fiendish murderer's nooses, wee worn shoes set diabolically in a row, parents whose grief is too deep for tears, surging crowds demanding quick vengeance—these dark thoughts swell today around the head of Albert Dyer, yet still he smirks. The pathetic tragedy of tiny lives snuffed out for lust, the enormity of his crime seem (sic) to have little effect upon him. Cooly (sic), he discusses the horible (sic) details of how he murdered and then attacked the three babes of Inglewood. It is the surging throngs of enraged Inglewood residents who terrify him. It was his fear of the crowd's threats that brought about his confession of the murders. Now in his cell, he waits justice as swift and sure as the throngs' demand.

Caption (lower left page 207) His face solemn, Dyer is shown being fingerprinted by Bog Rogers, county expert. Dyer repeated his confession after being given a chance to deny it if he thought he had been forced to admit the killings.

Caption (lower center page 207) Here is a closeup of the hands of Dyer. Once trusted by the three little girls to guide them through traffic, the hands were turned by a fiendish mind to snuff out the lives of the babes. First, Dyer said he strangled the girls with his bare hands and then slipped nooses around their necks "to make sure the girls were dead." Now he says he strangled them with nooses, his hands fashioned.

Caption (lower right) Dyer is shown above being "mugged" by the police photographer after his detailed confession. Today the slayer was being kept in seclusion in his closely guarded cell in the "high power" tank.

Herald Express August 4, 1937

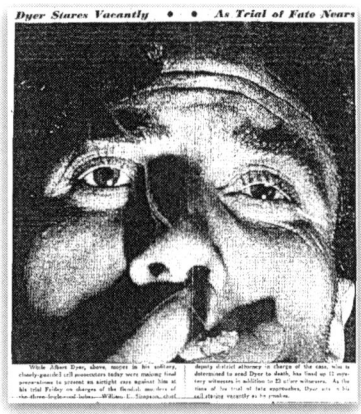

While Albert Dyer, above, mopes in his solitary, closely guarded cell prosecutors today were making final preparations to present an airtight case against him at his trial Friday on charges of the fiendish murders of the three Inglewood babes. William Simpson, chief deputy district attorney in charge of the case, who is determined to send Dyer to death, has lined up 12 mystery witnesses in addition to 23 other witnesses. As the time of his trial of fate approaches, Dyer sits in his cell, staring vacantly as he smokes.

A childlike Albert Dyer posing for the Press

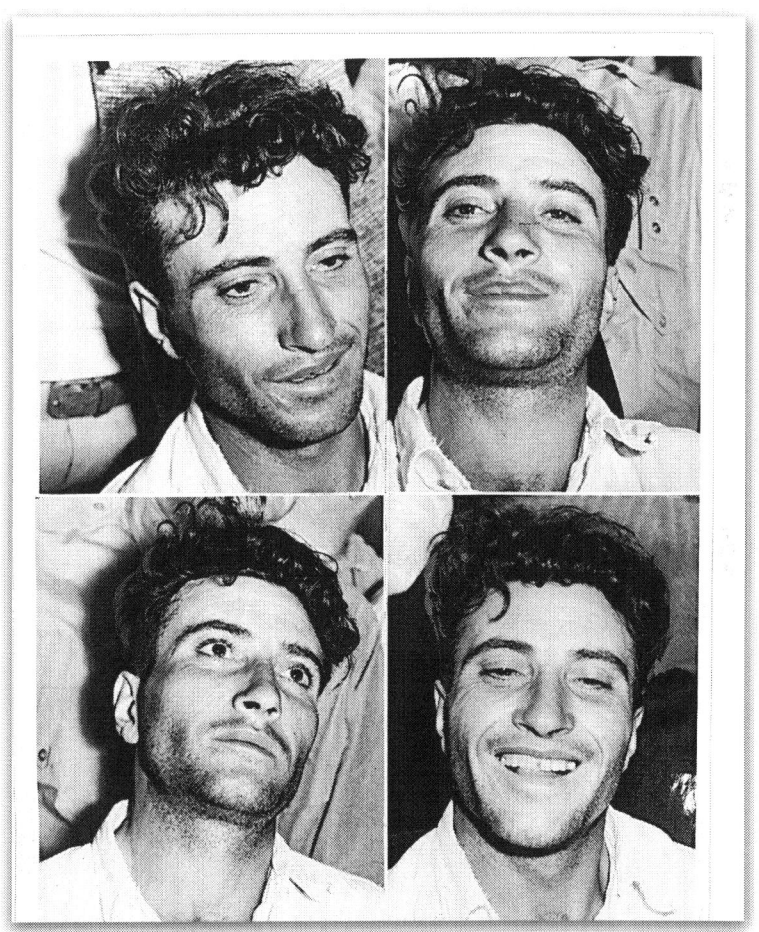

"Come on, Al baby, Big Smile for the camera."

Keyhole View of Dyer Case Newspaper Publicity

Thousands of Press Clippings Generated June - August 1937

MY ANALYSIS

Did Albert Dyer kidnap, rape, and strangle to death the three Inglewood Babes?

I think not.

Were officers from the Los Angeles and Inglewood Police Departments along with the press equally responsible for conducting a wrongful investigation and public influencing that combined to result in the execution of an innocent man?

I think yes.

The Death Penalty - SKH Personal Opinion

In the year of my retirement from LAPD (1986), a Gallup poll was taken that revealed most Americans (56%) favored the death penalty over life imprisonment.

That same survey was taken in October 2020 and showed a national reversal with 60% favoring Life Imprisonment with no possibility of parole and 36% favoring the death penalty.

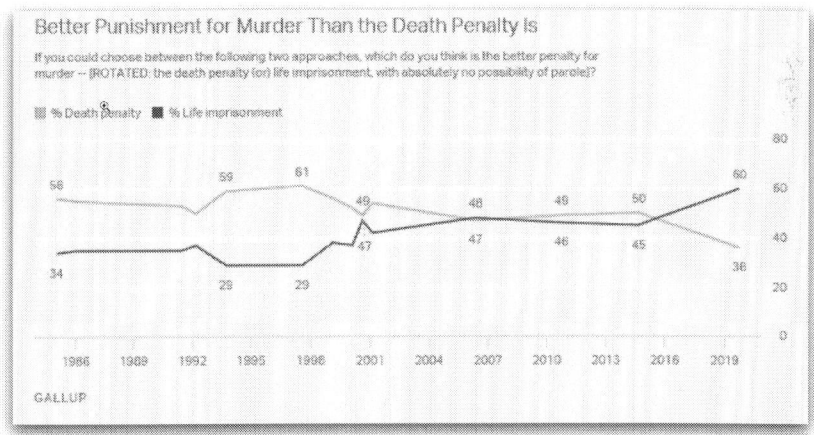

While I am unaware of any official poll taken in the law enforcement community, I would expect that the numbers would be exceptionally high. My guesstimate would be somewhere around 90% pro-death penalty.

This position is understandable as they remain on the front lines of victim abuse and see the daily brutality of the innocents.

Women and children raped, tortured, and murdered. Conscienceless thrill kills. Unimaginable domestic crime scene horrors that equal any battlefield brutalities.

No wonder that most of those officers, standing alone in the shoes of the dead victims, as their sole advocates for justice, demand "an eye for an eye."

As most of my readers know, I have been a homicide detective for fifty years now.

My training as an LAPD rookie detective began in 1969 after six years in uniform patrol.

During my service as an LAPD Hollywood Detective, I conducted over three hundred murder investigations. Several of my convicted killers remain to this day on death row in California prisons.

Despite the "been-there-done-that," I am strongly opposed to the death penalty.

My reason is not based on compassion for the killer, nor on any religious grounds.

It is based SOLELY on the possibility of WRONGFUL CONVICTION.

Current conservative statistics estimate that about 4% of all incarcerated prisoners in the US have been wrongfully convicted. As of 2019, the prison population in the US was **1.4 million.** If that 4% statistical estimate holds true, that could mean, the US Justice System has incarcerated some **56,000 wrongfully convicted** persons.

Per the Criminal Justice Project, there are currently **2,620 on death row** in the United States. According to the 4% statistical estimate, **105 of those awaiting a death may have been wrongfully convicted.**

In this just-published two-volume set of *The Early Years* Part I (The 1920s) and Part II (The 1930s), we have seen dramatic examples of what I believe were unquestionably wrongful convictions.

The first being the wrongful conviction and imprisonment of the elderly nightwatchman, S.C. Stone, in the 1927 Martin Sisters murders. Imprisoned for fourteen years and eventually pardoned by the governor of California.

The second was the wrongful conviction and execution of Albert Dyer, the severely retarded twenty-eight-year-old crossing guard, with an "eight-year-old mentality" for the 1937 triple rape-murders of the "Three Inglewood Babes."

Setting aside whether George Hodel and Fred Sexton were the actual killers of the Martin Sisters and the later Everett sisters and Stephen's girl, there can be no doubt that both Stone and Dyer were innocent.

Speaking both from a personal and professional position, I gladly join the now majority of Americans in opposition to the death penalty and support LIFE IMPRISONMENT WITH THE POSSIBILITY OF PAROLE.

Steve Hodel
Los Angeles, California
December 28, 2020

San Quentin Inmate Intake - September 5, 1937

Fingerprint Classification 31 - II / 32 - OL / 15

Fingerprint Reference

Age 32
Eyes Hazel
Hair Dark Brown
Complexion Med
Weight 131 ½

Nat. N. Y.
Teeth Fair
Chin Sq
English Height 5' 2 ½"
Build Med

Description taken at San Quentin SEP 5 1937, 19____, by Mull

Police and Witness Description
suspect in park was "5-10"

Albert Dyer was 5'2"

When you look at the case objectively, nothing really fits.

Without going into a long dissertation and without the benefit of all the official police reports and witness interviews, below are a few bullet points which, in themselves, would be enough to create an exculpatory finding, and if not that, then certainly enough to form a "reasonable doubt."

- As initially described, **suspect was a man of 5'-10"** in height and **150-60 pounds** in weight.

- According to his Inmate Intake at San Quentin, **Dyer was 5'2" and weighed 131 pounds**.

- Multiple witnesses who saw the suspect with the three girls eliminated Dyer and affirmed in the trial that "He was not the man with the girls at the park on the day they were kidnapped." Dyer's positive elimination included the Centinela Park Director, who saw a man with the victims on the day of their disappearance.

- Multiple witnesses testified in court and provided formal sworn affidavits that they had seen Dyer in his neighborhood at different hours "noon," "2 p.m.", "5 p.m.," effectively ruling him out as the suspect seen with the girls.

- Dyer had no vehicle and could not drive, and the witnesses clearly established and testified that they were with the victims and saw them get into the suspect's vehicle at Centinela Park and drive off to "go rabbit hunting."

- The prosecution's claim that Dyer walked a block ahead, and the girls followed him from the park to the

Baldwin Hills area on foot, which is highly questionable as the distance is over five miles.

- The LAPD fingerprint expert claimed he obtained "clear, identifiable fingerprints" from the crime scene, but then at trial, they claimed the opposite, that they were "not clear." Leads one to suspect the fingerprints originally obtained were not those of Dyer; therefore, somebody may simply have *round filed* them?

- Coroner Dr. Wagner testified that suspect sperm was obtained from all three victims. Those slides could/ should have been analyzed for blood type and RH factor and compared to Dyer's blood. There are three possibilities: this analysis was done and it did not match Dyer, the test was done but "no match" was found to any suspect, or no such test was performed.

- The fact that all three victims were sexually assaulted, and that male ejaculate was found in each of their bodies argues strongly in support of more than one perpetrator. It is highly likely at least two suspects were involved in the sexual assault of the three young girls. Based on the location, and time restrictions, it is hard to imagine that one man could have strangled, raped and performed three separate sex acts to climax all within the documented short time span.

- "Nine separate confessions" were obtained by law enforcement. These "confessions" contained numerous contradictions. The transcript introduced at trial, as previously noted, contained "leading questions" and only required a simple "yes" or "no" response from the suspect.

- Before Dyer's arrest, positive identification by percipient witnesses, including Olive Everett, were made, and APBs (All Points Bulletins) were issued for the separate suspects, each of whom had an ironclad alibi.

- Based on the facts, it is doubtful that a single suspect could have committed all three crimes without a second suspect's aid to assist. There were mentions of "a second possible suspect," but no follow-up was ever released to the public.

- At least six different psychologists tested Albert Dyer, and they agreed his IQ was in the 55-60 range, which in the terminology of that day was equal to that of a "Moron." His mental age was found to be that of an "8-10-year-old boy."

- Dyer recanted his "confession" and claimed he only made it because he was terrified when the officers told him they "would release him to the angry mob of a thousand persons who were yelling 'hang him' and were ready and willing to lynch him then and there on the steps of City Hall."

- They promised Dyer they would not turn him over to the yelling angry mob and would protect him if "he confessed" to killing the three children.

- All of the above is well documented, and "what we know occurred." What else was said or done to the little man with the handicapped mentality, presumed to be the child rapist/killer of three innocent children, while in police custody (physical harm, threats, sleep deprivation, etc.), we can only guess.

Fred Sexton and or
Dr. George Hill Hodel as Suspects?

Could either of these men or both be the real kidnap/rape/murderers of "The Inglewood Babes?"

Yes, I think much exists that can potentially link one or possibly both men to the crimes through the physical description and MO (Method of Operation).

It is my personal belief, in considering all the known facts, that the "Eddie the Sailor" description seems to fit more closely to Fred Sexton, based on clothing, his actions, and demeanor, possible vehicle, etc., than it does to George Hodel.

That said, the physical comparison of Hodel to suspect Othel Strong (shown below) cannot be ignored, as it is almost "picture perfect."

Let's take a look.

Physical Description

We recall that witnesses at the park, as well as Olive Everett (sister to two of the victims), positively identified both Othel Strong and Fred Godsey (at separate times) as being the suspect, "Eddie the Sailor." She claimed this was the same man who had her go obtain a length of clothesline from a nearby store and then showed all of the girls rope tricks and who later in the morning took her two sisters and Jeanette "rabbit hunting."

Author's Note - I seriously question whether Olive's story did occur, that she went to a store and purchased a rope. While the police report to confirm this may exist somewhere, I have not seen it. The incident as described may well have been the child's fantasy, which could and should have been easily confirmed by contact with the store owner.

George Hodel and Fred Sexton

George Hodel 1936-7   Fred Sexton 1932   Fred Sexton 1944

Hodel   Strong   Sexton   Godsey

George Hodel compared to Othel Strong compared to Fred Sexton compared to Fred Godsey

Both George Hodel and Fred Sexton closely fit the circulated "Wanted Suspect" composite description of the killer.

George Hodel -

Male, age 30, 6' 150, black hair, mustache.

Fred Sexton -

Male, age 30, 5-10, 150-60, black hair, mustache.

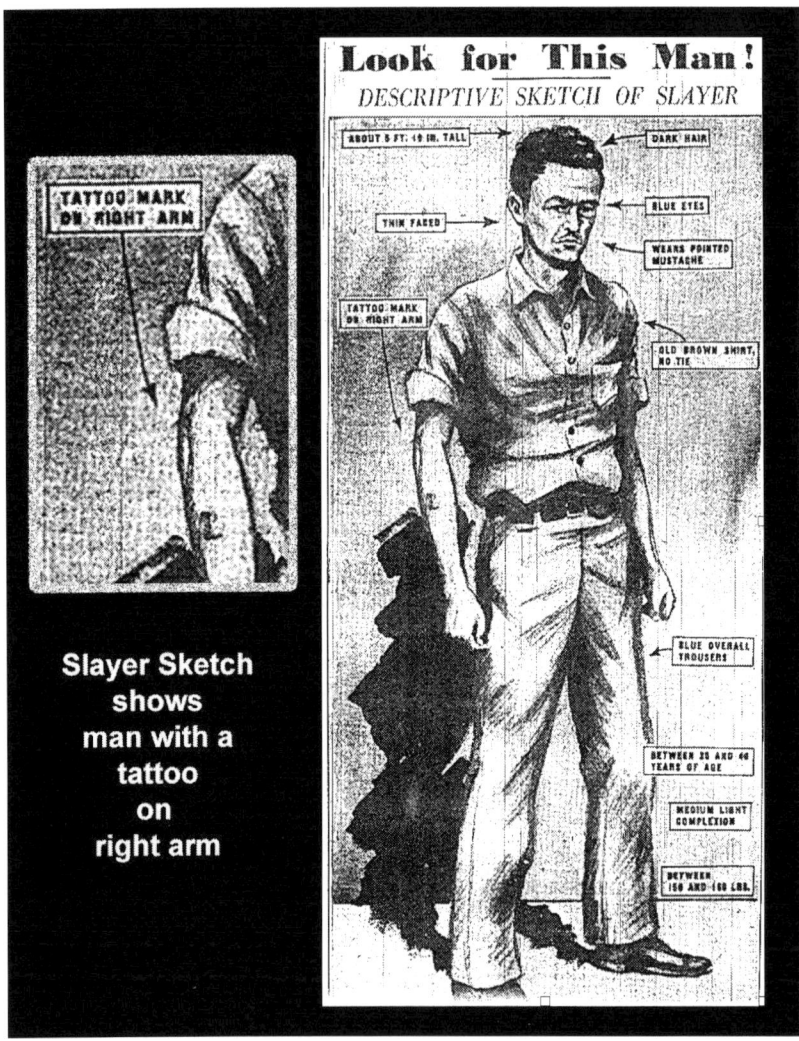

Author's Note - Blow-up (on left) of right arm from "DESCRIPTIVE SKETCH OF SLAYER" inserted above for clarity. **Question**: Where is the testimony that Dyer or any other "suspect" had a "tattoo mark on right arm" as indicated in the newspaper sketch shown here (above) and on page 157.

Earlier in this chapter (page 194), I included an article from *The Record* (Hackensack, New Jersey, June 30, 1937) entitled, *"Witnesses Offer New Evidence In Triple Crime; Two Girls Who Escaped Describe Him."*

It contained the following paragraph.

> **"Various children who play in the park know a man who has frequented it only as Eddie the Sailor. Olive (Everett) recalled the man once told her he had helped build the park swimming pool last year. Police found it was built by seven men as a WPA project and sought the seven for questioning."**

During my 1999-2001 investigation I interviewed Joe Barrett, a family friend of my parents, who lived and rented a room in our home in Hollywood during the 1940s.

Barrett knew Fred Sexton, who was a regular visitor and good friend of my father, George Hodel.

In one of my interviews with Joe (there were many), I attempted to obtain as much background information on my father and his good friend, Sexton.

I knew Sexton had been involved and arrested by LAPD, along with my father, George Hodel, for the 1949 sexual molestation of my half-sister, Tamar, who was then just fourteen years old.

I also knew from an earlier interview with Fred Sexton's daughter (referred to as "Mary Moe" in *Black Dahlia Avenger*) that he "had sexually molested her from age eight to eleven." (The same ages as the three "Inglewood Babes.")

During my interview with Joe Barrett, he mentioned that "Fred had worked at the film studios as a 'prop man,' and before that, during the Depression, he had done various jobs working for the WPA and had worked at a park in Inglewood."

My current recollection was that Barrett had indicated something about Sexton, an accomplished artist of note, "doing artwork on the park buildings." Still, my memory is unclear on that point.

That piece of information had no real meaning to me then. However, in light of what Olive Everett stated in the above article in 1937, "that the suspect told her he had helped build the swimming pool," it is certainly within the realm of possibility that his name just might have been one of the seven names referenced back then.

Physical Evidence

The Ligatures

All three of the victims were manually strangled to death using a clothesline's precut length tied tightly around their necks.

A photograph (top of page 223) of one of those ligatures as displayed during the courtroom trial of Albert Dyer. The testimony was that the ligature was "tied in the back with a double hitch knot."

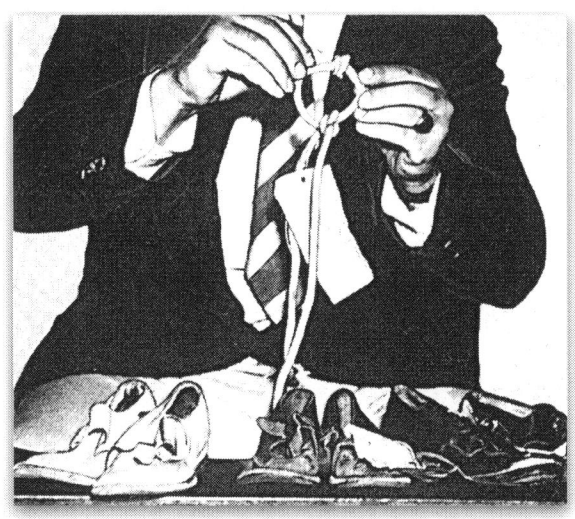

[see: https://www.101knots.com/two-half-hitches.html]

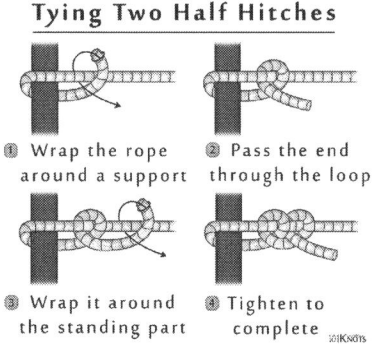

Tying Two Half Hitches

① Wrap the rope around a support

② Pass the end through the loop

③ Wrap it around the standing part

④ Tighten to complete

A "double hitch knot" comprises two half hitches.

Now let us compare this to the type of ligature used in the later known serial crimes of George Hodel and Fred Sexton.

The photographs (on 224) show the clothesline ligatures with "double hitch knot" used to strangle Chicago child kidnap/murder victim Suzanne Degnan, age 8 in 1946, and adult victim Louise Springer in 1949.

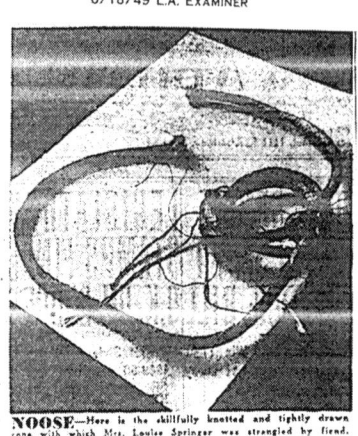

SPRINGER KNOT
6/18/49 L.A. EXAMINER

NOOSE—Here is the skillfully knotted and tightly drawn rope with which Mrs. Louise Springer was strangled by fiend.
—Los Angeles Examiner photo.

Degnan noose 1/8/46
Chicago

police bills in 5's & 10's."
—Associated Press wirephoto.

CLEW—This soiled piece of a clothes line is believed to have been used in the gruesome killing of Suzanne. It was found in the basement of building in which Hector Verburgh, the suspect, served as a janitor.

Precut clothesline brought and used in 1969 Lake Berryessa murder

Author's Note - Ligature strangulation was the method and cause of death in most of George Hodel and Fred Sexton's serial murders through the decades. (25 crimes to date). Most of the ligatures were not included as press photographs in the newspapers. But, I expect nearly all of them followed this unusual MO of bringing precut clothesline with them to use on their victims.

"The Little Shoes"

As previously noted, all three victims' shoes were neatly "posed" next to their bodies.

Posing was an essential part of both George Hodel and Fred Sexton's crimes.

Both men would expect their horrific crimes to terrorize the public and thus used them as public taunts to the police and the press, in particular, because such acts got them "above the fold" headline publicity.

Photo of "Inglewood Babes" shoes posed by their bodies.

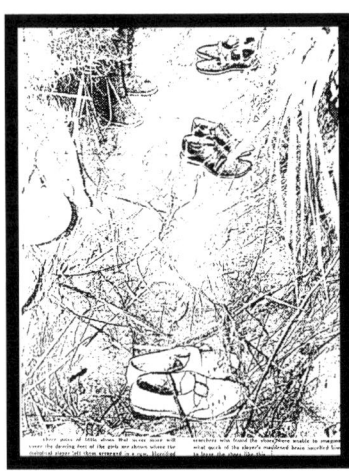

The "posing" in many of George Hodel and Fred Sexton's later serial crimes was likely not made public in all cases.

However, in the 1947 murder of Los Angeles victim Jeanne French, one of their more dramatic forms of posing was made public.

In that crime, George Hodel posed the badly beaten nude body of his victim in a vacant lot, and using lipstick from her purse, he wrote on the victim's body a taunting message for police and press that read, "FUCK YOU, BD."

**Victim's shoes posed in 1947 murder of Jeanne French
by George Hodel and Fred Sexton**

Additional posing in the Jeanne French murder consisted of putting her clothing and fur coat carefully on top of her nude body and ***removing her shoes and meticulously placing them on each side of her head, ten feet from the body,*** as reported in the *Daily News* article below.

Daily News - February 10, 1947

Were George Hodel and or Fred Sexton responsible for the kidnapping and murder of these three innocent children?

Absent fingerprint or DNA linkage, it is impossible to include or exclude them as possible suspects.

But, as we move forward through the next chapters, let us at least keep an open mind and reserve judgment.

And also, as I close this chapter, let us consider the following as part of the "Big Picture."

The Thad Brown, William Simpson Connection

Thad Brown
LAPD
Chief of Detectives

William L. Simpson
LA County
District Attorney

The "Inglewood Babes Murder" investigation was in the year 1937.

We have learned that LAPD Detective Thad Brown was actively involved in this investigation.

More than that, Thad Brown was credited publicly with "following his hunch" after being tipped off by a teenager that Albert Dyer was "acting strangely."

Lieutenant Brown, accompanied by his partner, Lt. Leroy Sanderson, made "the first contact" with Dyer and ordered his wife to have Dyer come in for questioning.

We know where it went from there. The fact is, there likely would never have been any Albert Dyer arrest had it not been for the "hunch following" of Lieutenants Brown and Sanderson.

Also, let us recall that LAPD detective Thad Brown also played an active role in the investigation of Aimee Semple McPherson in both her "kidnapping" and then later in her 1944 death by "accidental overdose of Seconal."

Now back to the 1937 Dyer trial.

The man who ran the show for DA Buron Fitts and prosecuted Albert Dyer was Chief Prosecutor–Deputy DA William Simpson.

The Dyer conviction was a big win for Simpson, who effectively "made his bones" with the powers that be in LA County and with the public. So much so that Simpson would become "Mr. DA" for Los Angeles County. His administration would run from the years 1946 to 1951.

So, too, with his old buddy Thaddeus Brown, who rose quickly within the ranks of LAPD and was appointed, Chief of Detectives during Simpson's reign as District Attorney.

As documented in my book *Black Dahlia Avenger* both of these men were in power and were in charge of the Elizabeth "Black Dahlia" Short kidnap/rape/murder that occurred on January 15, 1947.

Both of these men were the "top law enforcement officers" that identified and would later privately acknowledge that Dr. George Hill Hodel was known to be the killer of Elizabeth Short, known to the world as the "Black Dahlia." Both men also knew that he had committed other "Lone Woman Murders" in Los Angeles during the 1940s.

DA Simpson and Chief of Detectives Brown oversaw and were aware of the "electronic tape-recorded confessions" George Hodel made—admitting he had killed Elizabeth Short and his medical clinic personal secretary, Ruth Spaulding. Both men knew Dr. George Hill Hodel had fled the country to avoid arrest and prosecution for those crimes.

Despite having a strong prosecutable case, these same two high-ranking officials decided not to obtain a warrant for his arrest or attempt to extradite him from a foreign territory or country.

Instead, it was Thad Brown and William Simpson who chose to lock away the LA DA Secret Hodel/Black Dahlia files and facilitate *the cover-up of what was most certainly a tape-recorded murder during the electronic stakeout of Dr. Hodel's residence.* (The crime involved Hodel and an accomplice going to the basement of the Franklin Avenue residence, beating a woman who cried out several times before she was knocked unconscious and likely slain. The two men were then recorded, saying,

"Don't leave a trace." See *Black Dahlia Avenger* for full details.)

Armed with the hindsight of these "Early Years" potential crimes, I am forced to ask myself this question—Is it possible that my father, perhaps after being informed by a "friendly" that he was about to be arrested in 1950 and "had been recorded," made contact with one or both of these two men?

That he then communicated either directly or through a confederate something along the following lines:

WAS THERE A DEAL?

Look, I am leaving the country and will never return. I will become invisible.

However, if I am arrested and charged with any crime, I will reveal what I know and have known since the 1920s and 30s. I know who did what and when to whom.

Also, you know that 1937 triple murder that you tried and won a conviction on? Well, guess what? You executed an innocent man. Albert Dyer didn't kill those little girls; I did.

I committed those crimes and will "tell-all" if I am taken down.

I have left a signed, sealed statement with my attorney "to be opened only in case of my death," which lays out all I know as relates to graft and corruption from the Twenties forward. I have named names and dates, and locations. If I remain free, then so do YOU. If I am arrested, all will be revealed. Choose wisely.

G. Hill Hodel, MD.

Author's Note - Granted, the above "deal" is speculative and may never have occurred, but knowing what we know, it certainly is within the realm of possibilities, or something close to it could well have happened.

I will close this chapter with a "thoughtprint" anecdote that I wrote about in *Black Dahlia Avenger* and then included on my blog site (www.stevehodel.com/blog) some eleven years ago, that adds a little more "meat to the bone."

LAPD Chief Thad Brown & Steve Hodel

But, as we move forward to the next chapters, let us continue to keep an open mind and reserve judgment.

1966 In front of—Parker Center "The Glass House."

**Officer Steve Hodel and Chief Thad Brown
From "The Squad Room Blog"**
(www.stevehodel.com/blog)

The 1966 Parker Center Photo

By Steve Hodel | December 26, 2009

Q: *I'm confused on how the LAPD Chief Thad Brown photograph taken with you as a rookie police officer connects to the Black Dahlia murder. Can you explain it?*

Yes. The above photograph (page 233) was taken in 1966, in front of what was then known as the LAPD's PAB. (Not long after this photo was taken, the Police Administration Building was renamed **Parker Center** in honor of Chief William H. Parker.)

Immediately after Parker's death in 1966, then Chief of Detectives Thad Brown was named as Los Angeles's interim chief of police. (This is common for a high-ranking officer to be selected and assume command while other staff officers prepare to compete for the exam, orals, and permanent selection.)

In 1966, with only three years on the job, I was a rookie officer working Hollywood Patrol and was sent, along with a dozen other officers from Hollywood, to attend Thad Brown's swearing-in ceremony in the police auditorium.

Immediately after the ceremony, **a photographer approached me** as I was walking out the front door and asked, "Would you like to have your picture taken with the new chief?" Surprised and honored, I readily agreed, and Chief Brown smiled as we walked out in front of the building where this photograph was taken. About three weeks later, I received this copy through the Inter-Department mails. I threw it in a box and forgot about it.

The photo had no real meaning or significance to me, other than the obvious honor of being with the chief.

However, we now know it had tremendous meaning and import to Thad Brown. He knew then what I would not discover for another 35 years. Thad Brown KNEW I was the son of the Black Dahlia killer, and it is obvious to me he just could not resist the "photo-op."

It would not be until after the completion of my investigation and the publication of my book that we would learn from an LAPD reserve officer about the conversation between Thad Brown and actor Jack Webb, his close friend who played LAPD's Sgt. Joe Friday.

In that confidential conversation, Thad Brown disclosed to Jack Webb, **"We know who killed the Black Dahlia. The case was solved. It was a doctor in Hollywood, who lived on Franklin Avenue."**

This was Chief Brown's independent and separate confirmation of what we discovered from the DA DAHLIA/HODEL Files.

Those files, opened in 2003 as a result of my investigation, revealed Dr. George Hodel to be the prime Black Dahlia suspect as of late 1949.

Chapter 5

The San Diego & Surrounds, Serial Crimes
1930-1947

This chapter covers the eight 1930s San Diego area murders (plus one in 1947) along with two northern Mexico area murders which together* span a period of seventeen years from 1930-1947. [*See map on page 3.]

San Diego law enforcement believes most or all these separate crimes were committed by the same suspect(s).

I here present these murders in the chronological order of their commission.

Murders No. 1 & 2 - Francis Conlon and Lois Kentle

Miami News, November 9, 1930

Below is a blow-up of the upper righthand section of *Miami News*, November 9, 1930 article, page (236), showing a photograph of the Conlon-Kentle crime scene at Ensenada Beach in Mexico, where the young couple was slain while they slept in their pup tent.

Tuesday, August 26, 1930

The bodies of Francis Conlon, age 24, and his fiancée, Lois Kentle, age 23, were found partially buried in the sand on an Ensenada Beach some sixty miles south of San Diego, California, in Lower (Baja) California, Mexico.

Both victims had been attacked while sleeping inside their small tent at the waterfront.

The killer(s) entered the tent and stabbed Conlon eleven times and stabbed his fiancée, Lois, seven times.

The bodies were then dragged a short distance and buried in the sand in shallow graves. Robbery was not a motive as both victims' valuables were untouched. There were no

VICTIMS OF STABBING

Lovers Slain While Asleep on Beach

LOIS KENTLE ~ AGE 23   FRANCIS CONLON ~ AGE 24

witnesses to the crime, and no physical evidence was found to assist in furthering the investigation.

Relatives from Pasadena, California, reported that the couple became engaged after meeting at a paint company where Conlon was employed as a salesman and where Lois worked in the office.

San Diego police assisted Ensenada Police Department officers in providing and gathering information on the victims, but all to no avail.

No solid suspects were ever identified, and the crime to this day remains unsolved.

San Diego police consider this double murder as possibly connected to other unsolved serial murders that followed in the 1930s and 1940s in the San Diego County area.

The suspect viciously attacked both victims with a long-bladed knife and then dragged and placed their bodies in shallow graves just fifteen feet from the tent.

Below is the section of *Miami News*, November 9, 1930, article showing an artist's rendition depicting the Mexican Bar's interior that the victims were believed to have visited the evening of August 25, 1930 before setting up their camp at a nearby beach.

PASADENA POST AUGUST 27, 1930

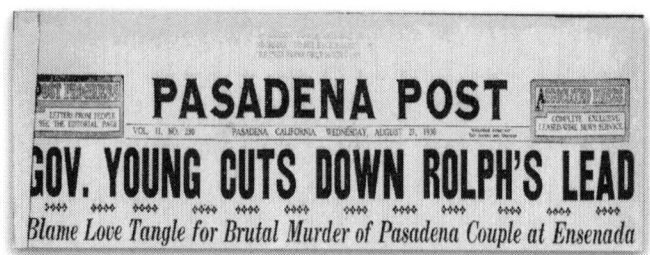

"BLAME LOVE TANGLE FOR BRUTAL MURDER OF PASADENA COUPLE AT ENSENADA"

Excerpts from THE PASADENA POST:

TWO NATIONS JOIN SEARCH FOR SLAYER

End of Honeymoon Book Found Near Girl; Lovers Planned Marriage

Jealousy today was blamed for the brutal slaying of Francis Conlon, former Pasadena high school football star, and his fiancée, Lois Kentle, stabbed to death as they lay asleep on the sand near Ensenada Monday night.

Working upon the theory that the murder of the Pasadena couple was the result of a love tangle, police authorities of two nations today began an intensive search for a third man reported to have been seen with the two lovers only a few hours before they were slain.

Scrutinize Past Lives

While Mexican police, border guards, and San Diego police spread a net around the border hills in an effort to trap the unknown killer, investigators here sought information concerning the past lives of the murdered pair and about any other admirers of Miss Kentle and their whereabouts at the time of the killing.

Neither Miss Kentle's jewels nor Conlin's (sic) pocketbook had been disturbed, exploding the theory that robbery might have been the motive for the crime.

Apparently, the slayer, maddened by hate, crept into the little tent in the dead of night and plunged his knife again and again into the hearts of his victims. Then dragging the bleeding forms from the enclosure, he partially buried them in the sand and fled.

...

The pajama-clad bodies were found at daybreak yesterday morning by the port captain.

In Miss Kentle's hand was clutched a copy of the book, "The End of the Honeymoon." (Italics/emphasis author's)

Sorority Leader

Miss Kentle was 23 years old and had been prominent in student circles at University of California at Los Angeles during her course there. She was president of the school's chapter of the Phi Mu sorority. Since her graduation from college, she has been an interior decorator for the Matthews Paint company's Pasadena branch.

Conlon also was an employee of that company and met Miss Kentle a year ago when both were working in the Pasadena store. Later he was made manager of the Monrovia branch.

...

Conlon was a member of the Southern California championship lightweight football team while attending Pasadena High School in 1924.

Additional information revealed that the killer had carefully posed Lois Kentle's body supine in a shallow sand grave and folded both arms over her chest, and then placed the book, *The End of the Honeymoon,* in her hand.

(**SKH Note** - It was later determined that Miss Kentle had borrowed the book, *The End of the Honeymoon,* from a friend before leaving on vacation.)

George Hodel Crime Signatures and MO

In this 1930s double homicide in Mexico, I see MO linkage to three of George Hodel's later crimes.

Let's examine the evidence:

A.

In his 1938 double murder of Hazel and Nancy Frome, as summarized in my book, *In The Mesquite* (Thoughtprint Press 2019), George, while in Sonora, Mexico, across the border from El Paso, accidentally runs into an ex-classmate/alumnus of his from his premed college days at UC Berkeley. The mother and daughter are seen dancing with him and a second male in the Mexican cantinas. Shortly after the victims return to their hotel in El Paso, they receive a letter and package and become terrified and flee the hotel in their touring car. Their bodies are found later posed side by side in the sands of West Texas. They had been tortured and burned with cigarettes, and a pair of doctor's rubber gloves were found near the bodies.

(See *In The Mesquite* for complete details.)

B.

In the 1966 "Zodiac" murder of eighteen-year-old former Ramona High School cheerleader Cheri Jo Bates, in Riverside, California, the killer waits for her to exit the college library in the dark of night, attacks and cuts her throat with a razor. He then mails a typed "Confession Letter" with the following excerpts:

"She was young and beautiful. But now she is battered and dead. *She is not the first, and she will not be the last.* I lay awake nights thinking about my next victim. ... *Maybe she will be the shapely* **blue-eyed brownett that said no when I asked her for a date in High School**..."

(Italics/emphasis - author's.)

C.

In the 1969 "Zodiac" attack murder/attempt murder of college students Cecelia Shepard, age 22, and her boyfriend, Bryan Hartnell, age 20, at the shoreside of Lake Berryessa, fifty miles northeast of San Francisco near Napa Valley we find:

"Zodiac," costumed and wearing a mask and armed with a long-bladed knife, threatens victims, claiming he needs to steal their car to go to "Mexico" and provides them with precut lengths of clothesline and orders them to tie each other up. They comply, and he viciously stabs both victims over a dozen times and leaves them for dead at the lakeside. (Both victims are found by a passerby and rushed to the hospital. Cecelia dies a day later, Bryan survives the attack.)

A 99-Year-Old Thoughtprint Provides the Linkage

In my initial book, *Black Dahlia Avenger: A Genius for Murder* in 2003, I coined the term "thoughtprint" and have presented examples of them throughout my many serial crime investigations and writings.

Here is my partial definition of a "thoughtprint":

> In all of our actions, each of us leaves behind traces of our self. Like our fingerprints, these traces are identifiable. I call them *thoughtprints*. They are the **ridges**, **loops, and whorls** of our mind.
>
> ...
>
> A collective of our motives, a paradigm constructed from our individual thoughts, these *elusive prints construct the signature that will* **connect** *or* **link** *us* **to** *a* **specific time**, **place**, **crime**, *or* **victim**.

Just as a fingerprint is comprised of numerous "points" (the whorls, ridges, and loops) that together lead to the identification of an individual, so, too, the points of this thoughtprint provide the linkage that leads to the identity of George Hodel.

My investigation into the 1930 Lois Kentle and Francis Conlon double homicide has revealed one of the best examples of how a thoughtprint can help solve a crime.

The "points" that reveal and link him to the Lois Kentle and Francis Conlon double murders are multiple and include: Points 1, 2, & 3.

(shown graphically here & below the graphic in text)

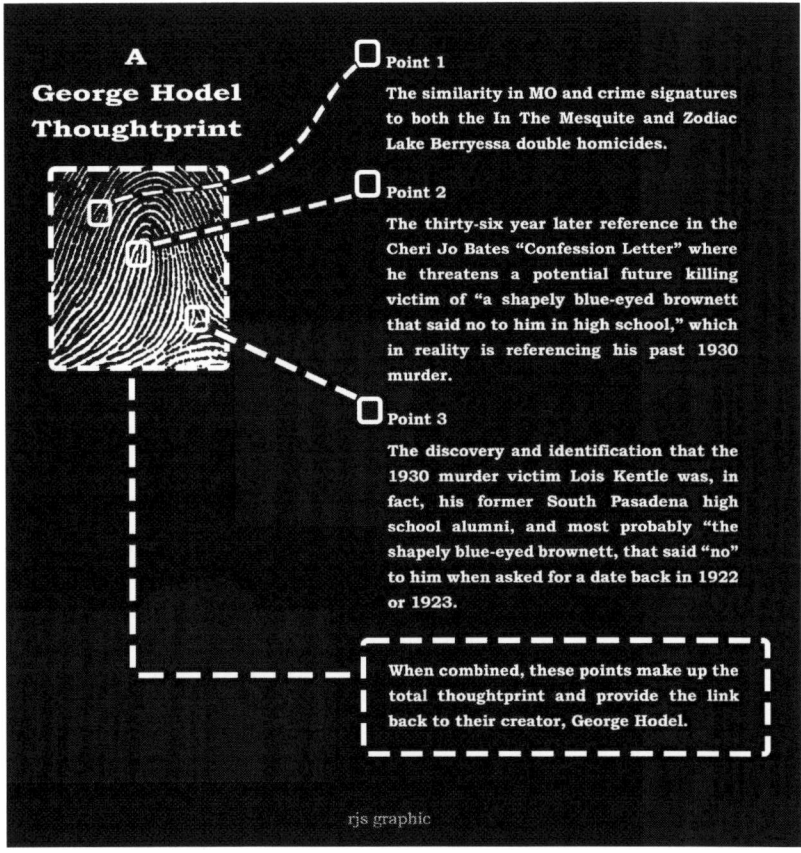

Point 1.

The similarity in MO and crime signatures to both the *In The Mesquite* and Zodiac Lake Berryessa double homicides.

Point 2.

The reference, thirty-six years later, in the Cheri Jo Bates "Confession Letter" where he threatens a potential future killing victim of "a shapely blue-eyed brownett that said no to him in high school," which in reality is referencing his past 1930 murder.

Point 3.

The discovery and identification that the 1930 murder victim Lois Kentle was, in fact, his former South Pasadena high school alumni, and most probably "the shapely blue-eyed brownett, that said "no" to him when asked for a date back in 1922 or 1923.

When combined, these points *along with others* make up the total thoughtprint and provide the link back to their creator, George Hodel.

...

In this case, this *thoughtprint*, and its multiple points, circumstantially connects and links the then 1930 premed student George Hodel to a previous: *time, place, crime, and victim.*

The time: 1922-1923
The place: South Pasadena High School
The crime: Double Homicide
The victims: Lois Kentle and Francis Conlon

Thoughtprint Points: QED
(quod erat demonstrandum)

A]
Below 1922 South Pasadena High School Yearbook (page 41) showing (see arrow points) both on the school's Honor Roll; George Hodel as (a junior) and Lois Kentle as (a sophomore)

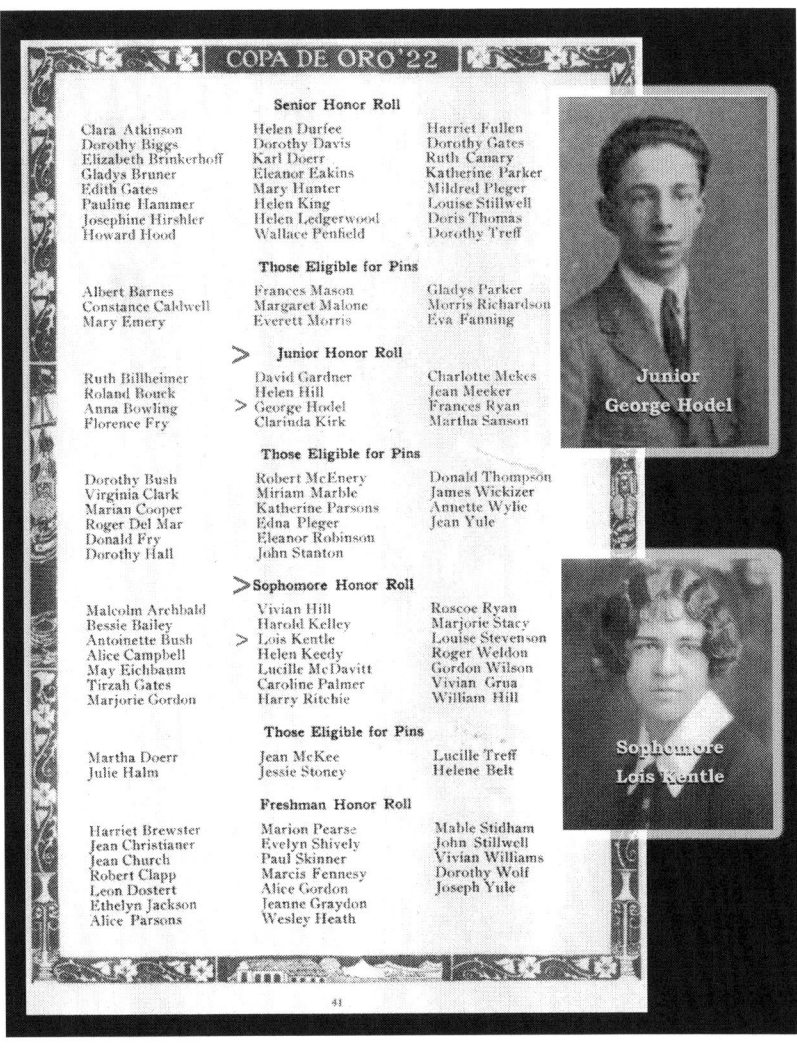

COPA DE ORO '22

Senior Honor Roll

Clara Atkinson	Helen Durfee	Harriet Fullen
Dorothy Biggs	Dorothy Davis	Dorothy Gates
Elizabeth Brinkerhoff	Karl Doerr	Ruth Canary
Gladys Bruner	Eleanor Eakins	Katherine Parker
Edith Gates	Mary Hunter	Mildred Pleger
Pauline Hammer	Helen King	Louise Stillwell
Josephine Hirshler	Helen Ledgerwood	Doris Thomas
Howard Hood	Wallace Penfield	Dorothy Treff

Those Eligible for Pins

Albert Barnes	Frances Mason	Gladys Parker
Constance Caldwell	Margaret Malone	Morris Richardson
Mary Emery	Everett Morris	Eva Fanning

Junior Honor Roll

Ruth Billheimer	David Gardner	Charlotte Mekes
Roland Bouck	Helen Hill	Jean Meeker
Anna Bowling	George Hodel	Frances Ryan
Florence Fry	Clarinda Kirk	Martha Sanson

Those Eligible for Pins

Dorothy Bush	Robert McEnery	Donald Thompson
Virginia Clark	Miriam Marble	James Wickizer
Marian Cooper	Katherine Parsons	Annette Wylie
Roger Del Mar	Edna Pleger	Jean Yule
Donald Fry	Eleanor Robinson	
Dorothy Hall	John Stanton	

Sophomore Honor Roll

Malcolm Archbald	Vivian Hill	Roscoe Ryan
Bessie Bailey	Harold Kelley	Marjorie Stacy
Antoinette Bush	Lois Kentle	Louise Stevenson
Alice Campbell	Helen Keedy	Roger Weldon
May Eichbaum	Lucille McDavitt	Gordon Wilson
Tirzah Gates	Caroline Palmer	Vivian Grua
Marjorie Gordon	Harry Ritchie	William Hill

Those Eligible for Pins

Martha Doerr	Jean McKee	Lucille Treff
Julie Halm	Jessie Stoney	Helene Belt

Freshman Honor Roll

Harriet Brewster	Marion Pearse	Mable Stidham
Jean Christianer	Evelyn Shively	John Stillwell
Jean Church	Paul Skinner	Vivian Williams
Robert Clapp	Marcis Fennesy	Dorothy Wolf
Leon Dostert	Alice Gordon	Joseph Yule
Ethelyn Jackson	Jeanne Graydon	
Alice Parsons	Wesley Heath	

Junior
George Hodel

Sophomore
Lois Kentle

41

[Photos added - Also see "B]

B]

South Pasadena High School
Senior Class Yearbook Photo & Activites

Senior Class of 1923

GEORGE HODEL

Adj.—Intelligent
By-word—Myself
Activities—**Honor Society**
1-2-**3**
Activities—**Latin Club**
1-2-**3**-4
Assembly
Class Programs 1-2
Debating 2-3-4
Short Story Contest 2-3
Spelling Contest 3
Economics Club 4
Senior Play 4
Tiger Staff 4
Jumbles 4

Senior Class of 1924

LOIS KENTLE—LOUIE

Annual Staff (4)
Girls' Athletic Club (1) (2)
(3) (4)
Latin Club (1) **(2)**
Art Club (1) (3) (4)
Spanish Club (3)
Operetta (3)
Class Assembly (4)
Class Play (4)
Honor Society (1) **(2)** (3) (4)

"The joy of youth and health
her eyes displayed,
And ease of heart, her every
look conveyed."

Common Activities in **Bold** show Potential for Social Interaction

Honor Society -   1922: George as Jr., Lois as Soph.
Latin Club -   1922: George as Jr., Lois as Soph.
Senior Class Play - 1923: George as Sr., 1924 Lois as Sr.

vjs graphics

1 or (1) = Freshman Yr.
2 or (2) = Sophomore Yr.
3 or (3) = Junior Yr.
4 or (4) = Senior Yr.

C]
**Lois Kentle was a Drama student during her years at SPHS.
Shown here in cast of her Senior Class Play in 1924.**

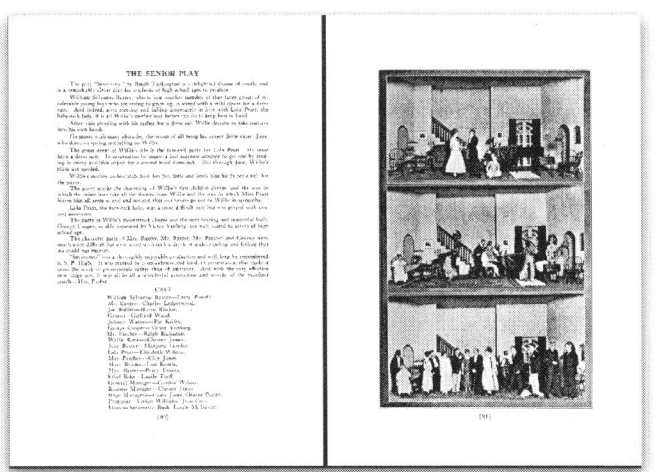

D]
Likewise,
**George Hodel was a drama student during his years at SPHS
Shown here in the cast of his Senior Class Play in 1923.**

E]
Below is a summary found in the South Pasadena Library describing Lois Kentle as a student at South Pasadena High School—Senior Class of 1924.

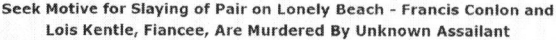

Lois Marion Kentle - Class Of 1924

Lois Kentle

1907 - August 26, 1930

Seek Motive for Slaying of Pair on Lonely Beach - Francis Conlon and Lois Kentle, Fiancee, Are Murdered By Unknown Assailant

Ensenada, Lower California, Mexico - A motive for the brutal slaying of Francis Conlon, 24, Monrovia, California, businessman and his fiancee, Lois Kentle, Los Angeles sorority girl was sought by Mexican and American authorities today.

The bodies of the couple, stabbed to death by an unknown assailant, were found on the beach August 26, 1930. Near the spot were evidences of a camping ground that evidently had been hastily broken up, according to the police. There appeared to be no motive for the murders, the American consul at the Lower California resort told the girl's relatives. They were strolling along the beach when their slayer crept upon them.

Mrs. William Kentle, mother of the girl, said the young couple had planned to be married. The port captain of Ensenada discovered the bodies, sprawled twenty feet from a tent they had pitched on the beach. Miss Kentle was president for two years of the national Phi Mu sorority chapter at UCLA. She was prominent in alumni affairs.

F]
Below is a summary found in the South Pasadena Library describing George Hodel as a student at South Pasadena High School—Senior Class of 1923.

George Hill Hodel Jr - Class Of 1923

George Hodel, born on October 10, 1907, in Los Angeles, grew up in South Pasadena on an estate on Monterey Road. He was identified as a child musical prodigy and the Hodel home was even visited by famed composer Rachmaninoff. George Hodel was declared a boy genius after scoring 186 on an IQ test, purportedly one point higher than Einstein. George graduated early from South Pasadena High in 1923 and later that year at only age 15, entered Cal Tech.

George became a physician and hobnobbed with Hollywood socialites and became acquainted with Beat poet Kenneth Rexroth, writer Henry Miller, and surrealist artist, Man Ray. In 1949 Dr. George Hodel became a Black Dahlia murder suspect and the LAPD planted two microphones in the family home in Los Angeles. Dr. Hodel moved to the Philippines which was his home base for the next forty-years. Dr. Hodel was an early pioneer in market research and his company, INRA-ASIA was the most respected research firm in all of Asia.

In 1990 he returned to California to live in San Francisco. George Hodel died in his penthouse residence on Bush Street in San Francisco May 16, 1999. He was 91.

As referenced earlier, I expect that the *how* of the double murder of Lois Kentle and Francis Conlon, by George Hodel, came about much like his double murder of Nancy and her mother, Hazel Frome, in 1938.

That crime resulted from the chance meeting of an old alumni in a Mexican Cantina, "south of the border down Mexico way" in Juarez. (Nancy Frome could well have rejected him in college at UC Berkeley?)

The Colon/Kentle murder, likewise, could have resulted from a chance meeting, "south of the border down Mexico way", this time, in Ensenada in the Cantina that Lois and Francis were seen in hours before their murder.

George, partying and drinking in the bar, chances upon "the blue-eyed brownett" who rejected the nerdy fourteen-year-old at South Pasadena High School, is now seen in the company and about to marry Francis Conlon, the handsome Pasadena high school football hero.

Nobody rejects George Hodel and gets away with it! Even with a seven-year "water under the bridge" passage of time.

Regardless of *how* the crime unfolded, thanks to my discovery of this long-concealed thoughtprint, we now have the link that provides us with the Motive, the Opportunity, and the Means.

Murder No. 3 - Virginia Brooks

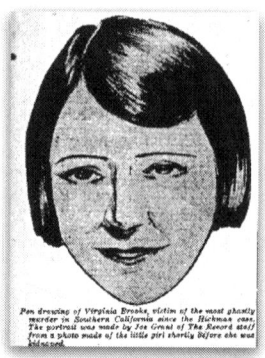

Pen drawing of Virginia Brooks, victim of the most ghastly
murder in Southern California since the Hickman case.
The portrait was made by Joe Grout of The Record staff
from a photo made of the little girl shortly before she was
kidnaped.

Sketch of Virginia Brooks, age 10

February 11, 1931

Virginia Brooks, age 10, disappears while on her way to
school in San Diego. Massive search efforts by authorities
are unsuccessful in locating the child or her suspected
abductor(s).

Los Angeles Record **March 11, 1931**

Caption: *Girl's Butchered Body Found*

Los Angeles Record caption (page 252) reads:

A month's search for Virginia Brooks, 10, ended when her horribly mangled body was found on Camp Kearney Mesa, near San Diego, Calif., Tuesday.

Inset: the murdered child.

Left: Edward Miers, criminal identification expert, shown examining the sack containing the girl's schoolbooks, found beside her body. Right: George Moses, the sheepherder, who found the body—which apparently had recently been exhumed and moved to the spot where discovered.

Author's Note - George Hill Hodel was a staff crime reporter for this, *The Los Angeles Record* newspaper, *just six-years earlier from 1924-1925.*

As reported previously, I believe that George Hodel and Fred Sexton were named as possible suspects in the 1924 kidnap/murder of the Martin Sisters.

In Chapter 6 of *The Early Years Part I*, I referenced that LAPD hired Dr. Elias Morgenstiern, the famous Russian criminologist known as "The Ferret of Europe," to assist in the investigation.

In *TEY Part I,* Chapter 6, I wrote,

"Dr. Morgenstiern used the opulent and newly built downtown Biltmore Hotel as his headquarters, and after weeks of interviews and investigation, provided authorities with both the motive and names of two young men who he believed committed the kidnap murders of the Martin sisters."

I will here provide significant excerpts from an article, *WHAT HAS HAPPENED, San Diego's Girl Murders A Succession of Horrors That Shocked West Coast*. It was printed in *The Daily News,* April 1, 1934, (three years after the Brooks and other San Diego murders occurred).

I will be presenting those crimes later in their chronological order. However, this article focuses on and provides an excellent summary of the still-unsolved 1931 Virginia Brooks child abduction/murder.

***Daily News*, April 1, 1934 - Photos in paper** (page 254)

Photo Upper right: **Where the hunt for Virginia Brooks ended. George H. Moses (second from left), who found body, kneels with officers at spot.**

Photo Middle: **The vacant chair in the Brooks home. Mr. and Mrs. John Brooks, parents of slain girl, sit down to dinner with their sons, Gordon and George (right), during search for missing child.**

Photo Lower left: **The late Virginia Brooks, who disappeared while on her way to school.**

WHAT HAS HAPPENED

San Diego's Girl Murders

A Succession of Horrors

That Shocked West Coast

By PETER LEVINS

SAN DIEGO - April 1, 1934

...

Ten-year-old Virginia Brooks, child of John Brooks, a skilled workman, was the first to die. She left her home on University Ave., San Diego, at 8 A.M., February 11, 1931, to attend the Euclid Ave. school a mile away. She never reached the school.

...

Investigation showed that she had last been seen by C.L. Chandler, owner of a nearby junk store. She had been tripping along University Ave., a few blocks from her home. Somewhere between that point and Winona St., half a mile away, she vanished.

The hunt began in earnest the next morning. The police broadcast a description—age, 10; weight, 75 pounds; brown hair and blue eyes; when last seen was wearing a white dress with a colored flower design, black shoes, and short socks. Virginia, who had been born in Indianapolis,[5] had two brothers, Gordon, 12, and George, 5.

An exhaustive search of the locality disproved[6] the theory that the child might have fallen into a canyon while picking wildflowers.

The theory that she might have run away was also abandoned, as[7] Virginia had been a normal, healthy, and happy child. Unfinished valentines and an unfinished letter to an aunt in Portland, Ore., were found in her school desk.

After no trace of the 10-year old was found on February 12, Mrs. Brooks, Virginia's mother, lay prostrate with fear while Virginia's father joined the search for her killer.[8]

A feeling of fear and horror clutched San Diego as thousands of citizens, soldiers, deputy sheriffs, Boy Scouts, and newspapermen of this city of 130,000 joined in the hunt. Parents kept close watch upon their children as the whole West Coast followed the story.[9]

---

[5] Ed.: Original (had been born in Indianapolis and had) changed for clarity.

[6] Ed.: Original text (disposed of) changed for clarity.

[7] Ed.: Original text (was also dropped, for) changed for clarity.

[8] Ed.: Original text augmented/re-arranged for clarity.

[9] Ed.: Ibid.

The territory within a five-mile radius of the Brooks home was combed. Police dragged all nearby pools.

As several days passed fruitlessly, the search was extended over all the Southwest. The police, as usual, received a great many false leads.

Goat Herder's Dog Finds Girl's Mutilated Body.

The next day an abandoned well 125 feet deep was discovered within three miles of the Brooks home. Quicklime filled the bottom of the well,[10] and it was thought the girl might be buried there. A search revealed nothing.

Hope of finding Virginia steadily waned. Police confessed they had practically nothing with which to work.

But on March 10, 1931, George H. Moses, a goat herder, was making his rounds on Camp Kearney Mesa, an unpopulated plain seven miles northeast of San Diego, when he saw his dog, a collie named Blakie, nosing at something. It was the mutilated body of Virginia Brooks, wrapped in a burlap sack. The exact location was three-quarters of a mile off the Escondido highway, two miles beyond the mouth of Murray canyon.

Mr. Moses drove to a telephone and called authorities. Several cars full of deputy sheriffs, police, and newspapermen went to the scene.

The appearance of the body was frightful. The head had been cut off, apparently to make it fit the sack; flesh and hair had been stripped from the head, which had also

---

[10] Ed.: Original text (it) changed for clarity.

been boiled in water, probably in an attempt to hide the girl's identity.

A post-mortem examination revealed that the remains of Virginia Brooks[11] had been there only about 48 hours. Death was due to strangulation. The arms were amputated, and the liver, intestines, and windpipe removed. *The killer appeared to have some knowledge of surgery.*

Automobile tire marks were found nearby the recovery site, showing that a car, which probably contained the body, was driven off the road and through the brush.[12]

If the murderer was attempting to hide the girl's[13] identity, however, he made at least one mistake.

The books Virginia was known to have carried to school the morning of February 11 were found in the brush a hundred yards away. Any further doubt as to the child's identity was removed after a conference with the child's parents and an examination of the teeth.

The following clues were considered the most important: (1) **a surgeon's glove found in the brush nearby;** *(emphasis mine)* (2) a man's blonde hair found on the right hand of the corpse; (3) auto tracks; (4) leaf mold in the bottom of the sack; (5) fingerprints on the books; (6) palm leaves in the sack.

---

[11] Ed.: Original text (the remains had been) augmented for clarity.

[12] Ed.: Original text (Automobile tire marks were found nearby, showing that a car which probably contained the body had pushed off the road through the brush.) changed for clarity.

[13] Ed.: Original text (to hide the identity) augmented for clarity.

One of the questions confronting authorities was where the body had been from February 11 to March 8, when it was placed on the mesa. A search for a "murder laboratory" was carried on—fruitlessly.

...

A suggestion was made that Virginia was the victim of a "black magic" cult, but nothing supported any other theory than that she was the victim of a degenerate about whom nothing was known **except that he was apparently a man with some medical training.** (emphasis mine.)

On March 12, San Diego papers offered rewards totaling $400. The State followed with $1,000, and private citizens volunteered enough to bring the total to $3300.

Gov. James Rolph took an active interest in the case ordering Harry Hickock and M.F. Burnenberg, experts attached to the State Bureau of Identification, to San Diego.

Two notes were received by the police in the week preceding the inquest, held March 20. One was signed "The Gorilla" and the other "The Doctor." Apparently from the same person, the notes declared that the writer had killed the Brooks girl and threatened to kill another girl soon.

THE NOTES

First Note mailed to police

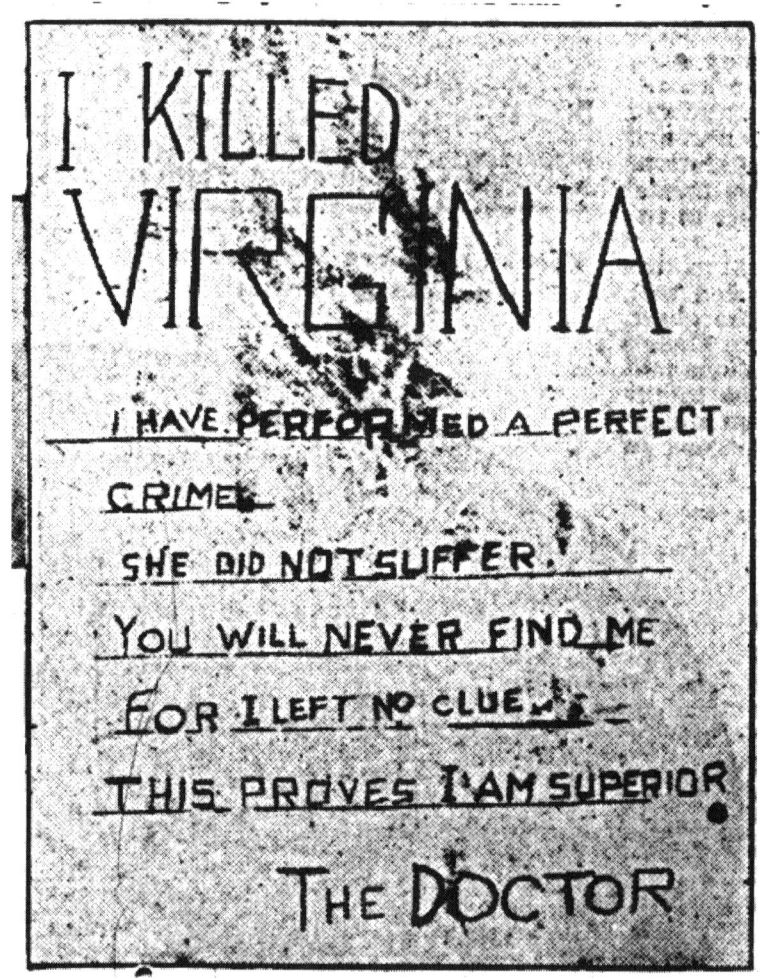

The second Note was not reproduced or shown to the public, but the text was released, and authorities indicated that "half the writing was in script and the second half printed and they believed that the handwriting/printing matched both notes and likely were written by the same individual."

The second note read:

I HAVE DEFIED YOUR EXPERTS.

H.A.! H.A.!

ANOTHER SCHOOLGIRL WILL

DISAPPEAR WITHIN A WEEK.

LET MOTHER'S BEWARE!

"THE GORILLA"

Author's Note - The "Ha! Ha!" verbiage seen here is used frequently by George Hodel in both his "Avenger" and "Zodiac" notes and letters which were written in the 1940s and 1960s.

Potential linkage of the Virginia Brooks MO and Crime Signatures to George Hill Hodel and Fred Sexton

- Police suspected a "man with medical training" performed the body dissections, removed organs, and the head's decapitation. In his final year of pre-med at UC Berkeley, George Hodel was preparing to cross the bay and attend UCSF for another four years, where he will obtain his M.D.

- A pair of rubber surgical gloves were found near the body.

  In the 1938 double homicide of kidnapped/ torture-murder victims, Hazel and Nancy Frome (mother and daughter), which I have attributed to George Hodel and Fred Sexton, a pair of rubber surgical gloves was also left next to the victim's bodies in isolated terrain.

- Two taunting notes were mailed to the police. At least one of the letters was written on "brown wrapping paper" identical to the brown wrapping paper used to mail the severed ear to the parents of the Chicago Lipstick Killer victim, little Suzanne Degnan, age 6. Suzanne was also kidnapped, and her body, according to the coroner, was disarticulated by a "skilled surgeon." Printed taunting notes were left at her crime scene. (G.H.H. graduated with his MD in 1936 and had been practicing medicine and surgery for ten years at the time of the 1946 Degnan murder.)

- In the Brooks notes, the writer states that he is "superior" and left no clues, inferring that he is a "master criminal" and is, as he claims in his later Zodiac mailings, "Crack Proof."

- Uses press to terrorize the public by speaking directly to parents of children promising "let mothers beware. Another schoolgirl will disappear in a week." In his 1967 "Zodiac" Cheri Jo Bates Letter, he will again threaten, "...keep your sisters, daughters, and wives off the streets...beware I am stalking your girls now... there will be more."

- Multiple national newspapers liken the crime to the Los Angeles 1924 Martin Sisters Kidnap-murder.

- Suspect in signing the first note gives a hint to his identity by signing it "The Doctor." (G.H.H. was, at the time of this murder, just completing his pre-med training to become "The Doctor.")

- Suspect(s) incorporate a theme from a popular "thriller movie" of that time as part of his taunting second note by signing it, "The Gorilla."

> George Hodel's later crimes include references from the following films: *Charlie Chan at Treasure Island (1939), The Most Dangerous Game (1932), Spellbound (1945), The Sniper (1952), etc.*

> I am surprised that nowhere in my research have I seen a police or public link to that movie, which had been released just a few months before the crime and would have likely been showing at San Diego area theaters at the time of the murder.

> Though, on the next page (264), the promotional advertisement dated in the upper left corner was "for December 1930," the film's release date was Nov. 2, 1930—three months prior to Virginia Brooks's murder on February 11, 1931.

"The Gorilla"

Thriller film released in U.S. November 2, 1930

"...mind of a master-criminal—lust cravings of a beast."

The copy on the movie's showcard below reads:

"Out go the lights! On go the thrills! Into the mystery-mansion stalks the 'Gorilla,' a *mind of a master-criminal—lust craving of a beast.* (Italics mine) In walk Mulligan and Garrity, the two-dumb-detectives, and then the fun begins. It shouldn't be missed."

IMDB "Storyline - A series of murders that take place in an old, dark mansion are suspected of being committed by an ape."

A scene from *The Gorilla* 1930

Ninety years later, the child kidnap/murder of Virginia Brooks remains unsolved. I understand that San Diego authorities believe it to be one of the many serial crimes committed by the same suspect(s) during the 1930s.

If any of the evidence still exists, there remains the possibility of solving this and the other suspected 1930s serial crimes through DNA comparison.

Murder No. 4 - Louise Teuber

April 19, 1931

GIRL FOUND HANGED AFTER WRITING SHE WAS LEAVING HOME

By Telephoto—
—International Newsreel.
MISS LOUISE TEUBER.

Evidence of Fight Found on Body of Girl Hanged Nude

Visalia Times-Delta April 20, 1931

San Diego, Calif.
April 20. (U.P.)

Louise Teuber fought desperately for her life, an autopsy revealed today.

Coroner Chester Dunn announced that bits of skin, evidently from the face of the slayer, were found under the girl's fingernails.

It also was determined that she was struck behind the left ear with a heavy weapon and then was hanged from the tree while still alive.

As Coroner Dunn made public the autopsy report, Sheriff Ed Cooper announced that investigators had found the girl's diary and some letters from young men giving about 20 names of male acquaintances.

SAN DIEGO, Cal. April 20.

The slaying of Louise Teuber, 17,[14] whose body was found hanging from an oak tree on Black Mountain, 10 miles from here, presented authorities today with the problem of deciding which of many motives was the right one.

Sometime after midnight Saturday, the girl was strangled with a hemp rope pulled across a limb and tied to a stump, and there, 12 hours later, a group of picnickers found her body dangling clad only in a brassiere and a pair of slippers.

Robbery and assault[15] were immediately discarded as motives by Sheriff Ed Cooper. An examination showed she had not been assaulted. Her purse was found in the underbrush, where the rest of her clothing was scattered.

---

[14] Ed.: Original text (Louise Teuber, 27) changed for clarity.

[15] Ed.: Original text (**Robbery and attach**) changed for clarity.

LETTER WRITTEN BY MURDERED GIRL

SAN DIEGO. Calif., April 20.

A letter written by Louise Teuber, 17, was delivered to her father hours after she had been murdered and her body suspended from the limb of a tree near Black Mountain, it was revealed today by the sheriff's office.

The letter read:

> "Dear Dad—I have tried for a long time to be satisfied with the way you are running the house, and I can stand it no longer. I am leaving home tonight, and I am not coming back."

The letter, a special delivery, was stamped at the post office at 7 P.M., Sunday, and had been mailed in San Diego. Sheriff investigators believe that Louise was struck on the back of the head and suspended from an oak tree about midnight Saturday.

Sheriff Ed Cooper declared that either the girl had mailed the letter at an out-of-the-way box, or the slayer, finding it after Louise had been killed, figured that its delivery to the father would keep him from becoming alarmed and possibly result in the body being undiscovered for days.

(Author's Note - *I would suggest a third possibility. Perhaps the killer(s) forced Louise Teuber to write the letter under threats of harm prior to her murder? Then after hanging her, he/they mailed the letter to her father.)*

William Teuber, the girl's father, is a well-to-do barber, owning his own shop here.

"I cannot understand it," Teuber told deputy sheriffs. "I knew of nothing serious between us. There had been minor disputes in the last few months—mainly because Louise wanted to go out nights more than I thought was right."

Shortly after Sheriff Cooper announced the letter clew, he revealed that three suspects, (whose names he would not make public,) were suspicious that Louise Teuber may have been hanged by a sailor. This idea was based on the knowledge that the *double half-hitch, a knot* known to all seamen, *was used in making the loop that choked[16] out the life of the young girl* who was a clerk in a local store.

She left the store late Saturday, telling a friend there that she expected to go away and that she probably would not communicate with the friend for several weeks.

This information led police to believe that she presumed she was going to live elsewhere with the person who murdered her.

Harry Hickok and Jack Nuremberg, criminologists from the State Bureau of Identification at Sacramento, who have been here since the Brooks girl was found slain at Camp Kearney Mesa, started to work on the Teuber slaying today.

EVIDENCE

A Mr. Tomas Martinez, his wife, and two children were picnicking at the foot of Black Mountain, eighteen miles northeast of San Diego. Reaching an oak grove, they were confronted with the spectacle of a girl's body hanging from a tree limb by a rope.

Louise's dress and undergarments had been placed in "a neat pile on an army blanket."

Author's Note - Here again, we have the "posing" of the victim's clothing consistent with many of George Hodel and Fred Sexton's serial murders.

While no suspect(s) were seen with the victim in the hours immediately before her abduction, one potentially

---

[16] Ed.: Original text (chocked,etc.) changed for clarity.

important piece of evidence was found at the crime scene - THE HANGING ROPE.

Pursuit of clues in the "love lynching" of Louise Teuber, 17-year-old San Diego girl, turned to the Bay District late today when it was learned that the piece of rope used to hang the nude victim had been made in San Francisco.

The rope was definitely identified, according to press dispatches, as the product of the Tubbs Cordage Company, Twenty-second, and Iowa streets.

Stuart Henshaw, sales manager of the firm, informed of the newest lead in the San Diego murder inquiry, declared the

company would render authorities every assistance possible in tracing the rope to its purchaser.

He explained that the product of his firm is easily identifiable through a number of markings used only by the Tubbs Cordage company. These consist of a white cotton string through the center of one type and a black and green cotton string through the center of second and third-grade rope, respectively.

...

The rope clue was considered of extreme importance by investigators, inasmuch as it narrows down the range of possibilities in tracing the source of the cord that strangled Miss Teuber.

Author's Note -

In 1931-1932 George Hodel was living and working in the San Francisco Bay area and, while attending UCSF Medical School, had two part-time jobs: 1) Driving a

Yellow Cab in downtown San Francisco and 2) Working as a journalist for the *San Francisco Chronicle*.

That newspaper, George Hodel's 1931-1932 place of employment, was located at 901 Mission Street, *just two miles from Tubbs Cordage Company, where the murder weapon/rope, used to hang[17] Louise Teuber, was made and likely purchased.*

The Louise Teuber murder was never solved and is believed by San Diego authorities to be one of the many crimes committed by the 1930s murder suspect.

Again, if any evidence remains in custody, we have a strong possibility of making a DNA connection through the "fingernail scrapings" obtained in 1931. Also, the possibility exists of getting additional samples by using the newly discovered "Touch DNA" method and attempting to obtain skin cells from the victim's clothing and or the hanging rope.

I have my father's full DNA profile available for comparison. Fred Sexton's familial DNA would have to be obtained possibly from his daughter, son, or other close relatives.

---

[17] Ed.: Original text (that slew) changed for clarity.

Murder No. 5 - Dolly Bibbens

April 23, 1931

Los Angeles Evening Express

San Diego, April 24. (U.P.)

The slayer of Mrs. W.B. (Dolly) Bibbens, whose pajama-clad body was found on a bed in her apartment late yesterday, returned to the scene of his crime before the crime was discovered, police believed today. Fruit, less than three days old, was found in her room.

Preliminary autopsy of[18] the body revealed the woman had been strangled to death, Coroner Chester Gunn announced.

The fruit, police pointed out, showed no sign of decay such as would be evident had it stood for any length of time, and on this fact, they based their supposition.

Strands of hair under the fingernails of Mrs. Bibbens, known as "Diamond Dolly," may lead to identification of her slayer, it was announced by police.

"We have definite clews which we believe will lead to the arrest of the slayer within a short time," was the announcement of Police Capt. Paul Hayes shortly after the autopsy.

...

DEAD SIX DAYS

Mrs. Bibbens had been dead at least five and probably six days when R.B. Brown, a plumber, made the gruesome discovery last night as he entered her room with a pass-key to make repairs.

A blood-smeared towel covered her face and was carefully tucked beneath her head.

---

[18] Ed.: Original text (autopsy over the body) changed for clarity.

(**Author's Note** - Here again, we have the "posing" common to almost every other crime George Hodel ever committed pre- or post-1931.)

Police revealed today that Mrs. Bibbens' automobile was missing, and police throughout the State were asked to watch for it, in the apparently well-grounded hope that with robbery as the motive, her slayer took her car as well as her jewelry.

...

STRANGLED WOMAN LINKED TO L.A. SUICIDE

A published photograph of Mrs. W.B. (Dolly) Bibbens, third victim of strangulation in San Diego, was identified today by Capt. Jack Trainor of Newton street police division, as that of the woman who obtained the personal property of W.B. Bibbins, [sic] 43-year-old negro, after he had committed suicide at 1138 East Forty-first street last September 16.

Bibbins fired a bullet into his head with a .45-caliber automatic pistol and left a note asking that Dolly Bibbens of the William Penn Hotel, San Diego, be notified of his death.

The Dolly Bibbens mentioned by the negro came to Los Angeles and obtained the personal effects of the suicide victim, which had been held by the police. In signing the receipt, she wrote the name, "Dolly Bibbens."

At the time of the investigation, police noticed that the suicide victim signed his name "Bibbins" and that the woman signed her name "Bibbens."

The San Diego woman was a white woman, according to Captain Trainor, who declared the picture published today was unmistakably that of the one to whom he gave the dead negro's personal belongings last September.

The discovery sent police on a search of police files, where they found that a Mrs. Dolly Bibbens had been arrested here on three occasions on morals charges.

(Author's Note- The "morals charges" were for "violations of rooming house ordinances" where "on April 19, 1929, she was arrested with a Negro and fined $50 or 30 days in jail, the record showed her age to be 35 years.")

Mrs. W. D. Bibbens is the third person to be found murdered in San Diego in the past few weeks. Her body was found in her apartment there late yesterday. She was the victim of a strangler.

Dolly Bibbens

(Ed. Victim is Mrs. W. B. Bibbens)

Caption under photo (page 277) of 'Dolly Bibbens' reads:

Mrs. W.B. Bibbens is the third person to be found murdered in San Diego in the past few weeks. Her body was found in her apartment there late yesterday. She was the victim of a strangler.

Victim Dolly Bibbens, age 44, resided at 1272 11ᵗʰ St., in San Diego. Her body was found lying across her bed. She suffered massive blunt force trauma to her face and body, and no suspect(s) was seen at her apartment.

Consequently, the only possible solution to this crime would be by way of DNA linkage. (Again, scrapings were found under her fingernails, like many of the other San Diego victims.)

Authorities believed her personal automobile was taken, which matches the 1944 strangulation murder of "LA Lone Woman Murder" victim Georgette Bauerdorf, whose car was stolen and abandoned in DTLA just a mile from George Hodel's medical office at 7th and Flower Streets.

I have found no reference from a search of 1931 newspapers that indicated that Dolly Bibbens's automobile was subsequently located. Still, it may well have been, and I was just unable to find the reference.

Author's Note - Just on a personal "gut feeling level," I am not convinced this murder is, in fact, one of the San Diego serial crimes. For me, it is a bit of a coin-toss. I would give it a fifty-fifty probability that it is connected to the other crimes.

As far as George Hodel and Fred Sexton are concerned, the "alleged robbery of her valuable diamonds" was never part of their MO They were sadistic, lust killers, but other than taking a possible "trophy," I am not aware of any actual robbery motive associated with any of their victims.

I have read newspaper accounts that "jewelry was taken" and others that claim "no jewelry was taken," so what to believe? If robbery was not the motive, then chances that the crime was serial to the others is, to my mind, much more likely.

To my knowledge, the Dolly Bibbens crime was never solved, and I believe that San Diego authorities still include it as one of their 1930s serial crimes.

Murder No. 6 - Hazel Bradshaw

Committed on May 2, 1931

Hazel Bradshaw, age 23

Los Angeles Evening Express May 4, 1931

WHERE FOURTH MURDER VICTIM WAS FOUND

In the shadow of an ancient stone hut, in the Indian village section of Balboa Park, in San Diego, the body of pretty Hazel Bradshaw, 23, was found by two small boys. She is the fourth murder victim there in months. The body was lying in grass two feet high, with 17 stab wounds in it. The above picture shows the spot where the body was found. (indicated by the arrow.)

The body of Hazel Bradshaw was found by two Boy Scouts lying near an adobe wall in the Indian Village built as part of San Diego's Indian village for the San Diego Exposition of 1915.

The victim was lying on her back. She was wearing a brown topcoat, which was open. She was stabbed seventeen times with a long-bladed knife, and a man's handkerchief had been stuffed inside her mouth. Her pocketbook was by her side and had been rifled.

The last known person to see her alive was her boyfriend, Moss Edward Garrison, age 35, a coworker with Hazel at the San Diego and Arizona Railroad Company. Garrison was a steward in the commissary, and Hazel worked there as a telephone operator.

Garrison walked into the San Diego Police station and readily admitted, he and Miss Bradshaw had dated and gone to a movie on Saturday night. He informed police officers, "We usually go to a movie every Saturday night. We walked through the park, past the merry-go-round and the Indian village to her home. I left her at the door at 11:55 P.M. and saw her enter before I ran to catch my streetcar home."

Police questioned Garrison's story, and he was placed under arrest for suspicion of murder. This ultimately resulted in a later trial; however, a jury quickly found him "not guilty," and later crimes led police to believe the actual killer was not Garrison and was, in fact, still at large.

There were no witnesses to the brutal, apparently motiveless knife attack of Hazel Bradshaw, and it, like the other crimes, remains "unsolved."

Author's Note-As documented in my previous investigations, in at least six of the serial crimes attributed to George Hodel and or Fred Sexton, *a man's handkerchief was found at the crime scene.* Also, in the 1969 Lake Berryessa "Zodiac" slaying of victim Cecelia Shepard, age 22, she was stabbed with a long-bladed knife more than a dozen times. Her boyfriend, Bryan Hartnell, was stabbed six times and survived the attack.

A potential source of DNA linkage would be possible from the man's handkerchief if that item is still booked in evidence?

Like the other San Diego serial crimes, this brutal murder remains "unsolved" as of this writing, some ninety years after it was committed.

Murder No. 7 - Mrs. Maud Detweiler

August 28, 1931

Coroner To Investigate Death By Asphyxiation

SAN DIEGO (U.P.) — Although convinced that Mrs. Maude Detweiler, 40, was accidentally asphyxiated by the fumes from a cleaning fluid, the coroner's office plans to hold an inquest into the death early next week, it was announced today.

Mrs. Detweiler, drug store clerk, was found dead in the bathroom of her apartment at 13th avenue and B street by Mrs. Florence Putnam, a friend, Friday.

Dr. F. E. Toomey, county autopsy surgeon, who performed the autopsy Friday night, said Mrs. Detweiler was asphyxiated. There was not evidence of foul play, investigators said.

San Francisco Examiner Sat. August 29, 1931

The reportage on the possible murder of Maude Detweiler, age 40, is minimal.

In researching the incident, I cannot determine whether her death was ultimately judged to be a homicide or accidental asphyxia.

The preceding article (page 284) suggests it was at least initially considered "accidental."

However, some years later, I found that her death was listed as one of the seven San Diego serial *murders* reported in the *Minneapolis Sunday Tribune, November 25, 1934.*

The excerpt from that newspaper lists her as the fifth victim in an insert-box entitled, "SEVEN ACTS IN THE DEATH PAGEANT." It reads:

"August 29, 1931—Mrs. Maud Detwiler [sic] wealthy divorcee, found slain in the bathroom of her apartment. Unsolved."

...

"On August 29, 1931, Mrs. Maud Detwiler (sic), wealthy and vivacious divorcee, was found slain in the bathroom of her apartment. Not a single tangible clue was unearthed to the crime, despite an exhaustive investigation by police."

Author's Note - I include this Maude Detweiler death investigation as possibly one of George Hodel's serial crimes primarily because it is identical to three later murders committed by him, as detailed in my previously published books, *Black Dahlia Avenger and Most Evil.*

Specifically, I refer to:

1) the 1944 "Bathtub Murder" of victim Georgette Bauerdorf. In that crime, a large cloth bandage was stuffed in her mouth, and she was placed in the bathtub of her apartment in Hollywood. A neighbor heard water running and discovered the body the following morning.

2) The 1945 bathtub murder of victim Josephine Ross, who had also been placed in her apartment bathtub after her killer cut her throat and then washed the body clean in the tub. He then removed her body to the bedroom, put adhesive tape over her facial wounds (more "posing"), and left the apartment. This was the first of his three Chicago "Lipstick Murders."

3) The 1945 bathtub murder of victim Francis Brown, also placed in her apartment bathtub after being shot and stabbed. The "Lipstick Killer," then using lipstick, wrote the following taunting message on the living room wall, "For Heaven's sake, catch me before I kill more. I cannot control myself."

The Maude Detweiler "bathtub" death could well have been a precursor to the three similar crimes that followed in the 1940s.

Murder No. 8 - Mrs. Mary Adams

March 4, 1934

On March 4, 1934, the bruised body of Mary Adams, age 23, was found by a motorist lying in a thicket of brush on a lonely by road.

No identification was found at the crime scene, but her mother, Mrs. Mary Dobson, later identified the victim.

Based on coroner's examination and toxicology, initial reports indicated the victim might have "been poisoned" and then her body thrown from a speeding automobile.

San Diego newspapers indicated the victim, known as "Tootsie," had been employed at "a raucous border resort in Tijuana, for some time."

Initially her husband, Wesley Adams, a sailor, was taken into custody and questioned.

According to his story, he and his wife quarreled Saturday night, and she threatened to "kill herself." Adams became intoxicated and "passed out," and friends put him to bed.

When he awoke, his wife was gone.

Here are excerpts from the *Los Angeles Times* article dated March 6, 1934:

WOMAN'S DEATH CAUSE PUZZLES

Police Follow Party Trail at San Diego

Owner of Car Transporting Body Sought

Officers Await Analysis of Stomach Contents

SAN DIEGO, March 5.

The "party trail" of Mrs. Mary Adams Saturday night, which ended when her lifeless body was dragged to the side of lonely Adobe Falls Road

and abandoned there, was followed by Sheriff's officers today on their hunt for the cause of death.

Three men who were with the woman Saturday night have been questioned, but none has thrown any light on the death of the 23-year-old woman.

The men are Wesley Adams, the dead woman's husband, Joseph Bridges, and Emerson Miller, close friends of the couple. All three men are firemen aboard the destroyer Kane.

...

VISIT TO CAFÉ

Evidence shows that Mrs. Adams left her home at 1733 First Avenue, Saturday night, after quarreling with her husband, and appeared later at the Fleet Café—a sailors' resort. From that place, no trace of her movements has been found.

Adams told officers he went to bed after his wife left their house in the company of Bridges, a close friend of the husband. Miller remained behind to "put Adams to bed."

Adams was "very drunk," it was stated. Miller then followed the couple to the Fleet Café.

Bridges asserted he left Mrs. Adams at the café but Miller told Sheriff's officers that Bridges and the woman left the café together, Mrs. Adams having stated that she was going home.

Meanwhile, Adams had been completely exonerated of any part in his wife's death. Bridges and Miller have been turned over to navy officials and are being held aboard the U.S.S. King.

ANALYSIS AWAITED

Officers are awaiting the completion of chemical analysis of the contents of the dead woman's stomach. That she died by "poison strangulation" was the opinion of Deputy Coroner Hebert. Liquor, with which her body was literally saturated, might have played some part in her death, it was stated.

But whether she died from liquor or accidental poisoning, or by self-administered poison, or was murdered is still an unanswered question.

Mrs. Adam's death leaves motherless little Catherine Margaret, her 30-month-old baby.

Author's Note - This death is a strange one. Though it varies significantly from the other serial crimes, I suspect that based on the fact that the body was discarded in the general area where several other victims were found, that may have been a factor for its inclusion?

In some respects, this crime is similar to the "LA Lone Woman Murder" of Laura Trelstad, that occurred in Long Beach, California, on May 11, 1947, which I attributed to Dr. George Hodel and included in my earlier publications. Ms. Trelstad had an argument with her husband, went drinking, became intoxicated, and was later found beaten and strangled in an isolated oil field.

I am unfamiliar with the coroner's reference to "poison strangulation," which was likely clarified as the investigation progressed.

Since the Mary Adams case was reported and named one of the 1930s serial crimes, I include it here.

Murder No. 9 - Celia Cota

August 18, 1934

Pomona Progress Bulletin **August 18, 1934**
Celia Cota age 16

Student Is Victim Of Strangler

Murder of 16-Year-Old Deepens Mystery In Crime Series

Pupil's Death is 7th Puzzling Slaying in San Diego

SAN DIEGO, August 18 (UP)

Convinced that the murder of Celia Cota, 16-year-old high school girl whose ravished body was found near Balboa Park today, was the work of a fiend, police today started a round-up of 50 known degenerates in the San Diego area.

Several grey hairs were clutched in the girl's hand when the body was found, furnishing the only tangible clue on which police have to work.

SAN DIEGO, August 18

An all-night search for pretty Celia Cota, 16-year-old high school girl who failed to return from a short walk last evening, ended today with the finding of her body behind a shed near Balboa Park.

She had been slugged and criminally assaulted, authorities said.

In reconstructing the crime, they said the girl had been strangled to death following the assault.

Celia's disappearance was reported to police at midnight by her parents, Mr. and Mrs. Edward Cota, when the girl did not return after leaving home at 8:15 P.M. for a "short walk."

CLOTHING IN TATTERS

The patrolmen found the body behind the shed and near a canyon's edge shortly after daybreak.

The girl was lying on her back when found, and part of her clothing had been ripped from the body.

The death of Celia Cota makes the seventh mysterious murder on San Diego police records within the past 42 months.

...

Determined that the death of Celia will not join this procession of unsolved crimes, police today called on all their resources to track down the slayer.

Police admitted, however, the clues virtually were non-existent.

Author's Note - This crime fits the MO of the previous crimes: abduction, violent attack, and strangulation. Again, no witnesses to the crime, so the only possible linkage would be a match to the suspect's DNA.

Murder No. 10 – Ruth Muir

August 1, 1936

Ruth Muir, age 48

The Arizona Republic September 3, 1936

Victim And Scene Of Crime

La Jolla crime scene

Sitting alone on a lover's lane bench overlooking the sea, Ruth Muir, daughter of a prominent San Antonio banker, was ravished and beaten to death to become the seventh victim in a series of shocking murders within the San Diego city limits during the last six years.

Photo above shows police seeking clues at the scene of the crime, where trampled weeds gave evidence of a violent struggle before the woman met death. Investigation yesterday took a startling turn. Scientific tests taken of hairs found in the victim's hand indicated they were from the head of a woman.

Author's Note -   Subsequent reportage that "the hairs found in her hand were that of a woman" were modified by San Diego Police Chief Sears, "We are giving strong consideration to the possibility Miss Muir was attacked by another woman."

This suggestion was later scoffed at by Detective Captain Harry Kelly, who was quoted as saying, "We don't know whether the hair was from the head of Miss Muir or someone else, whether it came from the head of a man or woman."

The known facts surrounding the victim's murder again were minimal.

Investigating officers stated, "She went alone to a bench overlooking the ocean. Two hours later, she was dead, her head battered by repeated blows from an unidentified heavy object, her clothing torn, and her body mutilated."

The autopsy surgeon, Dr. F.E. Toomey, testified at the inquest that Miss Muir had been criminally attacked, and the cause of death was due to blunt force trauma to the head.

New Clew in Death of Y.W. Secretary

LOS ANGELES, December 4. (UP)

A new suspect was disclosed Friday in the Ruth Muir murder case, unsolved since the 48-year-old Y.W.C.A. secretary was brutally slain at La Jolla the night of August 1.

Movements of a Los Angeles man were investigated by Detective Lieut. Leroy Sanderson, after receipt of an anonymous letter which named him as the slayer and declared he lost a pith helmet at the scene of the crime.

A helmet of this description was found floating in the La Jolla surf September 2. Dark stains on the headgear, submitted to chemical analysis, were classified as blood of the same type as Miss Muir's, police learned. Prof. J. Laudermilk, Pomona college scientist, subsequently denied that he had identified hairs clutched in the hands of Ruth Muir as those of a woman.

Author's Note - I find this 1936 newspaper article interesting. In his later serial murders, Dr. George Hodel (GHH) used the same MO of mailing anonymous notes claiming he knew the killer's identity.

He wrote one anonymous note in the 1944 Georgette Bauerdorf murder. In the 1947 murder of Elizabeth "Black Dahlia" Short, he sent in three separate messages claiming he "knew the identity of the killer." And yet a fourth note (a lengthy handwritten letter) "naming the suspect and his actions" was mailed to police in his 1948 Gladys Kern Hollywood *Lone Woman Murder*.

In the first Elizabeth Short anonymous note, GHH sent a modified photo of the alleged "werewolf killer." In the second note, he sent in a drawing of "the killer." In the third, he claimed the killer was a man named "Manuel L. Marino."

The fourth note/letter, which I identified as my father's handwriting and mailed just two blocks from George Hodel's medical office on February 17, 1948, was received two days before victim Gladys Kern's body was found. In that lengthy letter, the writer claimed he knew the killer's name as "Louis Frazer" and provided a description and detailed a witnessing of the stabbing, etc.

Here is a copy of the handwritten Kern Letter as reproduced in *Black Dahlia Avenger:*

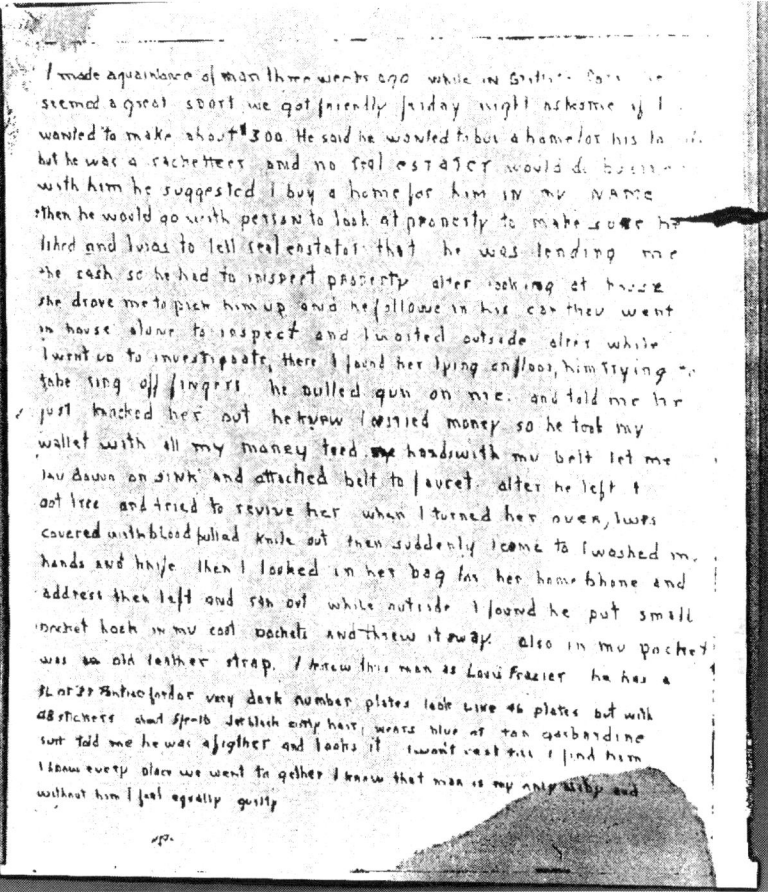

Dr. George Hill Hodel's handwritten "Kern Letter" sent to police in February 1948, naming the Gladys Kern killer as "Louis Frazer" and describing the stabbing/slaying of the victim. Letter mailed from letterbox just two blocks from Dr. Hodel's office in downtown L.A. and the same box location used to send a Black Dahlia note a year earlier.

To provide a complete understanding of how those later notes mimic the MO from several of these "early crimes," I am here providing a scan of those pages from *Black Dahlia Avenger II* (Thoughtprint Press 2014)—pages 380-390.

380|LAPD HISTORICAL SOCIETY: THE NEW EVIDENCE

LAPDHS Exhibit- The New Evidence

According to Chief Beck, "Given fiscal restraints," LAPD is unable to spare a detective to allot an hour's time to hear and be shown the new evidence.

Is the Chief right?

It is undeniable that we are living in fiscally tough times. If an LAPD Detective II in Robbery/Homicide Division is earning around $45 an hour and my presentation could run as much as ninety minutes, that could easily cost the Department $67.50.

Let's say the detective is convinced by my evidence and sends the evidence to be tested for DNA. That would require him or her to pick-up the phone and call SID (Scientific Investigation Division) to request the property be analyzed. That additional call for investigation could easily tack on an additional fifteen minutes. That raises the bill another $11.25.

We now have a total cost to the city of $78.75.

"Given the fiscal restraints on the city..." (Emphasis mine, sarcasm mine.)

381|LAPD Historical Society: The New Evidence

It's best I come directly to you, my readers, with the "new evidence." To be clear, you will be the first to see and learn the specifics of how and why I believe the 2012 LAPD Museum exhibit's evidence could forensically link my father, Dr. George Hill Hodel, to the Dahlia murder by way of DNA.

THE LETTERS

The exhibit displayed two letters that today's LAPD must have presumed were "crank letters," just a couple of samples of mailings from someone caught up in the Dahlia hysteria some sixty-plus years before.

I seriously question that. I believe at least one of the missives—possibly both—were mailed by the actual killer, Dr. George Hill Hodel.

Let's examine the evidence.

LAPD Police Museum Black Dahlia Exhibit May 2012

Page 382 *not used—unfocused images—the below montage stands in substitution.*

383|LAPD HISTORICAL SOCIETY: THE NEW EVIDENCE

George Hodel 1951

Letter No. 1 identifies the "Dahlia Killer" with a drawing that strongly resembles Dr. George Hodel, circa 1947. The hand-printed note also appears to resemble my father's handwriting. The extended letter "D" and the dotting of the capital "I" are both consistent with George Hodel's known handwriting.

Plus, in January 1947, the legitimate "Black Dahlia Avenger" sent an altered photograph of a young male in one of his many mailings. Signing the note as "A Friend," the sender claimed the photo was a picture of "the Werewolf killer." [That photo was later identified as Armand Robles, age 17, who later came forward to inform the police that just before the Dahlia murder he had been assaulted by a man fitting George Hodel's description.]

1947 anonymous mailing of "Werewolf Killer"

Unfortunately, the photograph I took of this exhibit is slightly out-of-focus, (due to shooting it through the glass cabinet) and we cannot now read the postmark. It is unknown by me if it was sent with the original batch of 1947 "Avenger Letters" or if it was mailed later.

Either way, we see this letter was addressed to the original and primary Dahlia investigator, Finis Brown, and contains three stamps. (Placing excess postage on his mailings was a common M.O. of the Black Dahlia Avenger.)

Based on all of these factors, I believe this letter and postage should be analyzed for the presence of DNA. If a viable sample is obtained, it should be compared to the existing DNA profile belonging to my father, George Hodel.

LETTER NO. 2

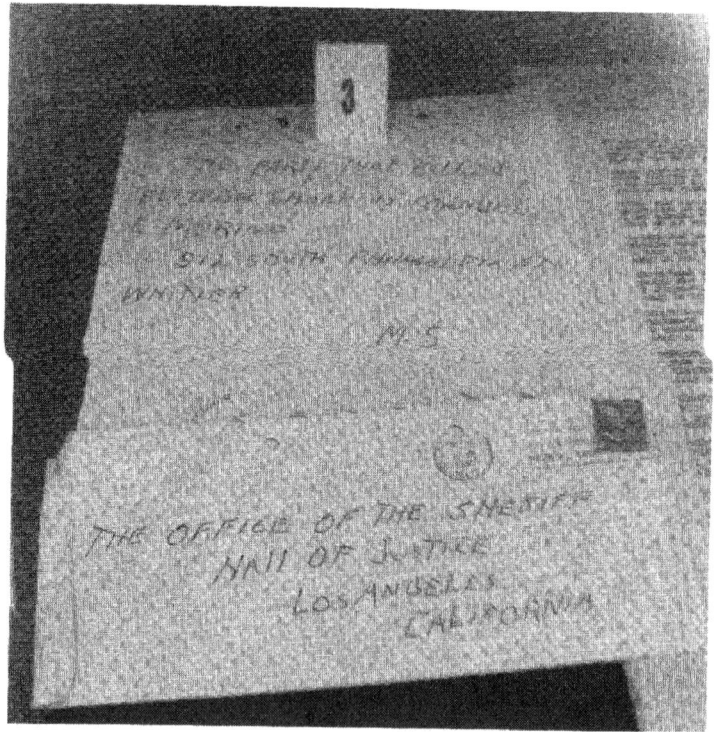

385|LAPD Historical Society: The New Evidence

Letter No. 2 [LAPDHS Exhibit 3] was mailed to sheriff's office at the downtown Hall of Justice. It reads:

Sheriff

The party that killed Elizabed Short is Manuel L. Merino.
512 South Philadelfia St.
Whitier

M.S.

It is written in the customary block printing with what I believe are deliberately misspelled words (Elizabed, Philadelfia, Whitier) that, as we know, are consistent with previous known and identified Avenger mailings.

However, what really caught my attention was that this letter was postmarked in 1950, some three-plus years after the murder. Why would anyone, be they a "crank" or the legitimate killer, send in information on the Black Dahlia murder long after it had fallen from the front pages and was no longer in the public eye?

Then I looked at the date of the postmark—*October 10, 1950*—and instantly made the connection. We know the Black Dahlia Avenger had a penchant for "anniversaries" and frequently used them in connection with his taunts. Significant dates were a real part of his M.O.

Recall the 1944 Bauerdorf Letter where the Avenger's typed note to LAPD promised he would appear in person at the Hollywood Canteen (the victim's former employer) on or near October 11, and specifically called it out as "the one-year anniversary of her murder." He signed off on that note by typing, "Let the Los Angeles Police arrest the murderer if they can."

Bauerdorf Anniversary Note from her killer
claiming the murder was "Divine Retribution."

387|LAPD HISTORICAL SOCIETY: THE NEW EVIDENCE

Letter No. 2's postmark of October 10 is not just any anniversary. Rather, it is a specific taunt. Another "Let the LAPD catch me if they can."

October 10th is the birthday of my father, Dr. George Hill Hodel.

George Hill Hodel Birth Certificate showing birth in Los Angeles on 10.10.07

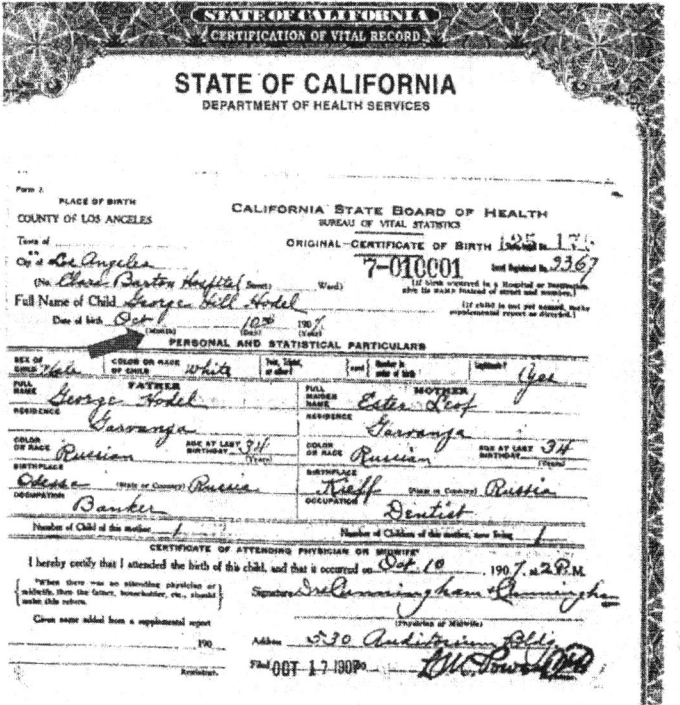

Based on our updated investigation, we know that while October,1950 had no real significance to the Black Dahlia investigation in general, it was especially time-specific to the then-prime suspect, Dr. George Hodel.

How?

Just five months earlier, as George was about to be arrested by LADA Lieutenant Frank Jemison, we know he fled Los Angeles, possibly to Mexico or to the Territory of Hawaii.

From the newly discovered Huston Letters, we also know my father was back at the Sowden/Franklin House with my mother for a brief period in August/September 1950. The reason? Maybe to collect his personal possessions and finalize the sale of the Franklin house before relocating to Hawaii and then Manila.

I believe my father mailed this birthday taunt to law enforcement as a slap in the face. Some three years later, he wanted to remind them he was still in control.

Let's examine the handwriting. Overall, it fits his usual printing style. However, there is one highly distinctive characteristic known to be used by my father that, for me, jumped off the envelope. It was the letter "c."

On occasion, George Hodel would write a lower-case "c" like a lowercase "e." Highly distinctive!

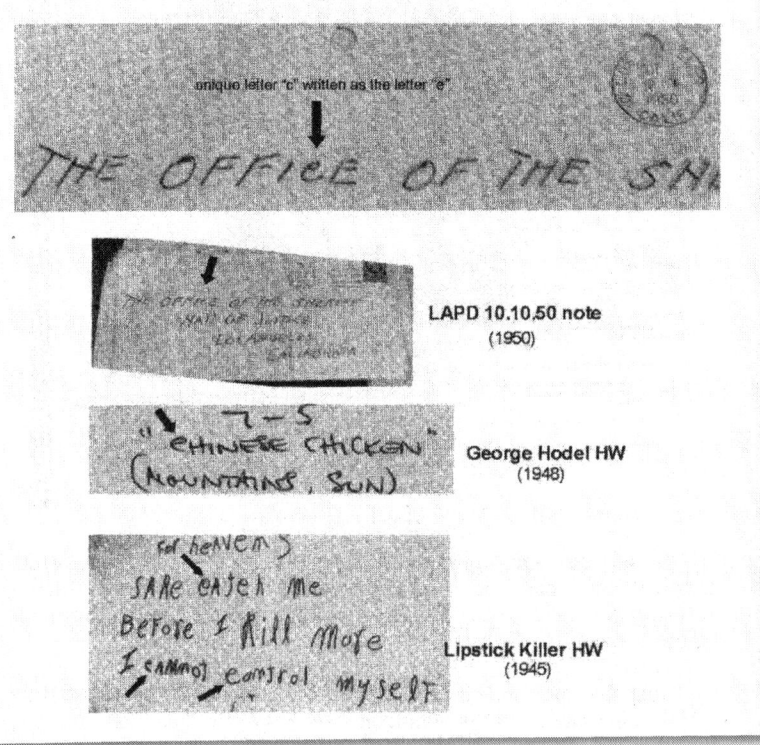

LAPD 10.10.50 note
(1950)

George Hodel HW
(1948)

Lipstick Killer HW
(1945)

389|LAPD HISTORICAL SOCIETY: THE NEW EVIDENCE

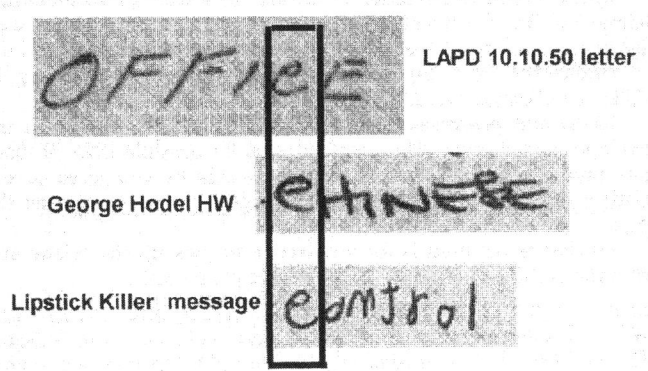

LAPD 10.10.50 letter

George Hodel HW

Lipstick Killer message

There are only three numerals on the October 10 letter—5, 1, and 2—written together as the address "512 South Philadelfia St."

Compare those to the same numbers found on a known envelope hand-printed by George Hodel in 1971. Although written twenty years apart, they look similar, especially the numeral 2.

George Hodel HW (1971)

LAPD EXHIBIT HW 1950

Based on this combination of factors, it's a strong possibility that George Hill Hodel is the author of Letter No. 2, mailed to the police on his birthday and, to a lesser degree, possibly Letter No. 1, too.

Unlike the other 1947 Avenger mailings, which according to LAPD, have "disappeared," these have not.

LAPD still possesses these two original letters, along with the envelopes and stamps. They can be tested for possible DNA. If those tests produced a DNA profile, it could easily be compared to the existing full DNA profile on George Hodel to identify him as the suspect.

All that is required is for a detective to pick up the phone and order the evidence to be tested. One simple phone call.

This 1936 "Lone Woman" Rape/Murder of victim Ruth Muir concludes what San Diego authorities believed was a series of crimes that were very possibly all committed by the same suspect.

For the most part, I am in total agreement.

I am not privy to any of the actual police files, so it is possible that in the intervening decades, one or more of these crimes could have been solved.

If it or they have, I am unaware and have not seen any public reporting of the solution.

It is also of interest that the series of San Diego murders stopped when George Hodel received his medical degree in June 1936 and shortly after that accepted a job as the sole surgeon at a CCC (Civilian Conservation Corps) logging camp in Arizona.

From 1936-1938 George Hodel was for the most part working out of California and serving as a District Health Officer in both Arizona and New Mexico.

That, however, did not stop his serial crimes, as documented in my book, *In The Mesquite: The Solving of the 1938 West Texas Kidnap Torture Murders of Hazel and Nancy Frome (Thoughtprint Press 2019)*.

I want to underscore that it is not me, the author of this book, that initially linked all of these San Diego murders as possible serial crimes.

No, it was the San Diego police and sheriff's departments and the press that made these links a decade before I was even born.

This was forward-thinking on their part, considering the term "serial killings" was not in use until the early 1980s. (Before that, the press and police generally called them "mass or chain murders.")

The Napa Journal, Friday, September 11, 1936

LATEST DEATH ADDS TO SAN DIEGO MYSTERY

Caption reads:

How long will shadowy death strike at women and girls in and around San Diego, Cal.? That is what police are wondering as they seek to solve the latest of the mysterious slayings—that of Ruth Muir, near La Jolla, a suburb, the seventh in the San Diego area in as many years. In each case, investigation has led to a blank wall. The dread toll of unsolved murder mysteries in and around San Diego includes the murder of Lois Kentle of Los Angeles and her fiancé, Francis Conlon, stabbed to death on the Ensenada, Mexico beach, August 26, 1930; Virginia Brooks, 10, abducted and slain at San Diego, February 14,1931; Louise Teuber, hanged near San Diego, April 18, 1932; Mrs. W.B. (Dolly) Bibbens, strangled in her San Diego apartment, April 23, 1931; Hazel Bradshaw, stabbed in Balboa Park, San Diego, May 2, 1931, and Celia Cota, 16, choked to death in San Diego, August 18, 1934. (Central Press)

1947

"Black Dahlia Avenger"
A San Diego Connection?

In my first publication, **Black Dahlia Avenger: A Genius for Murder** (Arcade 2003 hardcover edition), in Chapter 23, "*More 1940s L.A. Murdered Woman Cases*, I challenged the long-standing myth (perpetuated by LAPD) that "the Elizabeth Short, Black Dahlia murder was a standalone crime, none before and none after."

Here is the introduction of that chapter from page 293 the original *Black Dahlia Avenger* text:

Chapter 23

More 1940s L.A. Murdered Women Cases

BECAUSE OF THE SENSATIONAL coverage of the Black Dahlia murder in newspapers around the country in the late 1940s, most people who followed the case don't realize that Elizabeth Short's murder was only one of a series of crimes against lone attractive women from 1943 through the end of the decade. These cases bore striking similarities to one another, not only in the victims' profiles but in the nature and proximity of their crime scenes, the types of evidence that turned up, the descriptions of the men last seen with them, and the ways in which the police were taunted after the crimes·

In researching many of these crimes, some of which have already been examined by earlier researchers and authors, I found that law enforcement agencies other than the L.A.P.D., such as the Los Angeles Sheriff's Department, the Long Beach police, and the San Diego police, had also considered the possibility that these crimes were, in the newspapers' words, "Dahlia-related." Because of L.A.P.D.'s dogged resistance, and in some instances outright refusal, to share information with neighboring law enforcement, nothing came of the connections that to me seem readily apparent.

In 1947 San Diego detectives considered the possibility that the "Black Dahlia Avenger" suspect might well be responsible for the July 16, 1947, brutal San Diego murder of a 36-year-old divorcée named Marian Davidson Newton.

That crime occurred just six months after the "Black Dahlia" murder.

To their credit, they also asked themselves if there might be a further connection.

Might the Dahlia killer also be their decade-old serial killer who committed the horrific murders in their city in the 1930s?

Officers from San Diego, as previously indicated, met with LAPD detectives in 1947 but were turned away, with a "nothing to see here, not related."

Murder No. 11 Marian Davidson Newton (7.16.47)

In my now twenty-year-old initial investigation, I believed that San Diego's Marian Newton murder could well be connected to the other "LA Lone Woman Murders." I included that crime as "probably connected."

Here is my summary of that San Diego murder as initially presented in (*Black Dahlia Avenger* Arcade 2015 paperback edition), Chapter 31, *Forgotten Victims 1940s*, page 359:

Marian Davidson Newton (July 16, 1947)

Marian Newton, age thirty-six, was an attractive divorcée from Vancouver, British Columbia, who was vacationing in San Diego.

On the afternoon of Thursday, July 17, 1947, her body was discovered by a young married couple, Mr. and Mrs. Ward Robbins, who were on an outing to Torrey Pines Mesa just north of San Diego. While hiking in the afternoon, they discovered her body lying at the side of an isolated dirt road near some high brush.

San Diego homicide detectives responded to the crime scene and discovered that Marian Newton had been strangled to death with a thin wire or cord.

Bruises were found on her body, and she had been forcibly raped.

Tire tracks were visible nearby, and a coroner's examination estimated the time of death to be between midnight and 4:00 a.m. that day.

Two men's handkerchiefs were found nearby the body. One of them had stains; the other did not. *

The victim's purse and identification were later discovered on the sidewalk at University and Albatross Streets, near the downtown area of San Diego. The suspect had apparently thrown her purse out of his vehicle after he had disposed of the body.

Upon checking the last known movements and sightings of the victim, authorities were able to establish a description on the probable suspect and piece together the last hours of her life. Incredibly, her story would mimic—in details, actions, and words—the circumstances of Ora Murray's murder in 1943. From newspaper accounts and public records, here is a summary of what was known of her murder.

> *As referenced in our earlier investigations, this unusual "calling card" evidence corresponds to handkerchiefs also left at the French and Kern crime scenes.

On Wednesday, July 16, 1947, the victim, accompanied by Miss Edna Mitchell, whom she had met at the hotel where she was vacationing, decided to go to Sherman's nightclub. Sherman's was a popular military men's club and tourist attraction, famed for having nine different bars and the largest indoor dance floors in the world.

During the evening, the two women met and danced with a number of military men. Miss Mitchell told detectives that at one point, a civilian male began dancing with the victim. She described him as "tall, over six foot, thin, possibly in his thirties, with dark hair, wearing a tan sport coat and slacks, and a bright-colored tie."

The victim introduced him to Miss Mitchell, who could not recall his name for the detectives. When the suspect left momentarily, Mitchell told Marian Newton that she "didn't like the look of the guy" and warned her "not to get into any car with any man she met at the club."

Edna left the nightclub at 11:45 p.m. Witnesses there later confirmed that Marian Newton was seen leaving with a man who matched the description provided by Edna Mitchell.

Working in conjunction with San Diego FBI Agents, homicide detectives discovered that the description of this suspect closely matched that of someone previously known by them who had been frequenting downtown San Diego dancehalls and nightclubs in the weeks and months preceding the murder of Marian Newton. The suspect was believed to be using various names and aliases, including "Michael Vincent Martin." Representing himself at different nightspots both as an FBI agent and as a naval officer, the suspect was known to have used stolen and false identification in San Diego and had rented a vehicle using fake ID. A "Wanted Special Bulletin" was circulated within the law enforcement communities requesting information on the suspect.

Authors Janice Knowlton and Michael Newton (no relation to the victim) make reference to an interview, purported to have been conducted by Knowlton, of a retired sheriff's deputy, Thad Stefan, on July 12, 1993, during which Stefan referred to his original field notes dating from 1947. Stefan had documented an unusual incident that had occurred in Hollywood, at the Hub Bar and Café on Santa Monica Boulevard, in the sheriff's department territory. The incident was reported to him on January 26, 1947, and included a statement by a waitress, Dorothy Perfect, who reported that a man identifying himself as "George" came to the café and initially propositioned her, telling her, "I can fix you up with your own apartment on the Sunset Strip."

Dorothy Perfect described "George" as "a male Caucasian in his early forties, with wavy hair and glasses." She indicated "that while he did not appear drunk, he may have been under the influence of narcotics."

"George" identified himself as "an FBI agent assigned to work the *Black Dahlia* investigation," and informed Dorothy Perfect that "I can tell you who killed Elizabeth Short."

Deputy Stefan's notes included the fact that this same "George" had first come to the Hub Café on January 21, only six days after the discovery of Elizabeth Short's body. At the time, he had stayed in the bar area and was very talkative, informing the bartender he was "an FBI agent working on the Dahlia investigation." The bartender asked to see his agent's badge, at which point "George" mumbled something about "not being afraid of guns," and left the bar.

Other employees at the Hub confirmed that "George" had returned again on January 25, but left after only a few minutes, then returned one last time, on January 26, and was recognized by Dorothy Perfect from the prior contact, and she immediately summoned sheriff's deputies, but "George" left the bar before they arrived.

Initially San Diego detectives considered the possibility of a connection between their victim and the Los Angeles wave of killings of lone women, including that of Elizabeth Short, but again LAPD discounted and denied any connection.

Though the first known to occur outside of Los Angeles County, this crime is identical in MO to the Ora Murray killing. Coupled with the physical description of the suspect it must be included with the rest of the George Hodel's suspected serial killings.

Author's Note - I conclude Chapter 5 with a chronological listing of the 1930s San Diego murders that law enforcement suspected were serially connected and that I believe could well have been committed by George Hodel while living and attending medical school in California.

1. **Francis Conlon, age 24** *and*

2. **Lois Kentle, age 23, August 26, 1930, Ensenada, Mexico**

3. **Virginia Brooks, age 10, February 11, 1931, University Ave and Winona St, SD**

4. **Louise Teuber, age 17, April 19, 1931, Base of Black Mountain, SD**

5. **Dolly Bibbens, age 44, April 23, 1931, 1272 11th St, SD**

6. **Hazel Bradshaw, age 23, May 2, 1931, Balboa Park, SD**

7. **Maude Detweiler, age 40, August 28, 1931, 13th Ave and B Street, SD**

8. **Mary Adams, age 23, March 4, 1934, 1733 First Avenue, SD**

9. **Celia Cota, age 16, August 18, 1934, Balboa Park, SD**

10. **Ruth Muir, age 48, August 1, 1936, La Jolla Beach, SD**

Plus: I am also, here, including the eleventh San Diego murder that occurred in 1947 that I suspect is also serially connected to the earlier crimes.

11. **Marian Davidson Newton, age 36, July 16, 1947, Torrey Pines Mesa, SD**

Chapter 6

Kidnap Torture Murders of
Hazel and Nancy Frome

April 3, 1938

For Detailed Information
See the stand alone TrueCrime book:
In The Mesquite

Chapter 7

The Curious Case of Alfred "Bud" Lord

Murder or Suicide?

November 10, 1938

First, let me credit my original "source" on this investigation: "Seagull."

The unnamed woman goes by the name of "Seagull" and is a longtime contributor to the online website of Zodiackiller.com. The only information I have on her is that she joined that website in 2007 and has, to date, posted over 2400 "messages."

That website, run and maintained by Tom Voigt, and online for over twenty years, is pretty much the "go-to" Internet address for all things "Zodiac."

It was a significant source of my initial research on "Zodiac" and provided much of the documentation (police photos, crime reports, CA DOJ (California Department of Justice) reports, witness interviews, etc.) that assisted me in my investigation and linkage of my father, Dr. George Hill Hodel, as the serial killer who called himself, "Zodiac." (See my detailed investigations in my books, *Most Evil* (Dutton 2009) and *Most Evil II* (Rare Bird Books 2015).

Some years back, I chanced upon the following entry initially posted on the website in 2011 by "Seagull":

The Zodiac Killer -- Unsolved & Unforgotten
This is the discussion forum of Zodiackiller.com, online since 1998

Alfred M. "Bud" Lord's Death

Page 1 of 2

Seagull   Posted: 12:54 PM - Oct 01, 2011

I was able to find a copy of *Official Detective* magazine, June 1941, with the story of Bud Lord's death. It is a detailed account with many pictures. The magazine is large, about the size of a *Life* magazine so I had to do some serious surgury on it to include all the pictures and text. The headline spanned two pages and I could not combine them into one page. The same is true for the image of the pawn ticket which ended up being on pages 6 and 8.

The story is interesting and confirms much of what Howard has written about it with a couple of minor exceptions. It lays out how detectives came to the conclusion that Lord's death was indeed a suicide and not murder. Throughout the article the word "clue" is spelled "clew" as it is in the rest of the articles in the magazine!

As indicated above, "Seagull" posted her source, which was the article published in *Official Detective Magazine,* June 1941.

My thanks to "Seagull" for piquing my interest in this unknown and long-forgotten whodunit.

The Crime

Here is the headline and breaking story of the New Orleans murder as it appeared in the *Los Angeles Times* on November 12, 1938.

Los Angeles Times, **November 12, 1938**

NEW ORLEANS, November 11 (A.P.)

Police investigating the wharf slaying of a stylish, but penniless man they believe was Bud Lord of San Diego had a theory tonight he might have been shot to death by a person who followed him across the country for that purpose.

Pinned to the victim's overcoat was a pencil-printed note which read: "He accidentally knew too much, too bad." Beneath the printing was a cross within a circle.

Miss Shirley Jones of Wichita, Kan., whose name was found on a card in the dead man's pocket, said at her home that the description of the victim fitted that of Lord, 20, even to eyeglasses.

She said Lord, en route to this city to seek a job, stopped in Wichita to see her but left there Monday after telling her he had seen on the street a man who threatened to kill him in San Diego over a business quarrel.

Miss Jones, 17-year old daughter of a Wichita grain man, said Lord left by train for New Orleans with $40.

No money was found in the slain man's pockets, and he had a watch chain without a watch.

Police said Albert Boze, clerk in a small downtown hotel, identified the victim as the man who had registered with him Wednesday morning under the name of "Poudah Mannering, 200 Sixth St., Yuma, Ariz."

Father Says Son Made Trip to Seek Work

SAN DIEGO. November 11, 1938 (A.P.)

Frank B. Lord, father of Alfred M. (Bud) Lord, reported killed in New Orleans, today said he had received no information other than press dispatches.

His son left here Nov.3 to go to Wichita looking for work and to see Miss Shirley Jones. His family said they know of no enemies who might have slain the boy, who was 20 last August 14.

Photo showing the position of victim Bud Lord at the crime scene on the pier in New Orleans November 11, 1938

Author's Note - Seventeen (17) men (all but one, wearing hats) are lined up on the dock (many standing in/near/or on the crime scene). Where is the victim's hat?

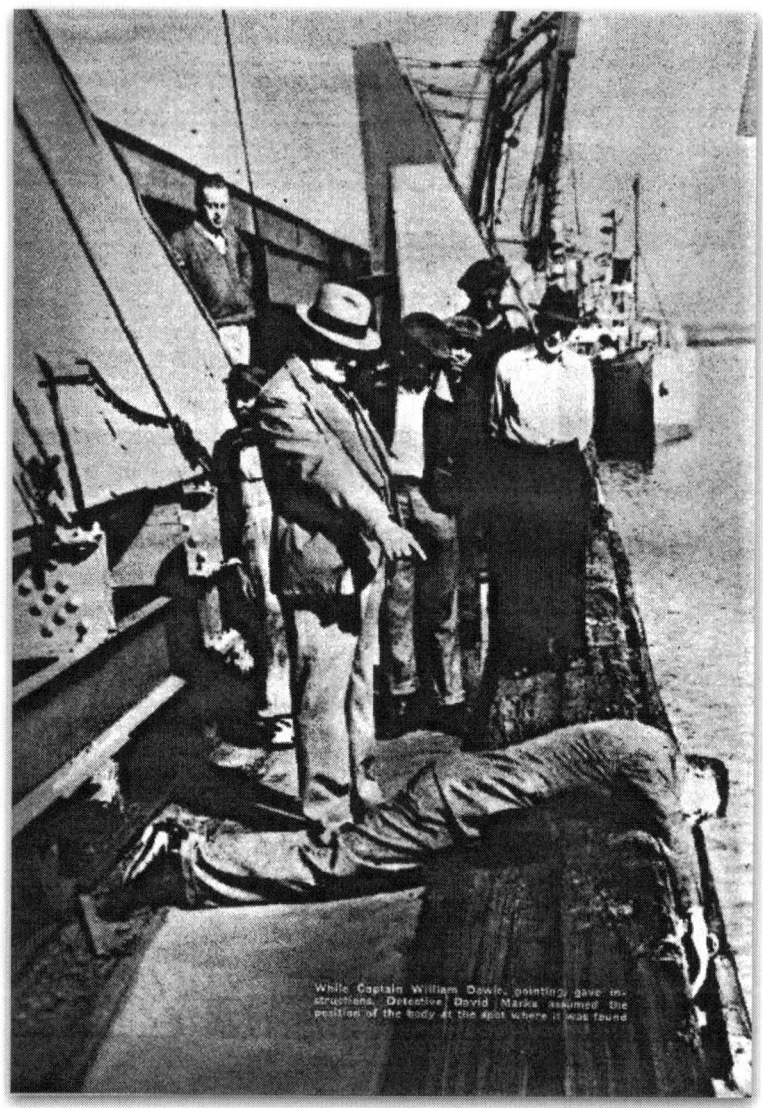

While Captain William Dowie, pointing, gave instructions, Detective David Marks assumed the position of the body at the spot where it was found

Reenactment by New Orleans Police detectives

The caption above reads: "While Captain William Dowie, pointing, gave instructions, Detective David Marks assumed the position of the body at the spot where it was found." Note: no mention of, or depiction of, the location of the victim's hat.

Albuquerque Journal Nov. 12, 1938

See Vengeance In Mystery Death

Theorize Assassin Premeditated Killing

The day after the murder, the following article appeared in the *Albuquerque Journal*:

**"See Vengeance In Mystery Death
Theorize Assassin Premeditated Killing"**

NEW ORLEANS, November 11

Police investigating the wharf slaying of a stylish but penniless man they believe was Bud Lord of San Diego, Cal. had a theory Friday night he might have been shot to death by a person who followed him across the country for that purpose.

...

Pistol is Found

Dr. C. Grenes Cole, coroner, terming the death a homicide, said the man had been shot through the top of the head, while wearing his hat, by a small-caliber bullet. No powder burns were discovered, and the coroner estimated the death weapon had been fired at least six feet away from the victim.

Police said Albert Boze, clerk in a small downtown hotel, identified the victim as the man who had registered with him Wednesday morning under the name of "Poudah Mannering, 200 Sixth Street, Yuma, Ariz."

Yuma authorities said the man was unknown there.

Crime Scene Investigation

"It is one of the most mysterious cases I have ever handled," said Chief of Detectives John Grosch, who revealed the belief Lord's assailant had followed him from San Diego to Wichita, Kans., and then to New Orleans.

Detective Grosch went on to inform the press that "the manner in which the card was attached to his clothing also was significant, as it was pinned to the back of the overcoat with a small piece of wire."

Chief Grosch was quoted as saying:

"The evidence, in this case, is most conflicting. We have been unable to establish any motive. We failed to find a single trace of powder burns, and if he had shot himself, we would have found some trace of powder. We will have to proceed on the basis that this is a case of murder."

The Victim

Alfred M.—Bud—Lord: His wedding plans weren't known to the girl he said he was going to marry

Alfred M "Bud" Lord, age 20

A day later, the "murder" suddenly becomes a "suicide" after officers found the gun in the Mississippi River's mud just below where the body had fallen.

The following excerpt from the *Blackwell Daily Journal*, November 14, 1938:

NEW ORLEANS, NOVEMBER 14 (U.P.)

Instead of being the victim of a "gang murder," 20-year-old Alfred M. (Bud) Lord of San Diego, Calif., took his own life, police said today.

They found the gun he used, a small-caliber revolver, in the mud of the Mississippi river. It dropped there from his fingers after he lay on a banana wharf, fully clothed, and fired one bullet into the top of his head.

Lord planned the death for a week, police said, after registering at a small hotel under an assumed name. He ripped identification marks from his clothing and pinned a note, "he knew too much, too bad," to his coat before shooting himself last Thursday midnight.

He put a picture of his high school sweetheart over his heart. She identified the youth but had no explanation for his death.

Author's Note - Clear example of a journalist taking "literary license" as the photo of his girlfriend was found in the victim's wallet. With what other "facts" did journalists take "literary license"?

Father Denies Son Took His Own Life

(By United Press)

SAN DIEGO, Nov. 14. — The father of Alfred (Bud) Lord, San Diego youth whose body was found on a New Orleans wharf under mysterious circumstances, expressed the belief today that his 21-year-old son did not shoot himself.

"Bud had no reason to take his own life," Frank B. Lord, his father, said. "He had everything to live for. He left here to marry Miss Shirley Jones, of Wichita, Kans., and he had great plans for the future. I know he couldn't have committed suicide."

Lord said he had requested New Orleans authorities to make a further investigation of the case.

The youth's body was found Nov. 11 by a night watchman. A note pinned to the coat said "he knew too much."

**Photo of Bud Lord and his girlfriend Shirley Jones
His wallet in his Senator Hotel room.**

This is the actual photograph found in the victim's wallet which gave police their first concrete clew and led to an amazing discovery

MYSTERY IN CLOSED CASE OF BUD LORD

Detectives Call it Suicide, Coroner Calls it Murder

NEW ORLEANS, November 14

Authorities prepared today to send to San Diego, Cal., the body of Alfred M. "Bud" Lord, 20, found Friday morning on the riverfront with a bullet in the head.

Officially, the death remained a mystery, as Chief of Detectives John Grosch declared it was a closed case of suicide on police records, while Coroner C. Grenes Coles listed it as a homicide.

...

A police diver Saturday recovered from the Mississippi river a .25 caliber automatic pistol directly below the edge of the docks where Lord's body lay.

Chief Grosch said after ballistics tests that this weapon fired the fatal bullet. "I think it likely that Lord printed the note himself to throw us off the track," he added.

Grosch said that Lord's hat, through which the bullet passed, was marked with powder burns. Coroner Cole declared he found no powder burns.

Lord's parents said last night in San Diego that their son left there for Wichita, expecting to marry Miss Jones.

His father, Frank H. Lord, expressed doubt that the young man had committed suicide. "He had great plans for the future, and I knew he couldn't have committed suicide," said the older Lord. "He had everything to live for."

WEAPON

A .25 caliber automatic was recovered from the riverbed, *identical* to the handgun pictured top of page 332. Officers claimed ballistics showed it to be the gun that killed Bud Lord.

The Note

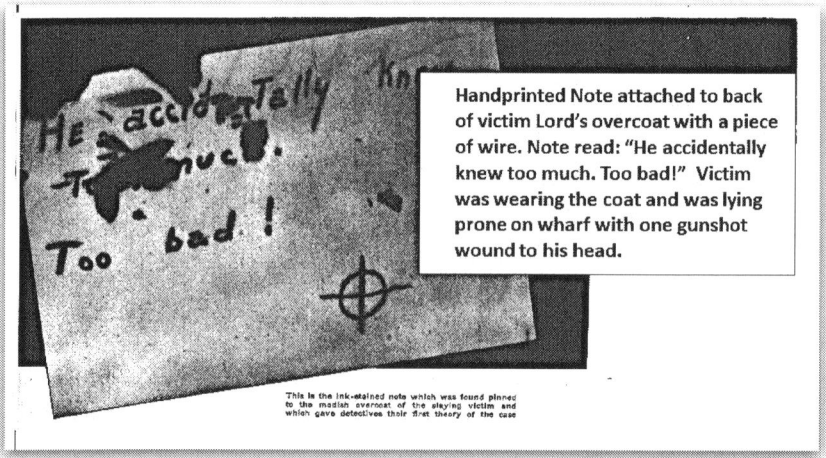

Handprinted Note attached to back of victim Lord's overcoat with a piece of wire. Note read: "He accidentally knew too much. Too bad!" Victim was wearing the coat and was lying prone on wharf with one gunshot wound to his head.

Small Caption Reads: "This is the ink-stained note which was found pinned to the modish overcoat of the slaying victim and which gave detectives their first theory of the case."

Sample of Lord's handwriting from Hotel Senator, New Orleans, where the victim registered and checked in on November 9, 1938, using the name "Poudah Mannering."

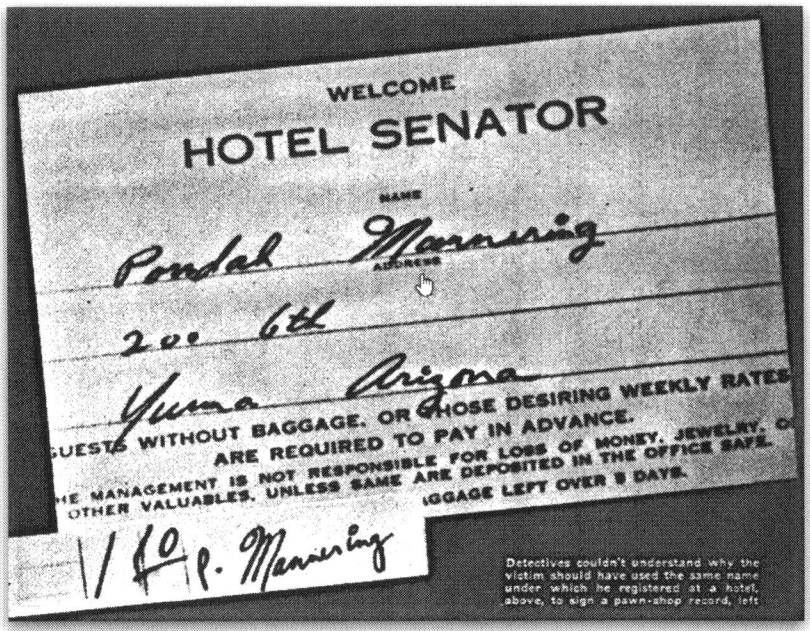

The caption reads: "Detectives couldn't understand why the victim should have used the same name under which he registered at a hotel, above, to sign a pawnshop record."

Chief of Detectives claimed, "Lord's handwriting matched that of the note." Really? Judge for yourself.

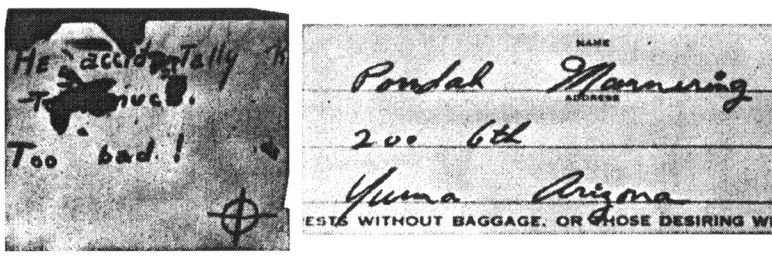

Within just a few days, the Alfred "Bud" Long case was "closed" and written off by New Orleans Chief of Detectives as "a suicide."

Some three years later, without any further investigation and the case being carried as a "routine suicide," an article appeared in the June 1941 edition of *Official Detective Stories*.

July 1941 edition of

Official Detective Stories magazine.

The Alfred "Bud" Lord investigation was reviewed in the June 1941 edition. The article introduced us to the three-year-old case as follows:

"Because He Couldn't Make Good."

"Could a Story of Phony Wedding Plans Told by This Youth Aid New Orleans' Detectives in Their Attempts to Solve His Mysterious, Midnight Slaying on a Deserted Wharf?"

By John J. Grosch

Chief of Detectives, New Orleans Police Department,

As told to Henry Jordan

As written by Henry Jordan, the article reads like a dime novel with Detective Grosch presented as a "super sleuth" ferreting out the mystery.

Additional information presented in the magazine article included:

- Locating the victim's hotel room at the downtown "Senator Hotel" and in checking his room discovering his clothing and a wallet with his girlfriend Shirley Jones's home address of 204 N. Graves Street, Wichita, Kansas, and a photograph of the couple. (Shown previously on page 330.)

- Contacting Shirley Jones in Wichita, Kansas, who identified the victim, including his real name of Alfred M. "Bud" Lord, with a home address of 6355 Imperial Highway, San Diego, California.

- A statement provided by Shirley Jones, age 17, indicated that Bud Lord visited her at her home on November 5, 1938. Lord told her "he had to flee San Diego as he had gotten into trouble with some man who threatened to kill him and that the man had followed him to Wichita." Miss Jones went on to say that Lord "left Wichita on the morning of November 9 because he had met the man who trailed him from San Diego and feared for his life."

- In the article, Detective Grosch then orders his fellow detectives to "bring me the hat worn by the victim." He then examined the hat and stated to his fellow officers, "There are faint powder burns on it; as far as I am concerned, this Bud Lord guy committed suicide." Grosch speculated that "Lord wrote the death note because he had a flair for the dramatic and probably thought it would look better if he would die as a mystery case."

- **Author's Note** - Where was the hat found? Not on the head of the victim? Crime scene and reenacted scene photos show the "victim" bareheaded. What are the probabilities that a man lies down on a dock, his head, neck, shoulders and arms hanging over the edge of the dock which is under his arm pits. With his head and arms dangling over, above the river, shoots himself through the "top of his head" (while wearing a hat) and after the shot drops the pistol out of his dead or dying hand into the river below the dock. Where is the hat? Still on his head? Why wouldn't it come off and fall in the water and be swept away? How tight would the man's hat had to have been around his head, to stay on after shooting himself in the top of the head—through his hat? Again, where was the hat found? And what kind of hat was it? The accounts do not say, only that Grosch told detectives to "bring me the hat worn by the victim."

- Grosch is then quoted in the article as saying, "I took the hat to the crime lab and fired four 'test shots' into the hat," claiming, "see faint gunpowder is left behind."

- **Author's note** - If Detective Grosch did fire "test shots" into the victim's hat, this action would be considered, in modern times, an unacceptable police procedure. Hard to believe he would even admit to doing such an act, but then again, it was eighty-two years ago, so?

- Grosch claims he then came up with the idea of searching the area and the water near where the body was found and the diver recovered the .25 caliber automatic.

- The pulp magazine article concluded with a claim by Detective Grosch that the handgun was supposedly traced back to a pawnshop in Wichita, Kansas, where a man bought the gun on November 7, 1938. The individual fit Alfred Lord's description. The pawnshop owner, Mr. Jacob Nathanson, described the purchaser as a "nice looking man, who said he was twenty-two years old and paid me ten dollars for the gun. I gave him a half dozen shells."

- Pawnshop owner Nathanson, when shown a photo of Alfred "Bud" Lord by Wichita detectives, said, he believed "he was the man that purchased the handgun."

- In the follow-up article, no documentation to support any of detective Grosch's claims was provided.

- All we know is that this information included in the Henry Jordan article came "as told by Detective Grosch."

- Based on what we know, I still am forced to ask, as relates to the Alfred "Bud" Lord investigation, "Murder or Suicide"?

30 Years Later - A Possible Zodiac Connection?

Enough factors have surfaced to include the "curious case" of Alfred "Bud" Lord as a chapter here in *The Early Years - Part 2* of my George Hodel investigations.

They are:

- The fact victim Alfred "Bud" Lord was reportedly "involved and recognized for his acting in plays in Pasadena." (We recall George Hodel was active in plays at the Pasadena Playhouse in the 1930s.)

- In the preceding chapters we saw how the city of San Diego became an integral part of our investigations and that Alfred "Bud" Lord lived in San Diego and was approached by a man who "threatened his life," which caused Lord to flee the city and use an "assumed name."

- The "**Zodiac Symbol**" and handwritten note "*He knew too much, too bad*"could well be related to our investigations presented in previous chapters. As a San Diego teenager, Alfred "Bud" Lord could well have "known too much" about one or more of the investigations presented.

Author's Note 1 - In *Most Evil (Dutton 2009)* and *Most Evil II* (Rare Bird Books 2015), I present the investigation and linkage identifying Dr. George Hill Hodel as the 1968-9 serial killer known as "Zodiac." *Not only is the symbol on the 1938 note pinned on the victim's clothing a virtual match to the handwritten symbol in the Zodiac Letters, but so is the handwriting. The block printing from 1938 is a close match to Zodiac's and George Hodel's handwriting from thirty years later.* This synchronicity of both symbol and handwriting (in each case) is so plausibly significant that any reasonable and well-trained investigator would see the connection and give it the appropriate weight of possibility.

Author's Note 2 - In *The Early Years Part 1 - 1920s (pages 353-357)* I made brief mention of the "Three Clue Signatory" ("Z", Ogham Cypher, and Zodiac "Cross & Circle") linking them to signage by George Hodel and to the spelling of his name. In this edition *The Early Years Part 2 - 1930s* and specific to the Alfred "Bud" Lord crime, I have chosen to expand on that analysis.

Alfred "Bud" Lord's note symbol compared to known "Zodiac" symbols - 30 years apart

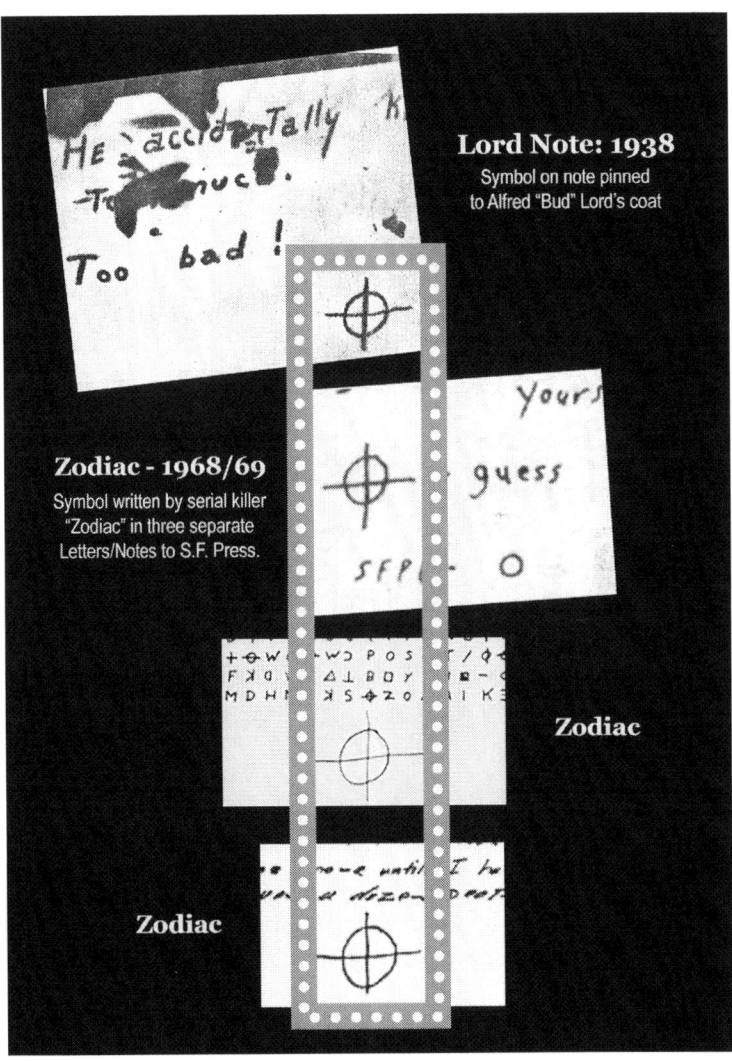

Lord Note: 1938
Symbol on note pinned
to Alfred "Bud" Lord's coat

Zodiac - 1968/69
Symbol written by serial killer
"Zodiac" in three separate
Letters/Notes to S.F. Press.

Zodiac Symbol as: Cypher, Sigil & Calligram

Cypher *noun*: a secret or disguised way of writing; a code.
Sigil *noun*: a seal, mark, or signet
> **Signet** *noun*: a seal used officially to give personal
> authority to a document *in lieu of signature.*
> (Emphasis mine)

Calligram *noun*: a design in which the letters of a word
(such as a name) are rearranged so as to form a
decorative pattern or figure (as for a seal) Merriam-Webster

In ***Most Evil II*** *(Rare Bird Books 2015),* **Chapter 10**,
one of the most remarkable findings in my GHH/Zodiac
investigation came from a reader from across the pond.

It was presented to me by Yves Person, a high-school
teacher in Paris, France.

Incredibly, Yves had "cracked the code" on a signet
cypher used by Zodiac in one of his mailings to the press
and police.

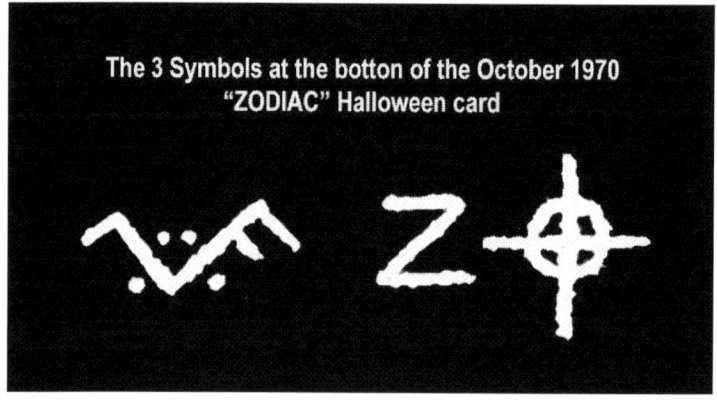

CHAPTER 10

Rosetta Stone

Fig. 10.0

ROSETTA STONE—An inscribed stone found near Rosetta (now called Rashid) in Egypt in 1799. Its text is written in three scripts: hieroglyphic, demotic, and Greek. The deciphering of the hieroglyphs by Jean-Francois Champollion in 1822 led to the interpretation of many other early records of Egyptian civilization.

(as noun) A key to some previously undecipherable mystery or unattainable knowledge.[33]

The Zodiac Rosetta Stone—Cracking the Cipher

"For tis the sport to have the enginer / Hoist with his owne petar."

—Shakespeare, Hamlet, *ACT III Scene iv.*

IT WAS WEDNESDAY, JULY 2, 2014; I had just begun preparing for a relaxing four-day holiday. No travel. No fighting traffic to and from the airport. Just some quiet time, at home, with the

---

[33]   Oxford Dictionary

anticipation of watching three or four good classic films, along with my July 4 traditional favorite, *Yankee Doodle Dandy*, starring James Cagney and Walter Huston. A welcome respite from writing and research. (Or so I thought.)

Just as I was closing down my computer, it happened. The sound of an incoming email. I glanced at my inbox and noted it was from France. I clicked on the new message:

Dear Sir,

Have you ever noticed that Zodiac's signature was a compound of two ogham "letters"? The letter on the left side is for "H" and the letter on the right side is for "L." The Irish name of the first "letter" is "beithe," that means "flash," "flame," and the other is called "uath," the old-Irish word for "scare." The dots remain mysterious.

I read your first book shortly after it was published, and it deeply changed my mind upon the real meaning of XXth century (namely, in the fields of ideology and culture).

Best regards from France.
—Y. P.

I responded with a few questions to "Y. P." and several follow-up emails arrived in quick succession from this anonymous Frenchman:

Encore-Ogham alphabet:

I'm back from my Celtic languages handbook: according to certain forms of writings (or engravings) the dots are for the vowels. Two dots = "O"; four dots = "E."

I refer to the signature that is drawn on the Halloween postcard and its envelope. (An inverted "L" on the left side, an inverted "F" on the right side and the four dots in the middle of the signature.) The inverted "L" is the Irish "letter" for "H"; the inverted "F" is the Irish "letter"

*for "L." There would be no "translation" into Irish, just a
cryptic game from an alphabet to another one.)*

A few of Y. P.'s words seemingly jumped off the page:

*Zodiac's signature a compound of two Ogham letters, "H"
on the left and "L" on the right? Celtic languages? Ogham
Alphabet? Cryptic game from an alphabet to another?*

I spent the next several days researching Y. P.'s references,
analyzing the material, and putting together a chart that,
I believe, "cracks the code" to Zodiac's mysterious Halloween
card symbol. The key to the symbol is just as "Y. P.," my
newfound *ami français,* had speculated. And, with this key—
the ancient Ogham alphabet—we can now, for the first time,
unlock, decipher, and read the signatory name of Zodiac.

See for yourself:

Ogham—The Key

Halloween Card   *Halloween Envelope*

Fig. 10.1   Fig. 10.2

*OGHAM /ˈɒgəm/—[1] (Modern Irish [ˈoːm] or[ˈoːəm];
Old Irish: ogam [ˈɔɣam]) is an Early Medieval alphabet
used primarily to write the early Irish language (in the
so-called "orthodox" inscriptions, 4th to 6th centuries),
and later the Old Irish language (so-called scholastic
ogham, 6th to 9th centuries).*

...

In Scotland, a number of inscriptions using the ogham writing system are known, but their language is still the subject of debate. It has been argued by Richard Cox in The Language of Ogham Inscriptions in Scotland *(1999) that the language of these is* **Old Norse**[34][35]

Ogham Writing on Standing Stone

Photo Courtesy of Jessica Spengler

Fig. 10.3

Author Note: Jessica Spengler's image: *'Fig 10.3'* (from page 160 of Chapter 10, *Most Evil II*) shows a standing stone with a carved image on the front and **Ogham writing on the stone's edge**. To draw the reader's attention to the carved Ogham inscription, a dotted rectangle has been added to the image.

---

34   Author's note: Emphasis mine
35   en.wikipedia.org/wiki/Ogham

The Ogham

The Celtic "Tree Alphabet" is a secret cypher of the Celtic bards and Druids, meant to make magical inscriptions on monuments. (Chart from McManus. *A Guide To Ogham*)

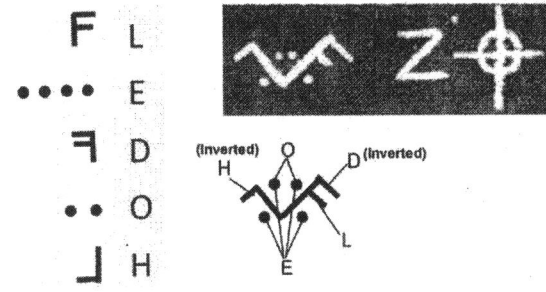

Fig. 10.4

Fig. 10.5

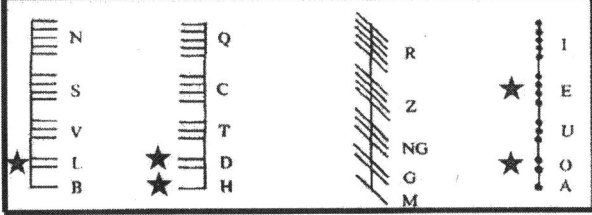

Fig. 10.6

162 – Steve Hodel

Below is shown a slightly more detailed rendering of the solution. (Courtesy of the artistry of my good friend, Robert "Dr. Watson" Sadler.):

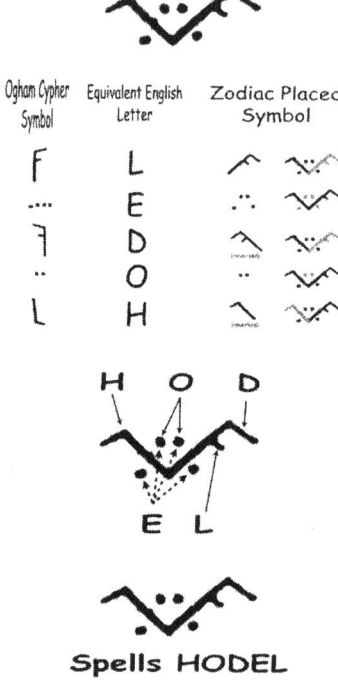

Fig. 10.7

The decryption is perfect. Zodiac's signature reads **H O D E L.** Nothing is missing. No additional letters have been added or omitted.

Based on this decryption, it is my belief that Dr. George Hill Hodel, thoroughly convinced that he was a "master criminal" and that his high-genius insulated him from detection—confident that his cleverness insured his cipher was "crack-proof"—wrote, as promised, on the front of his Halloween card, "...you ache to know my name, and so I'll clue you in." George Hodel threw all caution to the wind and signed his real name to the card.

Zodiac Halloween Card Deciphered

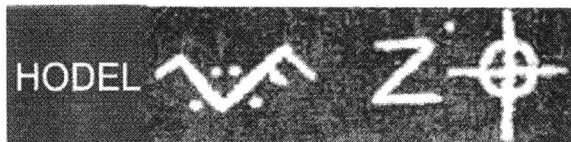

Fig. 10.8

The credit for this remarkable discovery must go to "Y. P." in Paris, France. I recently wrote and asked him if I might have permission to credit and use his real name, which he has just granted. "Y. P." is M. Yves Person, and to add a further ironic twist to our ongoing investigation, he teaches literature at a high school in the suburbs of Paris.[36]

M. Yves Person, Paris, France 2015

Fig 10.9

---

36   Many readers will recall that after the US military and intelligence experts were unable to solve Zodiac's original 1969 three-part cryptogram, a married couple, Donald and Bettye Harden, "cracked the code" after studying it for just one weekend. Their solution was confirmed by the Vallejo Police Department and published in the San Francisco newspapers. Donald Harden, like Yves Person, was also a high school teacher. Harden taught history and economics at North Salinas High School in Salinas, California.

Because of the importance of Yves' discovery and its potential linkage to this 83 year-old **sigil** or **signet** on the note pinned to the back of 1938 New Orleans victim Alfred "Bud" Lord, I am reproducing seven pages (157-163) from **Chapter 10, *Most Evil II*.** [See pages: 341-347].

As an introduction to the information in that chapter, here is a scan of the confirmed Zodiac "Halloween Card" sent to the press back in 1970. Note that Zodiac writes:

"You ache to know my name, and so I'll clue you in..."

Graphics courtesy of Robert J. Sadler

In my opinion, his "clues" are found in his signage, in the three signatures below the skeleton. The two hold the keys to his cat-and-mouse game "to know my name."

Three Zodiac signets enlarged (see page 340).

Cyphers and Sigils and Calligrams Oh My!

Cypher *noun*: a secret or disguised way of writing; a code.
Sigil *noun*: a seal, mark, or signet
Calligram *noun*: a design in which the letters of a word (such as a name) are rearranged so as to form a decorative pattern or figure (as for a seal) Merriam-Webster

Four years after Yves Person "cracked the Ogham cipher," a second equally remarkable discovery was made.

Again, it came by way of an email.

This time, it was not from a stranger across the sea but rather from a good friend I had been working with for several years in preparation for his plans to adapt my series of books to a television miniseries.

I refer to Robb Bindler, documentarian and film director, who at the time of this writing (May 2021) is actively engaged in the production, filming, and editing of the miniseries documentary, with an anticipated release in late 2022 or possibly 2023.

When I received the email below, the two of us had literally exchanged hundreds of emails, all related to different aspects of the investigation and ensuring our research was factually correct.

Like Yves Person's email, once the magnitude of Robb's discovery hit me, thanks to his roughly sketched diagram (page 351), I was stunned.

There it was AGAIN, like Poe's "Purloined Letter," hiding in plain sight.

Below is Robb's email to me from two years ago. (I have redacted his reference to named individuals for privacy purposes.)

On Mon, Aug 12, 2019, at 12:25 PM, S.R. Bindler wrote:

Steve —

Was reviewing ███'s comments on your blog, and he goes into Calligrams. Hadn't heard of these (but have seen them). I have heard and studied (when researching Jack Parsons a while back) occult sigils. I am pretty convinced the Zodiac crosshairs is a combo of a Calligram and a sigil that spells out HODEL. The fact GHH used the crosshairs like a signature (like the Ogham symbol) is even more persuasive. I wonder what ███ would say about it? Hard to prove, but it's hidden in plain sight!

I started playing around with sigils years ago and am pretty adept at creating them. When you start to play around with them, one tends to play with one's own name the most, trying to find a cool shape. Your eye quickly gets trained to find pleasing patterns. With everything I know about GHH's facility with images and language, I'm just convinced he was signing HODEL every time he used the crosshairs.

I know there is no smoking gun to be found here. Just saying.

Robb Bindler's first drawing in his email of Aug. 12, 2019

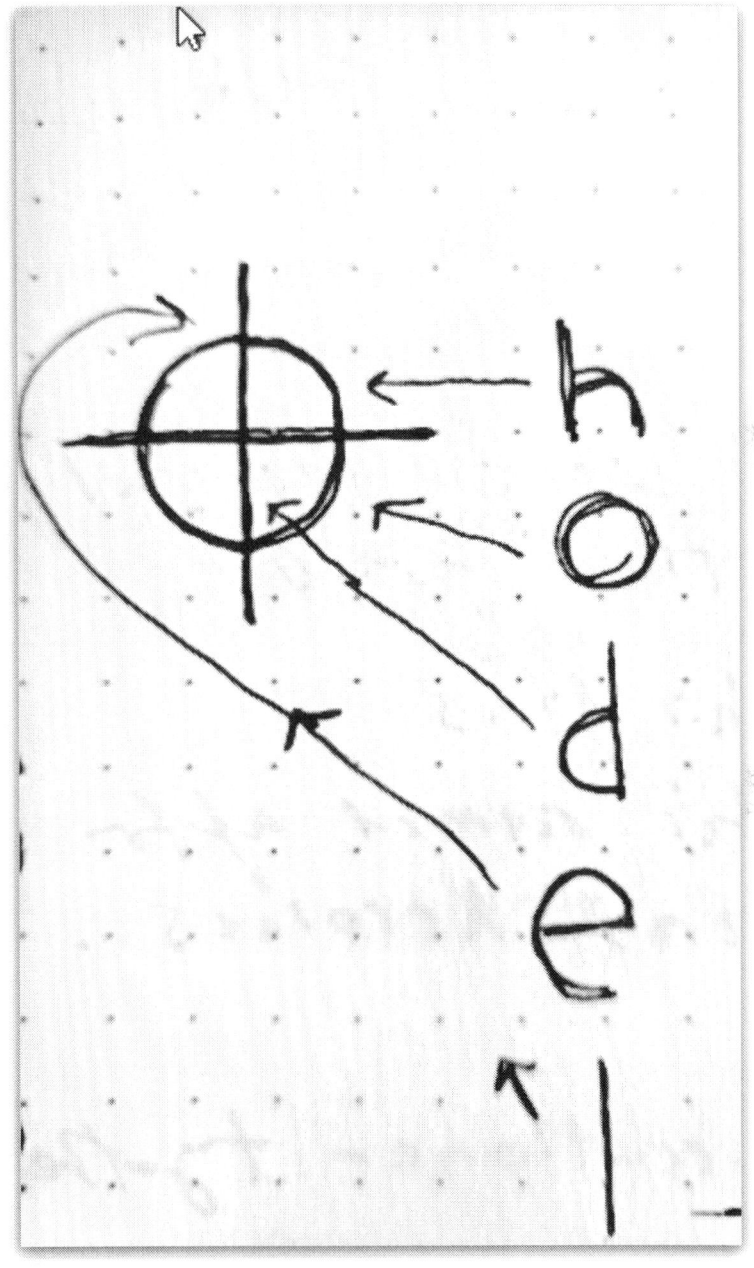

Robb Bindler's following diagrams show the result of his "cracking of the sigil." First as a vertical solution using the north-south alignment of the sigil. Second showing the solution on a horizontal east-west alignment.

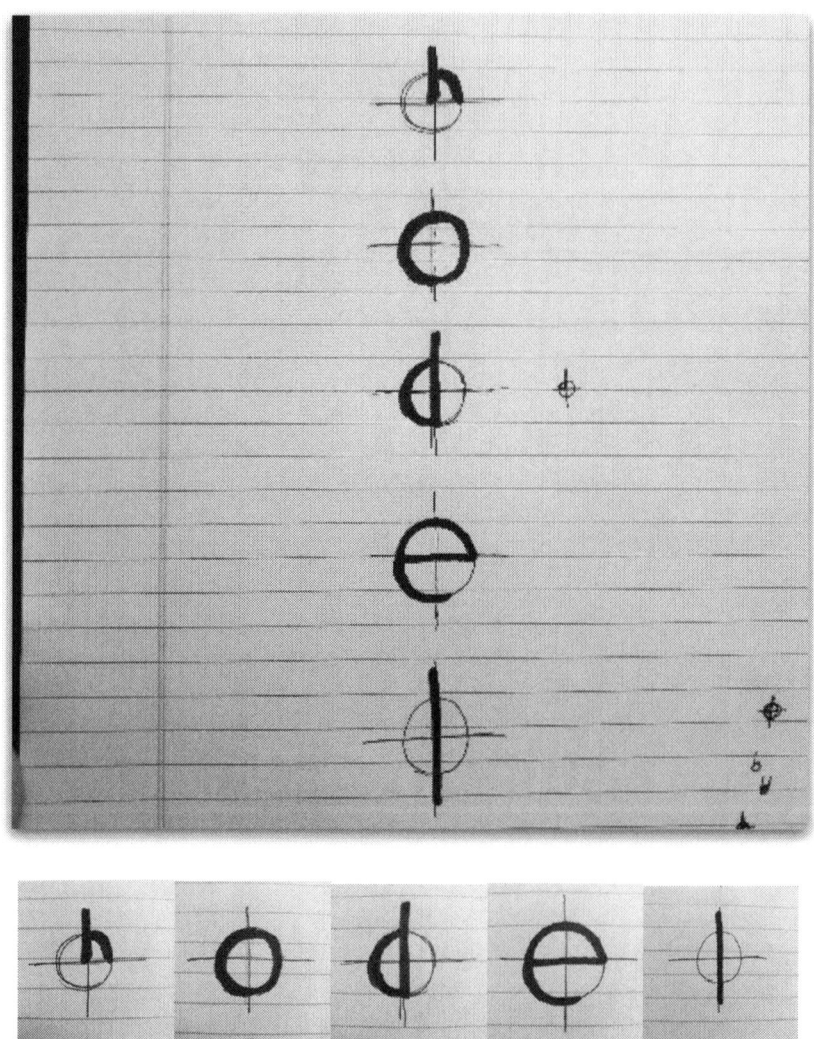

I must strongly disagree with my good friend Robb.

His discovery *is* just that—A SMOKING GUN.

A second smoking gun, as it directly corroborates both of George Hodel's Halloween Card "clues." ("You ache to know my name, so I'll clue you in." - page 340)

We now have both the Ogham HODEL cipher signature and the Zodiac Cross Hairs Circle HODEL **sigil** or **calligram** as signets—SIDE BY SIDE. (page 340)

Though separate and distinct, we have Robb Bindler in 2019 corroborating Yves Person's 2014 discovery by way of his independent code-breaking. Different sigils side by side, both were concealing the killer's actual name— HODEL.

Huge kudos to Robb for discovering the second "clue" that the rest of us missed seeing for over fifty-one years.

As relates to the 1938 New Orleans Alfred "Bud" Long death investigation, as documented earlier, I find it difficult to believe it was a suicide.

In my opinion, it was, in truth—a murder.

The victim's Pasadena and San Diego and sometimes "actor" connections just on their own create some degree of suspicion he could have known or met George Hodel.

The victim's statements to his girlfriend that "a San Diego man is following him and has threatened to kill him," is indicative of a GHH connection.

Add to this the crime signature of leaving a note, the handwriting, and the sardonic message, "He accidentally knew too much. Too bad!"

Finally, the note's circle and crosshairs symbol (page 331) which we now know contains the sigil letters HODEL, adds much weight to our circumstantial case.

All of this begs the question, "What did the victim know, and when did he know it?"

My initial thoughts were a possible connection to the Francis Conlon/Lois Kentle double murder, which was jointly investigated by the Mexican Federales and San Diego Law Enforcement. (Both victims from Pasadena etc.) But, that was almost ancient history—August 26, 1930. Seems a bit of a stretch that the victim would know about an eight-year-old cold case murder investigation?

The crime that immediately came to mind was much closer in time. Just months prior.

A different double homicide. What about the double murder of Hazel Frome and her daughter Nancy that occurred on April 3, 1938?

The Frome murders (April 1938) occurred just seven months before Alfred "Bud" Lord fled San Diego under a death threat (November 1938).

Could the victim, Alfred "Bud" Lord, have heard something connecting George Hodel to that much more recent murder investigation? A "loose lips sink ships" conversation in a bar?

We will likely never know.

But, based on the MO and known facts, I certainly cannot rule out the possibility of a connection between Dr. George Hill Hodel and "The Curious Case of Alfred 'Bud' Lord."

According to John Vaillant, in his book *The Tiger: A True Story of Vengeances and Survival*, "the impact of an attacking tiger can be compared to that of a piano falling on you from a second story window. But unlike the piano, the tiger is designed to do this and the impact is only the beginning."

Dr. George Hill Hodel could be compared to a feral tiger, a wild beast, a maneater, stalking his prey through the jungles of the human forest consuming man, woman, and child for 50 years, before at age 91 leaping into the abyss.

The Tyger

by William Blake - 1794

Tyger Tyger, burning bright,
In the forests of the night;
What immortal hand or eye,
Could frame thy fearful symmetry?

In what distant deeps or skies.
Burnt the fire of thine eyes?
On what wings dare he aspire?
What the hand, dare seize the fire?

And what shoulder, & what art,
Could twist the sinews of thy heart?
And when thy heart began to beat,
What dread hand? & what dread feet?

What the hammer? what the chain,
In what furnace was thy brain?
What the anvil? what dread grasp,
Dare its deadly terrors clasp!

When the stars threw down their spears
And water'd heaven with their tears:
Did he smile his work to see?
Did he who made the Lamb make thee?

Tyger Tyger burning bright,
In the forests of the night:
What immortal hand or eye,
Dare frame thy fearful symmetry?

Chapter 8

The Execution Murder of Cabdriver Ray Davis
"The Second" Pre-Zodiac Crime?

April 11, 1962

[First Call]

Anonymous Male telephone caller to Oceanside
Police Department on **Monday, April 9, 1962**

"I am going to pull something here in Oceanside and you will never be able to figure it out."

At 1:45 a.m. on Wednesday, April 11, 1962, Oceanside P.D. officer Terry Stephens was on patrol and, while cruising in an alley at the rear of former Oceanside Mayor Joe MacDonald's residence at 1926 South Pacific Street, discovered a body of a male lying in the middle of the alley.

The officer immediately determined that the victim was dead and had been shot in the back of the head. Patrolman Stephens radioed police communications to report the murder and request that detectives respond to the crime scene.

The victim was later identified as Ray Davis, a 29-year-old cab driver for Checker Cab Company, from identification found in his abandoned cab.

RAY DAVIS
Murdered

After dumping the body in the alley, the killer drove the victim's cab just 1.5 miles away, abandoning it in the 400 block of South Pacific Street.

Just days after the murder, *two more threats* were received from an anonymous male caller.

[Second Call]

Anonymous Male calls directly to Oceanside
Police Department on **Sunday, April 15, 1962**

**"Do you remember me calling last week
and telling you I was going to pull a real baffling
crime… I killed the cab driver
and I'm going to get me a bus driver next."**

'Oceanside Bus And Taxi Drivers Warned Of Killer

OCEANSIDE (UPI) — Bus and taxi drivers Tuesday continued to work despite an anonymous warning from a man who told police he killed a cab driver and planned "to get a bus driver."

Police have revealed that a man telephoned headquarters the night before the murder of cab driver Raymond Davis, 29, on Wednesday. The case is unsolved and police said they are unable to uncover a motive or clues.

Davis was shot in the back and temple. His body was dumped in an alley of the exclusively St. Malo residential district.

Police said another telephone call was received Sunday night from a man who asked:

"Do you remember me calling last week and telling you I was going to pull a real baffling crime . . . I killed the cab driver and I'm going to get me a bus driver next."

The 25 bus drivers of Oceanside Transportation S y s t e m were advised of the warning and a military policeman from Camp Pendleton was assigned to each bus operating on the base after dark.

Police took the call seriously and went so far as to place armed, uniformed military guards from nearby Camp Pendleton aboard the evening bus routes servicing the military base to protect the civilian bus drivers.

[Third Call]

Anonymous Male calls unidentified
Oceanside woman on **Tuesday, April 17, 1962**

"Tonight is the night I'm going to kill that bus driver. Tell the police."

New Threat to Murder Busman Told

OCEANSIDE (UPI)—A woman told police Tuesday that she had received a telephone call from a man who warned, "Tonight is the night I'm going to kill that bus driver."

Precautionary measures already were in effect as a result of a similar call to police headquarters Sunday night from a man who said he murdered cab driver Raymond Davis, 29, last week and planned "to get me a bus driver next."

Officers said no additional precautions were planned as a result of the latest threat.

Police did not disclose the name of the woman who made the report. They said she told them the caller refused to give his name but told her to relay his message to police.

Raymond Davis Autopsy

An autopsy was performed on the victim's body at the Seaside Mortuary in Oceanside on April 11, 1962. Oceanside Coroner surgeon, Dr. L.H. Fairchild, performed the autopsy and provided the following information:

1. Small bullet hole entry at the left side of the head with powder burns.

2. A second bullet hole entry to the back of the chest also contains powder burns.

3. Small spent slug removed from the body and given to Oceanside P.D. Detective Floyd R. Flowers and subsequently booked in evidence.

4. Dr. Fairchild determined the Cause of Death to be: "Massive intrathoracic hemorrhage due to perforated wound through right pulmonary vein due to bullet wound through the chest." Additionally, contributing Cause of Death was a "Bullet wound through the brain and rupture of right middle cerebral vein."

5. Blood specimens were submitted to the medical laboratory and subsequent toxicological analysis revealed they were "negative for blood alcohol and barbiturates."

The Murder Weapon

Oceanside P.D. determined the murder weapon was a .22 caliber handgun, and the ammunition was .22 long rifle.

The .22 caliber round, called a ".22 short" was first developed for small handguns in 1857 and the ".22 LR" or ".22 Long Rifle" round was developed in 1871. A weapon (handgun or rifle) chambered for .22 LR can fire a .22 Short, but a weapon chambered for .22 Short cannot fire a .22LR round. Thus the murder weapon had to have been chambered for .22 LR.

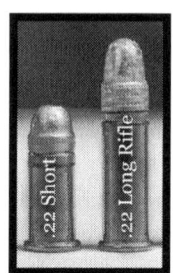

[**NOTE**: the term 'LR' or 'Long Rifle' does not indicate the LR cartridge/round is used exclusively in rifles.]

SKH Note-

The caliber of gun and ammunition used to kill cab driver Raymond Davis was identical to that used by Zodiac six years later in his December 20, 1968, Lake Herman Road double homicide of teenage victims Betty Lou Jensen and David Faraday.

(Obviously a simple ballistics comparison would establish whether he used the same gun in both crimes. However, based on prior law enforcement inactions, I would suggest that readers not hold their breath, hoping that a comparison will be made.)

1968 Zodiac Lake Herman Road victims

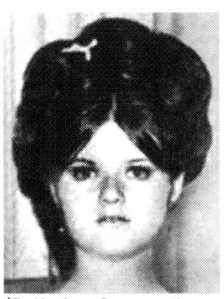

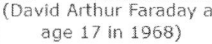

(David Arthur Faraday at age 17 in 1968) | (Betty Lou Jensen at age 16 in 1968)

Weapon: .22 caliber
Ammunition: .22 Long Rifle

~

Suspect's Physical Description
(Ray Davis Murder)

There were no known witnesses to this crime. However, unidentified fingerprints were obtained from the victim's cab. It is unknown if those prints belong to the actual shooter or were left by some previous customer and are unconnected to the crime.

If Oceanside detectives obtained a voice age guesstimate from any of the three telephone calls, that information has not been made public. Public description released only as "Male caller." It is unknown if police attempted to or did trace the phone calls to determine their origin, (whether local or outside the local exchange) or requested the CNA (Customer Name & Address) of call origin.

DNA Evidence

No DNA was obtained as this crime occurred some twenty years before discovering and collecting DNA from crime scenes. However, there is a remote possibility that "touch DNA" could yet be obtained from the victims' clothing scrapings if they still exist in police custody. (The suspect was known to pull the body from the vehicle and dump it in the alley, which would suggest the possibility of DNA skin cell transfer to the victim's clothing.)

Comparison of Crime Signatures/MO
to other George Hill Hodel serial crimes

- Hails cab from downtown and has cab driver drive to location across town.
- Shoots victim from rear seat "execution-style" with a handgun and .22 long rifle ammo.
- Pulls dead body from behind driver's steering wheel and across the front seat of a vehicle.
- Telephones and informs police before the crime that he is "going to kill in their city."
- He follows up by committing the crime and calls again after the murder to take credit.
- Specifically threatens to target passengers and driver on a city bus next time.
- Steals victim's car and abandons it on a city street a few miles from the shooting scene.
- Robbery is not a motive, and suspect in his threats makes clear he is an "urban terrorist."
- Suspect claims to be a "master criminal" and says he is "crackproof" or "uncatchable."
- Commits crime in San Diego County, where it is believed he killed seven prior victims.

Kristi S. Hawthorne
President of the Oceanside Historical Society

Ms. Kristi Hawthorne, President Oceanside Historical Society

Full credit and huge Kudos go to Kristi S. Hawthorne, the president of the Oceanside Historical Society, for making the first probable connection of 1962 Oceanside victim Raymond Davis to the later crimes (1966-69) of the killer known as "Zodiac."

Ms. Hawthorne first made the connection in her personal "Histories and Mysteries" blog initially posted on January 7, 2020, entitled: "The Murder of Ray Davis: Shades of the Zodiac?"

SKH Note-

I, and apparently the rest of the "Zodiac community" as well as all law enforcement, missed it—Kristi did not.

Based on all the known crime signatures and MOs used by George Hill Hodel, it is my professional opinion that my father very likely committed this 1962 murder on one of his many return visits to the US in that year.

For example, consider the "dot-connecting" quote from the Zodiac letter sent to the *Los Angeles Times* in 1970:

"I do have to give them credit for stumbling across my riverside activity, but they are only finding the easy ones. There were a lot more down there."

Zodiac letter - 1970

This is the Zodiac speaking
Like I have always said
I am crack proof. If the
Blue Meannies are evere
going to catch me, they had
best get off their fat asses
& do something. Because the
longer they fiddle & fart
around, the more slaves
I will collect for my after
life. I do have to give them
credit for stumbling across
my riverside activity, but
they are only finding the
easy ones, there are a heep
of a lot more than those.
The reason that I'm writing
to the Times is this, They
don't bury me on the back pages
like some of the others.
SFPD — 0   ⊕ —17+

Chapter 9

Fred Rafael Sexton ~ 1907 - 1995
Artist, *Assaulteur Sexuel*, Accomplice & Killer?

The author prepared the following biographical timeline in 2007 and updated it in 2013 on his blog site: www.stevehodel.com/blog and presented it as an **FAQ**. (**F**requently **A**sked **Q**uestion.)

FAQ 47

Q: There doesn't seem to be much information on Fred Sexton, who you claim was your father's accomplice in some of the murders. Any new evidence? I don't see anything to connect him to any crimes.

Well, perhaps if we provide a brief overview and chronology of what is known and documented about Sexton's life, it will put things in a better perspective. The chronology is a compilation from friends, family members, official police, DA, and other documents. (**Potential triggers and actual criminality highlighted in bold.**)

Fred Rafael Sexton 1907 - 1995

- 1907 June 3, born in Goldfield, Nevada. According to his daughter, Sexton was of "Irish, Jewish, Italian decent."

- 1920 - At age 13, young Fred witnessed police drag his father from their home on Christmas Eve (arrested for bootlegging) and, according to his daughter, "develops a lifelong hatred of police and authority."

- 1920s - Friend/acquaintance with John Huston and George Hodel. Sexton ran and "made good money" from a "floating crap game" in Los Angeles. Believed to have associated with known gangsters such as LA political boss Kent Kane Parrot and bootlegger, gambler Tony Cornero.

- 1920s - Sexton has an affair with an unnamed San Francisco newspaperwoman, and as a result, a son is born. The romance and birth of the son are kept secret until his daughter (born in the early Thirties) becomes an adult, and for the first time, discovers she has a "half-brother." (No further information.)

- 1920s - Sexton becomes relatively well known in the Los Angeles area as "an artist with talent."

- 1932 June 13 - Marries Gwain Harriette Nott in Santa Monica, California.

- 1932 July - Fred & Gwain depart for France. Fred contacts artist Morgan Russell and studies painting under him for an undetermined period of time. Gwain returns to the US, arriving in NY on December 17, 1933, followed by Fred's return to the US a month later, on January 18, 1934.

- 1933-4 Daughter born to them in France, unknown date. (To protect her privacy, I refer to this daughter in BDA as "Mary Moe.")

- 1937 - Sexton purchases a residence on White Knoll Drive in Elysian Park area of Los Angeles, just north of Sunset Boulevard., one mile west of downtown.

- 1938 - George Hodel with his two Dorothy's (my mother, Dorothy Huston Hodel, and Tamar's mother, Dorothy Anthony) move into residence next door to Sexton's house on White Knoll. Remain neighbors in the Elysian Park area for one to two years.

- 1939 - Sexton employed at Columbia Pictures Corp., at 1438 N. Gower St., Hollywood. Designs sets and does artwork for the studio.

- 1939-40 - Hired by his longtime friend, John Huston (now a screenwriter & director at Warner Bros.) to sculpt the "Black Bird" for the film *MALTESE FALCON (1941)*. Sexton casts the mold and creates the famous falcon now immortalized as "the stuff that dreams are made of."

Bogie in photo from 1941 film
with Sexton's Maltese Falcon

- 1940 October - Sexton's artwork was exhibited at Perls Galleries Exhibition including several Sexton paintings owned and loaned to the gallery by John Huston and Edward G. Robinson.

L.A. Times article October 6, 1940

ART PARADE REVIEWED

FRED SEXTON'S best past canvases—the monumental sunflowers, magnolias and other flower pieces together with several of the charming small heads of girls and the deep-toned, gleamingly colorful still lifes of fruit—are shown again in the exhibit of his work now at the Perls Galleries. With these are new pictures of foliage, painted with colors finely tempered to establish the depth in space of each part of the design. These new pictures, strange at first, grow on the beholder. Edward G. Robinson and John Huston loaned several of the Sexton paintings. . . With the Sexton pictures are shown, for the first time, small terra cotta figures modeled by Muriel Pulitzer. These are relaxed, natural in form and poetic in attitude. Here is a sculptress to watch and to collect. (To Oct. 15.)

- [2006 September 18] *Exquisite Corpse: Surrealism and the Black Dahlia Murder* authors Mark Nelson & Sarah Hudson Bayliss have posted this short Fred Sexton bio (below) in their Exquisite Corpse Book Map section.[19]

"Teenage friend of George Hodel's and John Huston's, Sexton was an accomplished artist in his day. He was given his debut exhibition by Earl Stendahl in 1935, and he designed the statuette of the Maltese falcon for Huston's 1941 film of the same name. An Arthur Millier column in the *Los Angeles Times* of May 12, 1940, noted that Edward G. Robinson had "bought and hung among his famous Cezannes, Van Goghs and Renoirs three new paintings ... from the brush of Los Angeles artist Fred Sexton." Another article in the *Los Angeles Times* of September 5, 1948, noted that Sexton was the first California artist asked to join the roster of Associated American Artists Galleries and that his work was in the collections of Edward G. Robinson, John Huston, Paulette Goddard, Ruth Maitland, Alfred Wallenstein, and Mrs. John J. Pike. Fred Sexton was accused along with two other adults of participating in sex acts the night that George Hodel was alleged to have had intercourse with his daughter Tamar."

- 1940-1944 - Sexton, during the war years, continues working for the film studios, drives a cab, and works in the Naval shipyards. Sexton exempt from the war because he had to care for his wife, Gwain, who was bedridden. (Dr. George Hodel was her personal physician, and gave her "gold injections" to treat her illness, presumably, severe rheumatoid arthritis.) Sexton commits incest with his 8-year-old daughter and

---

[19] http://www.mapbuilder.net/users/exquisitecorpsebook/24595

repeatedly molests her during this next three-year period, until she is eleven.

- **1948 - Sexton again attempts to have sexual intercourse with his daughter at the White Knoll residence. The daughter threatens to run away unless he leaves the home.** Sexton moves out and lives with John Huston and Paulette Goddard in West Hollywood.

- **1949 July - Involved with George Hodel in the sexual molestation of Tamar Hodel (age 14) at the Franklin House. Agrees to be a witness for LAPD and to testify for the prosecution. At the December 1949 trial, "admits being in the room with George Hodel & Tamar along with two female adults and to kissing Tamar, removing her blouse and attempting to have intercourse with the 14-year-old, but claims he did not penetrate her." (California law requires penetration for the act of statutory rape to be complete. Tamar testified before the jury that Sexton did complete the act.)**

- **1949 (approx.) - Sexton has an art studio at 2nd & Spring Sts., downtown LA and is having an affair with a married woman. Husband discovers it and comes after Sexton "intending to kill him." Sexton flees his 2nd story studio and jumps from roof to parking-lot, which resulted in a severe injury to his leg. Sexton was incapacitated**

for several months. George Hodel treats the leg injury and provides Sexton with a handgun, which Sexton's daughter reported: "was kept in a cigar box for protection in case the jealous husband showed up."

- **1950 - Sexton, with his now 18-year-old daughter present, admits to his wife, Gwain, to having had sexual intercourse with his daughter when she was a child.** (Previously, he had continued to deny his daughter's allegations.)

- Sexton is hired as an art instructor at Herb Jepson Art School, 7th & Hoover, near downtown Los Angeles. Begins to instruct students in art. **Half or more of the young females quit his class, complaining that Sexton had attempted to sexually molest them. Sexton was fired but refused to leave the campus and had to be forcibly ejected by the owner, Herb Jepson, and a couple of his friends.**

- 1950 January - Fred Sexton and Man Ray's artworks are exhibited simultaneously at the new Frank Perls Gallery opening at 350 N. Camden Dr., Beverly Hills. (Also exhibited were works by Picasso, Georgia O'Keeffe, Matisse, Miro, and many others.)

- **1950 - Sexton informs his daughter, "Man Ray was talked to by LAPD regarding George Hodel's arrest for incest" and tells her, "Man Ray would have been arrested, but he got a letter from his doctor saying he was 'impotent.'"** (**SKH Note** - Presumably for the misdemeanor charge of, "contributing to the delinquency of a minor" related to taking the nude photographs of her at age 13, as Tamar never alleged any sexual activity with Man Ray.)

- 1950-1960 - Sexton separates from his wife, Gwain, and travels and lives in Mexico. Travels back and forth between Mexico and California.

- 1961 (approx.) - In Mexico, he meets and marries his second wife, a successful artist. They move back to the US and live in Palos Verdes Estates (a beach town fifteen miles south of Los Angeles) with her three children from a former marriage. (Two sons and a daughter.)

- **1960s (mid to late 60s) - Sexton sexually molests his 11-year-old stepdaughter at their home in Palos Verdes. The daughter discloses it to her mother, who obtains Sexton's handgun from a dresser drawer and puts it to his head while he is sleeping. She attempts to pull the trigger, which won't operate. (Apparently, the safety was on, and she admitted she was "unfamiliar with guns.") Sexton awakes, grabs the gun from his wife, runs from the house, empties her sizable bank account, and** flees to Mexico. There, he removed all the cash from her second bank account. (It is believed the combined total cash taken from the two accounts amounted to $500,000. A fortune in 1960s dollars—two fortunes in Mexico.)

- **1969 - Sexton provides his daughter with a list of various LA banks where he had used different names on different accounts. One of the aliases she recalled was—"Siegfried Raphael Sexton." Sexton also showed his daughter his passport, where he was using the name "Robert Sexton." (His deceased brother.)**

- 1969 - Wife refuses to pursue criminal prosecution for the molestation of her daughter or the grand theft out of concern for the "harm and disgrace it would bring to her family." She obtains a divorce from Sexton in the US while he remains safe and untouchable in Mexico.

- 1971 - Sexton, at age 63, marries a teenager in Guadalajara, Mexico.

John Huston and Fred Sexton in Mexico circa the 1960s

- Sexton's activities and movements during the final twenty-four years of his life are unknown. It is believed he traveled back and forth between Mexico and the US One reliable source who contacted me indicated he thought there was mail correspondence between Sexton and George Hodel's ex-wife, Hortensia, then living in the Philippines.

- 1995 September 11 - Sexton dies in Guadalajara, Mexico. (Just before his death, **Sexton orders** his third wife to **"destroy all of his personal effects**." She complies, destroying everything.)

Author's Note - This is **the exact order** that Dr. George Hill Hodel gave to his wife, June, four years later, upon taking his life at age ninety-one by an overdose of Seconal. "June, **destroy all of my personal effects**."

from *Black Dahlia Avenger*—page 225

FRED SEXTON: "SUSPECT NUMBER 2"   225

Exhibit 34

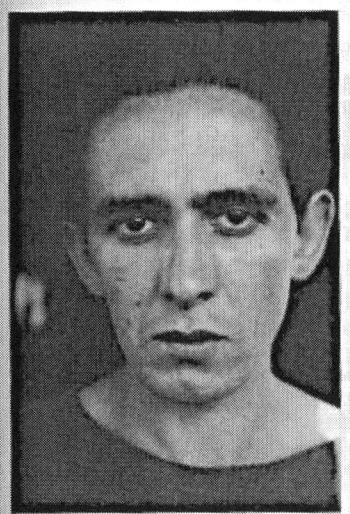

Fred Sexton, circa 1947

Fred Sexton's swarthy looks would easily have allowed someone to take him for an Hispanic, Italian, or Portuguese. A self-educated and intelligent bohemian, Sexton had penetrating eyes and a menacing cold stare.

We have been told he was fluent in both Italian and Spanish. With his smoldering good looks and brooding demeanor, he looked a lot like one of the stars of the silent movie era. At thirty-nine years old, six foot one, 180 pounds, and with sleek, slicked-back hair, Sexton, who also wore a mustache and a goatee from time to time, was as much of a womanizer as my father.

Fred Sexton was fluent in both Spanish and Italian and had a dark swarthy complexion

Chapter 10

Murder as a Fine Art

A New Fred Sexton Thoughtprint

Murder: Considered As One of the Fine Arts
Essay by **Thomas De Quincey** (1785-1859)
Blackwood's Magazine
1827, London

"People begin to see that something more goes to the composition of a fine murder than two blockheads to kill and be killed—a knife—a purse—and a dark lane. Design, gentlemen, grouping, light and shade, poetry, sentiment, are now deemed indispensable to attempts of this nature. Mr. Williams has exalted the ideal of murder to all of us; and to me, therefore, in particular, has deepened the arduousness of my task. Like Aeschylus or Milton in poetry, like Michelangelo in painting he has carried his art to a point of colossal sublimity; and as Mr. Wordsworth observes, has in a manner 'created the taste by which he is to be enjoyed'."

Thomas De Quincey 1846 portrait National Galleries of Scotland

In his *Blackwood Magazine's* essay of 1827, *Murder: Considered as one of the Fine Arts*, De Quincey, with wit and irony, introduced his readers to the *Society of Connoisseurs in Murder*, who meet to critique homicides "as they would a picture, statue, or any other work of art."

The Surrealists of the 1920s (which included George Hodel) fully adopted De Quincey and his writings which coincided with their own over-the-edge fantasies.

In my previous investigations I have presented this "Murder As a Fine Art" theme as an ongoing Thoughtprint/crime signature in George Hodel's five decades of spree killings.

I will not here attempt to restate all of those important linkages, other than to point out that as relates primarily to the 1947 Elizabeth Short "Black Dahlia Murder" well-known surrealist artists Marcel Duchamp, Man Ray, and William Copley, each separately paid *hommage* (French for tribute) to their friend, Dr. George Hill Hodel, by creating multiple artworks, *after the fact.*

Author's Note - In-depth discussions regarding "Murder as a Fine Art" crime signatures are found in six of my previous publications:

Black Dahlia Avenger I, II & III
Most Evil I, II
and
In The Mesquite

It is my opinion that these separate art works all created after the infamous 1947 "Black Dahlia Murder" were secret acknowledgments (winks and nods) to show their kinship to their fellow surrealist, and to honor George Hodel and his "masterpiece" which, to borrow De Quincey's words, "has carried his art to a point of colossal sublimity."

Let us begin with George Hodel's surreal masterpiece as he posed and presented it on the morning of January 15, 1947.

This, Dr. George H. Hodel's "colossal sublimity," was laid out for the world and for his fellow *Surrealist Society of Connoisseurs in Murder,*

"To be enjoyed as they would a picture, statue, or any other work of art."

January 15, 1947 10:30 AM "JANE DOE #1"

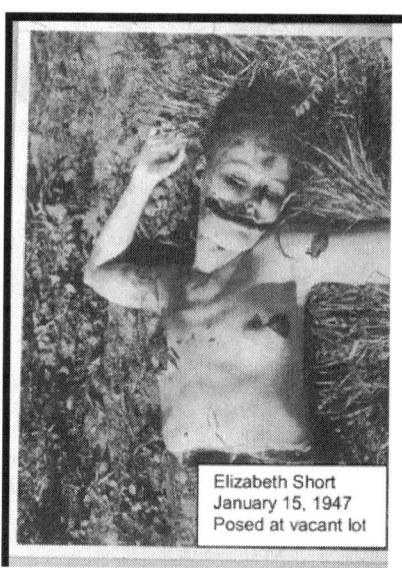

Elizabeth Short
January 15, 1947
Posed at vacant lot

BDA "Skyhorse/Arcade 2015" - page 486

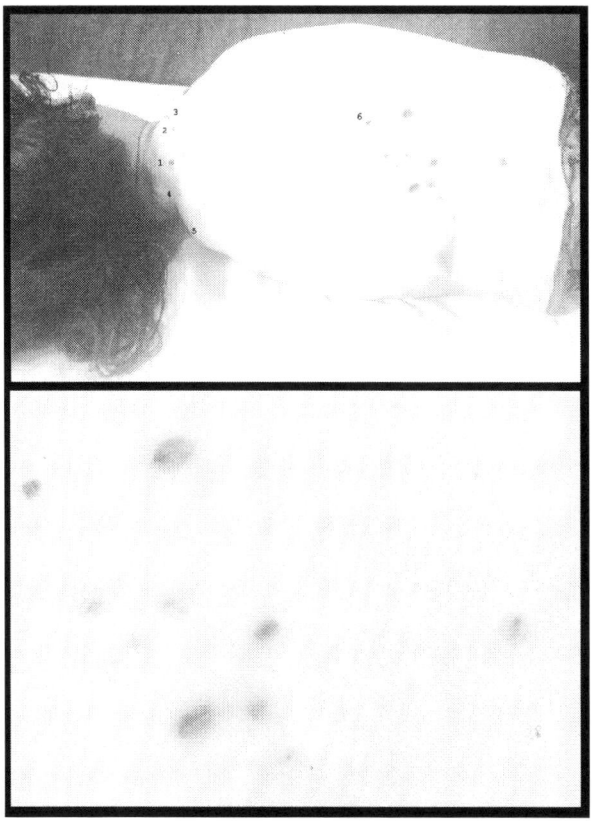

Exhibit No. 86—Cigarette burn marks (8 or 9) to victim's back

As independent review of the above photographs by nationally respected forensic expert and cardiologist Dr. D.P. Lyle, MD, provided the following opinion:

"...The lesions on the mid-back appear to be traumatic in nature. They appear to be cigarette burns, which are partially healed. They could be only hours old but are more likely 1 to 3 days old, since they seem to display some degree of healing in the central portion of each."

Surgical trauma inflicted on Elizabeth Short's body
both pre and postmortem.

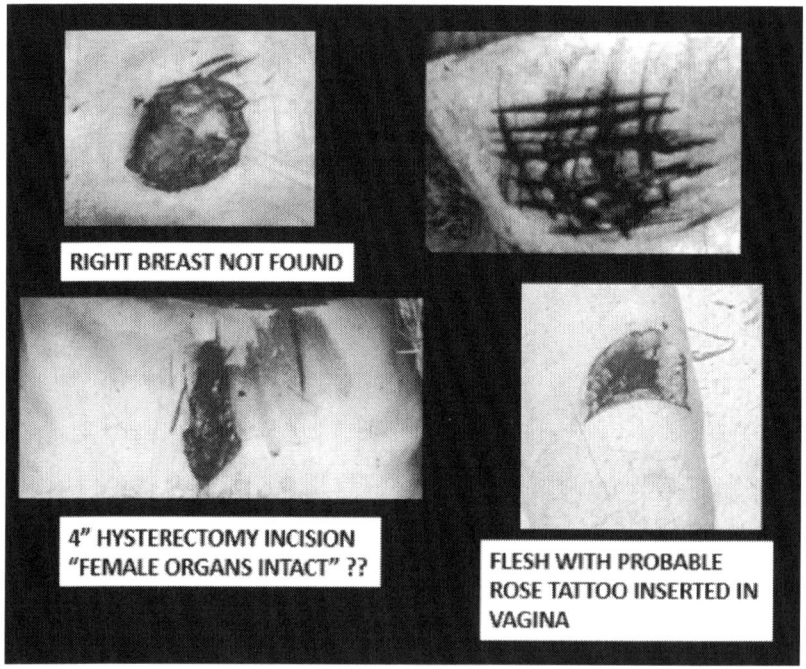

GHH surgical bisection and cutting to face inspired by his good friend Man Ray's "Minotaur" (a woman's body surgically cut in half at the waist with arms posed above her head in what surrealists deemed "The Minotaur position.") Dr. Hodel also used a scalpel to cut from ear to ear to represent Man Ray's painting and photograph, "The Lovers Lips."

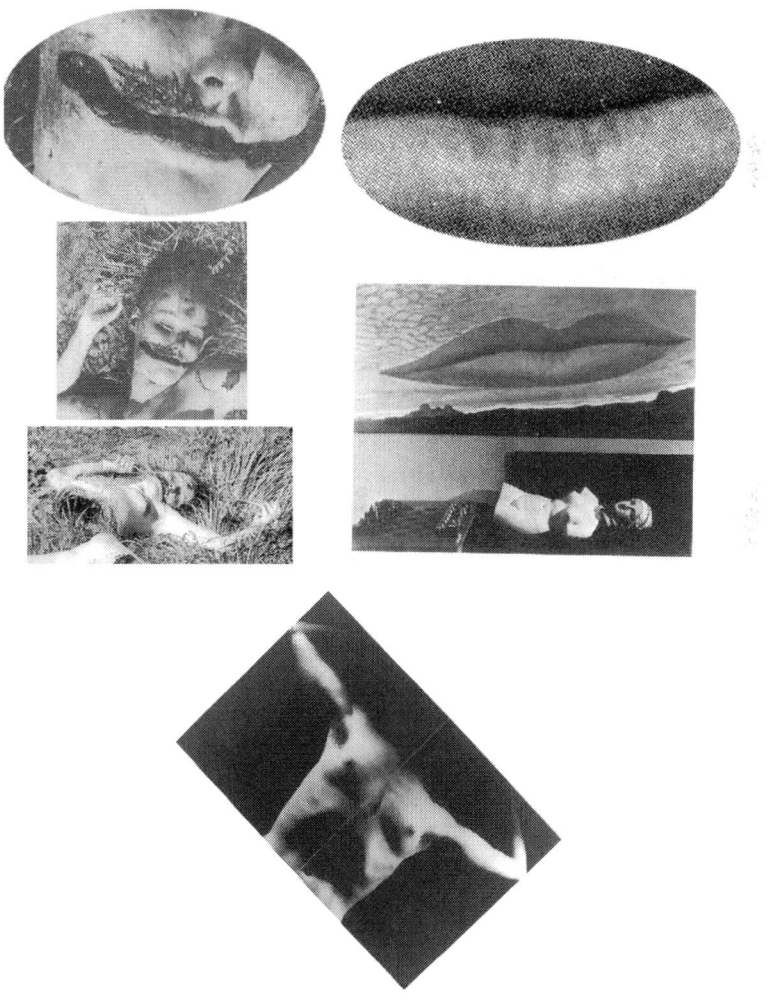

Murder as a Fine Art Montage

Surrealists Honor and Pay Hommage to Dr. George Hodel's "Masterpiece"

Marcel Duchamp's - *ETANT DONNES*

Per Marcel Duchamp's bequest, his sculpture was first installed and shown to the public at the Philadelphia Museum of Art one year after his death in 1969.

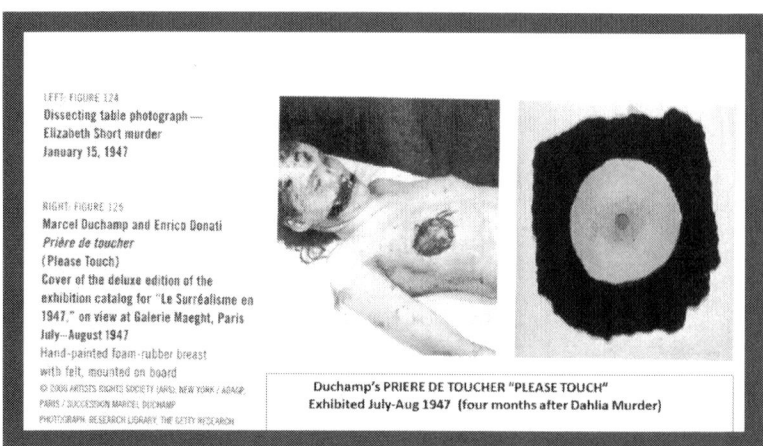

LEFT: FIGURE 124
Dissecting table photograph —
Elizabeth Short murder
January 15, 1947

RIGHT: FIGURE 125
Marcel Duchamp and Enrico Donati
Prière de toucher
(Please Touch)
Cover of the deluxe edition of the
exhibition catalog for "Le Surréalisme en
1947," on view at Galerie Maeght, Paris
July–August 1947
Hand-painted foam-rubber breast
with felt, mounted on board
© 2006 ARTISTS RIGHTS SOCIETY (ARS), NEW YORK / ADAGP,
PARIS / SUCCESSION MARCEL DUCHAMP
PHOTOGRAPH: RESEARCH LIBRARY, THE GETTY RESEARCH

Duchamp's PRIERE DE TOUCHER "PLEASE TOUCH"
Exhibited July-Aug 1947 (four months after Dahlia Murder)

Author's Note - Crime scene photos showing above trauma had allegedly been taken at the crime scene before LAPD's arrival by *Los Angeles Examiner* newspaperman Will Fowler and his photographer, Felix Paegel. Fowler (son of famed screenwriter Gene Fowler) would have shared these "first photos" with his coterie of Hollywood friends, including his father, and screenwriters Steve Fisher and Rowland Brown. (Brown, at that time, was having an ongoing affair with my mother, Dorothy Hodel.) Noted editor of the *Los Angeles Times* Aggie Underwood, in her memoir, *Newspaperwoman* (1949) claims that she was the first to arrive at the vacant lot. Regardless, untouched photographs depicting the full trauma were in circulation and available to the "inner circle" irrespective of the original source.

William Copley's,
It's Midnight Dr. _____. (1961)

Copley lying in "Minotaur position" next to letters Glove/Hat
"G.H." (George Hodel?) (1971) - *rjs graphics*

Man Ray's *Les invendables* Minotaur (1969)

Female posed in "Minotaur" position with blood flowing
out bisected half to form the bull's body and feet.

Man Ray's Objet de mon affection-L'Oculiste 1944 Sculpture

Exhibited at The Circle Gallery in 1944

Gifted by Man Ray to George Hodel in 1944

My father placed this artwork in a 1999 Butterfield & Butterfield auction but kept his identity anonymous. The piece was identified only as, "The Property of a Gentleman." George Hodel died just weeks before the auction date and sale. Sculpture auction price $30,000-$50,000.

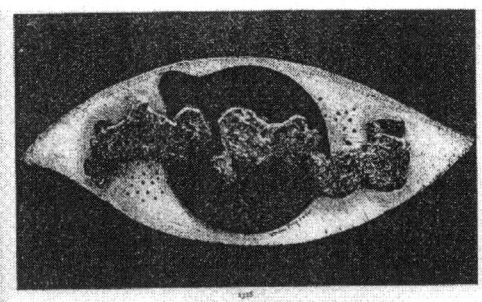

1) Human ribcage and vertebra

2) Woman's Lips

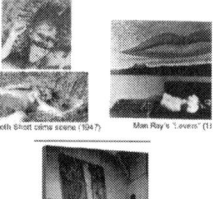
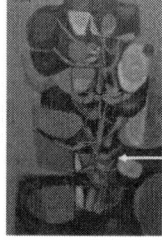

Elizabeth Short crime scene (1947)   Man Ray's "Lovers" (1)

3) Excised woman's breast

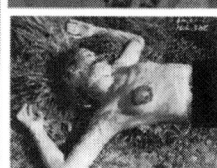

Duchamp "Please Touch" July 1947 *   Black Dahlia crime scene January 1947

Duchamp's "Please Touch" was published just six months after the murder and posing of Elizabeth Short's body on the vacant lot in Los Angeles, California. See my 2016 blog "Were Marcel Duchamp and Man Ray's 1947 "Priere de toucher" (Please Touch) Artworks Inspired by Dr. George Hodel's Surrealist Crime Scene Masterpiece?" HERE.

4) Woman's Lips

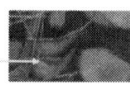

Elizabeth Short crime scene (1947)   Man Ray's "Lovers" (1)

Man Ray's - **Letter Q** for **quarrel** - Hodel Sowden House Courtyard 1947
(Below) *Les tours d' Elaine* - Man Ray 1939

Steve Hodel

More Man Ray

MAN RAY The Equivoque 1943 Tempera on cardboard
35x28cm Courtesy of the Marconi Foundation

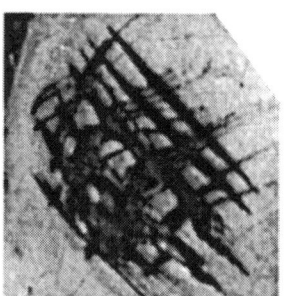

Cuttings surgically carved into right hip of victim
Elizabeth "Black Dahlia" Short by her killer in 1947

"To be, or not to be,..."

I have examined these "tributes" to GHH in length in my previous publications; interestingly, however, I found no acknowledgment from George Hodel's fellow surrealist and lifetime friend, Fred Sexton.

Why not? - "...**that is the question**."[20]

Was it because Sexton was an actual accomplice to the Black Dahlia Murder with a history of crimes/murders going back with George Hodel from the 1920s forward?

Did he choose to exercise his "Miranda Right" to remain silent?

Actually, NO.

The answer came in 2019.

I had just missed it.

On, page 398, is Fred Sexton's *hommage* or confession in his 1955 painting titled *Death of Monalita* which we can now add to his fellow surrealists' artworks that honor George Hodel.

---

[20] "To be, or not to be, that is the question." Shakespeare: Hamlet, Act 3, Sc 1

Death of Monalita **by Fred Sexton** - **1955**
This modernist painting becomes the 7th post-Black Dahlia
related art work believed linked to the murder.

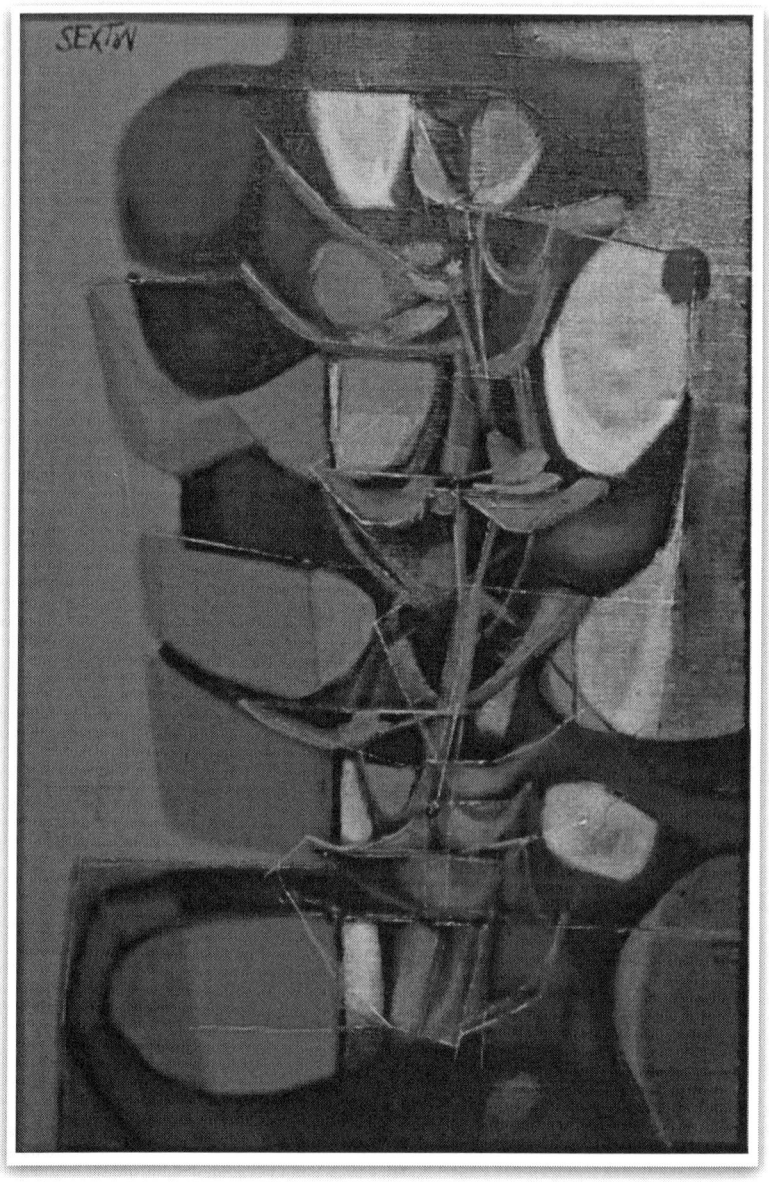

As outlined in Fred Sexton's biography, we discover that before he painted the *Death Of Monalita* in 1955, Fred Sexton was involved in the sexual abuse and molestation of his own pre-teen daughter (ages 8 to 11) from 1940-44.

In 1949 Sexton testified in court to being an accomplice, with his good friend Dr. George Hodel and two adult females, in the sexual molestation of my then fourteen-year-old half-sister, Tamar Hodel.

In 1950, Sexton also admitted to his wife, Gwain Sexton, to having had sexual relations with his daughter when she was a child.

Sexton divorces Gwain, marries artist Gemma Taccogna and commits additional and separate child molestation acts with his new stepdaughter in the late 60s. And after reportedly removing a half-million dollars from Gemma's bank account, Sexton flees to Mexico to avoid arrest. There, at the age of 60, he marries a teenager. He dies in Guadalajara at the age of 88 in 1995.

A Critical Examination of Fred Sexton's
Death of Monalita (1955)

Who was Monalita?

I do not know.

The name Monalita can be translated as "Little Mona." As the general rule, diminutives, according to numerous sources, are accomplished by adding "ito/**ita**" to the ending of a word indicating either smallness or affection.

To date, I have no background information on Sexton's painting other than it was reportedly created circa 1955. And at one time was believed offered for sale at the Calabi Art Gallery.

Sexton created the painting in 1955, approximately eight years after the murder of Elizabeth "Black Dahlia" Short in January 1947. His good friend, Dr. George Hill Hodel, fled Los Angeles in 1950 to avoid arrest for the crime.

Since "art" *is* said to be *in the eye of the beholder*, I will describe what I behold—what I AM SEEING—within the painting of *Death of Monalita* on page 398 is:

1) The center of the painting appears to be a skeletal structure showing what seems to be human vertebrae and ribcage.

2) Next, my eye is drawn to a figure whose upper torso is bisected at the waist, with arms extended in the "Minotaur position."

3) There is a woman's breast, which appears excised from the body.

4) I see a pair of woman's lips and lower jawline.

Are these depictions merely random, or is the artist presenting "clews" to an infamous crime that he would have been directly aware of, if not actually involved in, as an accomplice to the murder?

A Second Opinion: Graphics and Text Summary by
former Dallas PD Officer Robert J. Sadler

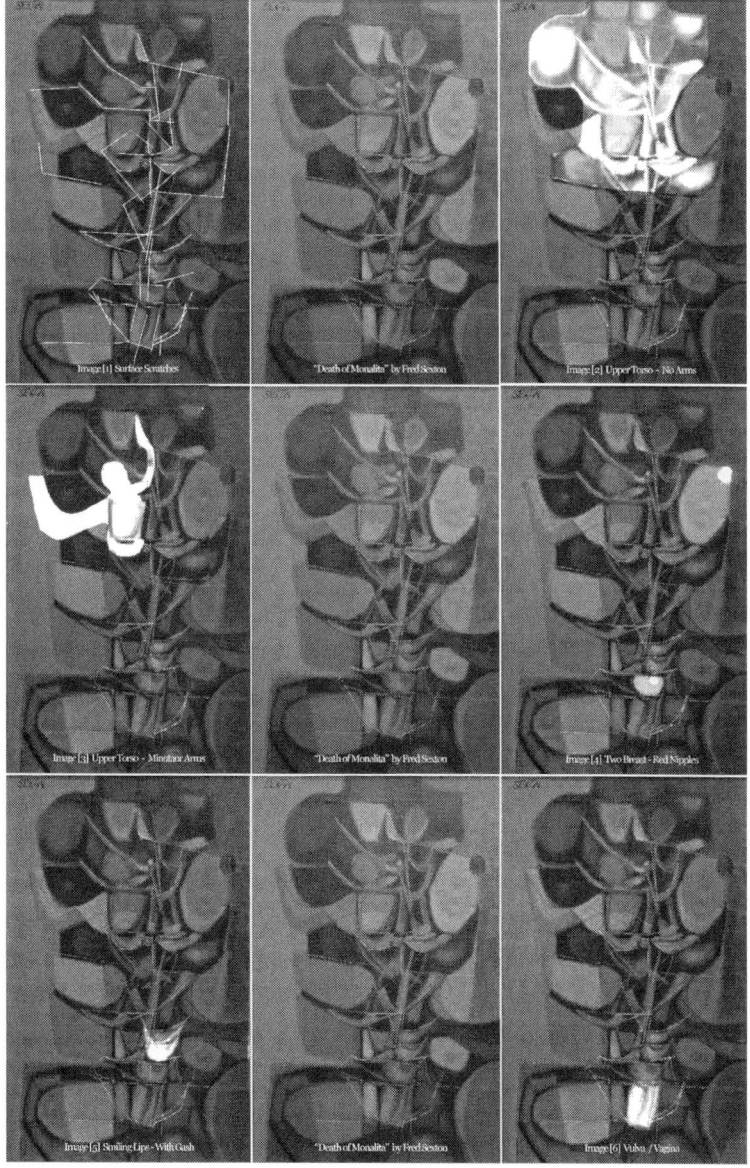

rjs' Interpretation of Sexton's *Death of Monalita*

This is a visual interpretation of images perceived to be and isolated within the Fred Sexton painting titled *Death of Monalita* circa 1955 and are purely subjective.

These graphics were intended to be viewed in color[21], alas, in this book you will see shades of grey and will therefore have to rely more heavily on the text.

These perceptions are based on my knowledge of the investigations of Steve Hodel and the association of Sexton with Dr. George Hill Hodel and Sexton's first-hand or second-hand knowledge of the torture and dismemberment of Elizabeth Short and possibly of other dismembered bodies to which Sexton may have been a party.

The "modernist" style of Sexton's painting is reminiscent of both Cubism and Surrealism. Both modes of painting often refracted or deconstructed the human form with its "parts" reconstructed to please the artist's esthetic or intention. The Surrealists often went one step further by separating the human form as if bisected (cut in half) or truncated: torsos without arms or leg for example.

Additionally the Surrealists inveigled with one another to create hidden meanings or messages in their works often using various images within the work or the work itself to pay *hommage* or tribute to someone.

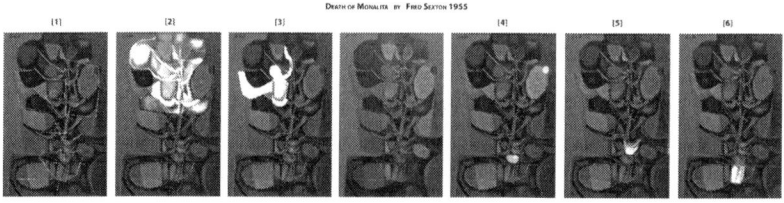

DEATH OF MONALITA BY FRED SEXTON 1955

[1] [2] [3] [4] [5] [6]

21 **You can view the painting and these graphics in color** on Steve's 9.26.2019 Blog: https://stevehodel.com/2019/09/26/fred-sextons-macabre-painting-death-of-monalita-revisited-a-footprint-thoughtprint/

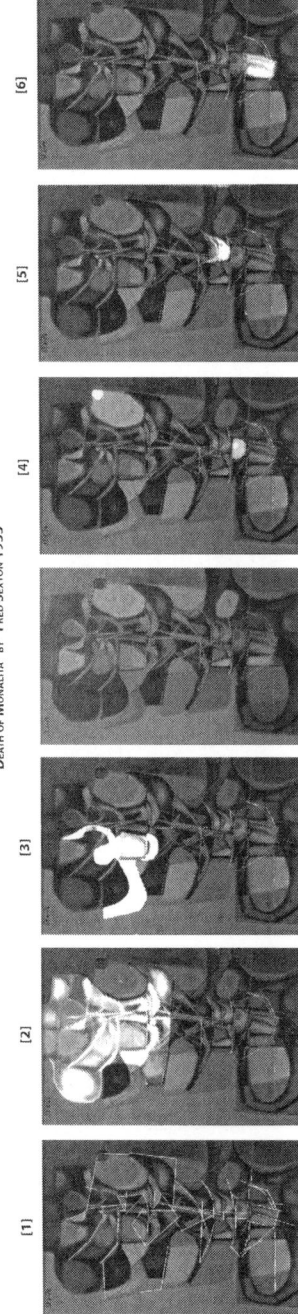

DEATH OF MONALITA BY FRED SEXTON 1955

Ed. Note - Images [1-6] on page 402 & enlarged on page 403.

In Image [1] the artist employed an object to scratch through the surface of the paint. Though the lines are ragged in terms of depth or line continuity most are remarkably straight, as if a straight edge or ruler were placed over the painting to guide the artist's hand in making these scratches. There're some anthropomorphic interpretations that can be made of these scratches—suggesting perhaps the arms, spine, and pelvis.

In Image [2] the highlighted area suggests a headless upper torso with neck and shoulders which have no arms.

In Image [3] the highlighted area suggests a head and upper torso with two arms bent at the elbows suggesting the Minotaur pose.

In Image [4] the highlighted areas suggest in the upper right a breast with a prominent red nipple and at the center bottom is a second potential representation of a breast with prominent areola.

In Image [5] the highlighted area is suggestive of a woman's red lips with a dark curved area above that could be interpreted as the smile-like gash imposed on Elizabeth Short's face. As well as a potential nod to Man Ray's *Lover's Lips*.

In Image [6] the highlighted area is suggestive of a woman's vulva and vaginal opening.

In review, the following *four* Surrealist paintings are now linked as "ThoughtPrints"—establishing the connective tissue, in the form of an artistic *hommage,* of these *four* separate artists' knowledge of Dr. George Hill Hodel's "Murder As A Fine Art 'Sculpture'."

SKH NOTE - The additional surrealist artworks used as "inspiration" by Dr. George Hill Hodel are not shown in this summary, which is limited to the surrealists' works created **after the murder and acknowledging their awareness of and linkage to the Black Dahlia Murder and her killer.**

1) Fred Sexton's "Death of Monalita" (1955)   2) William Copley's "It is Midnight Dr. _____." (1961)

4) Man Ray's *Les Invendables* (1969)

3) Marcel Duchamp's, *Etant Donnes* (1969)

Those individual artworks inspiring and related to the
Black Dahlia crime include:

> Man Ray's - *The Minotaur*
> Man Ray's - *L'Equivoque*
> Man Ray's - *The Lover's Lips*
> Man Ray's - *Juliet Stocking Mask*
> Man Ray / Copley's - *Alphabet for Adults*
> Man Ray's - *The Occuliste*
> Duchamp's - *Prière de toucher* (*Please Touch*)

~

HODEL, HUSTON, SEXTON
THE THREE AMIGOS

As previously documented, George Hodel, Fred Sexton,
John Huston were close pals from their high school years
and forward through the decades. Huston had Sexton
sculpt his "Black Bird" for *The Maltese Falcon* in 1941.
(Currently appraised at $4 million.)

George Hodel - John Huston - Fred Sexton

Of Interest:

Below is a link to an excellent article published in *Vanity Fair* in 2016, documenting Sexton's sculpture's history and mystery.

BELOW PHOTO OF FRED SEXTON'S SCULPTURE OF "THE BLACK BIRD" USED IN JOHN HUSTON DIRECTED 1941 "THE MALTESE FALCON."

DIGITAL COLORIZATION BY LORNA CLARK, LEFT, BY PAUL SCHRAUB/THE COLLECTION OF HANK RISAN; RIGHT, FROM THE EVERETT COLLECTION

VANITY FAIR- HWD
The Mystery of the Maltese Falcon,
One of the Most Valuable Movie Props in History

A statuette from the John Huston-Humphrey Bogart classic, *The Maltese Falcon* is one of the most recognizable and sought-after pieces of movie memorabilia in history. In fact, Steve Wynn paid $4.1 million for it. But was it the genuine article? Bryan Burrough tracks down a flock of Falcons, with links to both Leonardo DiCaprio and a famous Hollywood unsolved murder.

By BRYAN BURROUGH

https://www.vanityfair.com/hollywood/2016/02/mystery-of-the-maltese-falcon#5

Coda

With the completion of this two-book set, *The Early Years Part 1 & 2*, barring any unexpected developments, I see my investigation (into the "Life and Crimes" of my father, Dr. George Hill Hodel), as now complete.

It began in May 1999, as a 2,700-mile long-distance telephone call with my half-sister Tamar in Hawaii and our conversation about "what a remarkable father we had" and our shared reflections on "the great man's passing."

That conversation quickly, with just one sentence from my sister's lips, instantly and unbeknownst to me, became the catalyst that would consume my life for these past twenty-one years.

That sentence of nineteen fateful words would start me on a true-life odyssey more incredible, to me, than the Greek myth of Odysseus & his twenty-year journey home.

> "Well, you know Steven,
> the police suspected our father
> was the Black Dahlia killer,
> but he didn't do it."

Or did my journey begin much earlier?

Were Tamar's words the Hand of Fate reaching out to spark an unsuspected but preordained journey?

Was I, Telemachus, about to begin searching for his dead father, Ulysses (Latin for Odysseus), in the Underworld?

As noted in *Black Dahlia Avenger*, my mother named me after the character Stephen Dedalus in James Joyce's *Ulysses*. Though she so loved that book and named me Stephen, she chose to spell my name with a "v" as in S-t-e-v-e-n. In her words she "preferred the more manly spelling."

In his (Knopf NY, 1980) biography, *An Open Book-John Huston*, John who had been married to my mother, Dorothy Harvey, for seven years (1926-1933), wrote this about their honeymoon. Page 59:

> We rented a beach shack up near Malibu Colony, and there the marriage came together. I think we were both happier than we'd ever been—perhaps happier than we'd ever be again. During this time, Mother went to Europe and, upon her return, smuggled in a copy of Joyce's *Ulysses,* which was banned in the United States. Dorothy read it aloud while I painted. It was probably the greatest experience that any book has ever given me. Doors fell open.

Was her naming an homage because she so loved James Joyce's *Ulysses,* or because her hero/author had died earlier that year in January 1941?

I suspect it was both.

And then there is my middle name, Kent, which I addressed in an earlier chapter. I suspect this was my father's contribution in homage and respect for his acquaintance and friendship with Kent Kane Parrot, LA's early crime boss, and the historically acknowledged power behind many of LAPD's politically positioned high ranking officers.

There are no coincidences!

By my count, by the time I was born in November 1941, my father could have already taken more than two dozen lives that included men, women, and children.

My mother KNEW and was aware of at least some of these crimes.

Could it be that Happenstance is the reflection of Destiny as seen through a mirror darkly?

Dorothy Harvey Huston Hodel

What I am about to address and examine now is difficult for me. Very difficult.

I loved and love my mother deeply.

Perhaps this is true of all sons? A given? A commandment, "Thou shalt honor thy mother."

My mother instilled in my brothers and me strong core values.

> "Love the Good, The Beautiful, the True." "Treat all peoples, all races, with respect."

> "Judge no one." "Be compassionate and forgiving."

> "Love Nature." "Be Honest and True to Your Self and Others."

My mother was a gentle, loving soul. And these were her constant beliefs—when sober.

But there was another side to her nature. One that I only saw appear when she was drinking. Let's call that part of her—Mrs. Hyde.

Mrs. Hyde was dark, hostile, and violent. Her nature was to destroy. She hated the sweet, intelligent, beautiful "Dorothy Jean" side of her, who all men loved and worshipped almost as a goddess.

I do not recall ever meeting Mrs. Hyde as a small child. If any, those young memories have been erased.

However, Mrs. Hyde was present, as evidenced by my brothers and I being placed in "protective custody" at L.A. County Juvenile Hall and temporary foster homes in 1943 and 1945, and 1949.

On those several occasions, our mother was arrested and sent to the county jail for thirty days for drunkenness and child neglect.

But, somehow, Dorothy Jean managed to always take back control from her wicked-sister side.

Mother would find her boys and keep us together as "The Three Musketeers," and we would start over in Rancho Mirage, Santa Monica, Pasadena, and Van Nuys—on the move from rental to rental through our teen years.

Always on the move.

I attended Santa Monica High School, then Van Nuys High, and then Glendale High.

In my senior year there, just months before graduation, days after turning seventeen in November, I had my mother sign the papers, and I joined the Navy, and I was off to boot camp by January 1959.

Now to the hard part.

Just over four years ago, on September 1, 2016, I wrote down my thoughts on what I then termed an "epiphany."

Let me start by presenting some of those thoughts I committed to paper in a letter to an unnamed acquaintance (a well-known film director/screenwriter) with whom I anticipated possibly developing a script/screenplay miniseries to tell the Hodel story.

Author's Note -

The above-referenced director/screenwriter is not Robb Bindler, who I have been working with in recent years and is currently moving forward in making the miniseries.

I anticipate our current project will have been released by the time this two-book set of *The Early Years* is published.

Here is that letter as written in 2016:

September 1, 2016

Since roughly the beginning of this year, I've found it difficult to move forward on my writing of Book V, "The Early Years." I don't get "writer's block," so I was not sure what the cause might be?

(As I think you know, "The Early Years" covers GHH's crimes from the 1920s and 1930s, of which there are by my current count, approximately-twenty, or an average of one a year.)

Last week I had what one could call an "epiphany" or maybe more correctly, "a lightning bolt to the heart."

I'm sure I'm right on this and want to share it as I think it is another critical piece of the Big Puzzle and because it is so important on a personal level and how it is presented in our telling of the story.

Will try and keep it brief here, so this summary won't include all the "evidence" that leads me to my conclusion. Much of it (evidence) predates the LA Lone Woman Murders of the 1940s, so it will not be included in our miniseries.

BDA's "Mystery Woman"

My investigation revealed that a "mystery woman" was present on and at a number of incidents and witness sightings.

In BDA, these include

1) January 7, 1947, in San Diego, where a neighbor observed a late-night visit by "two men and a woman" who were seen exiting a car and door knocking the San Diego residence where Elizabeth Short was staying. Here's the description from BDA:

> Both he and the French's repeatedly said that Elizabeth "was living in fear of a jealous boyfriend." Mrs. French described to the police an "alarming" incident that had taken place the night before Elizabeth's departure. It had been witnessed by Mrs. French's neighbor, who remains to this day unidentified.
>
> The neighbor told Mrs. French that at a very late hour on the night of January 7, 1946, she observed: "three individuals, two men, and a woman, drive up, park a car, then walk to the front door of the French residence and knock." Possibly because it was so late, the neighbor kept watching. "The three waited for a few minutes, then all three of them ran to the parked car and drove off." The following morning, after her neighbor told her what she had seen, Mrs. French asked Elizabeth what she thought. Elizabeth said she too had seen the nighttime visitors: she had peeped through the window when the three had come to the door, but she had made no move to answer the door or acknowledge their presence.
>
> Mrs. French described Elizabeth's alarm over the incident to detectives, telling Lieutenant Haskins that "Elizabeth was constantly in fear of someone and was very frightened when anyone came to the door." Mrs. French tried to find out what or who Elizabeth was afraid of but was unable to, simply saying, "Elizabeth was very evasive and would not talk to me about the people, so finally I just gave up asking."

One week later, the second incident occurred, and I am confident it was the same three individuals as in San Diego.

2) January 14, 1947, downtown Los Angeles, 5th & Main. LAPD uniform officer Myrl McBride on foot patrol is approached by

Elizabeth Short, who she described was "sobbing in terror" and told the officer, "a man, a former suitor, just threatened to kill me." Officer McBride accompanies her to the nearby bar, but the man is gone, and they recover Elizabeth's purse.

A few hours later, Officer McBride sees Elizabeth Short a second time exiting another bar accompanied by "two men and a woman." McBride stops her and asks, "Are you all right?" Short responds, "Yes, I'm going to meet my father at the Greyhound bus station." McBride continues her foot patrol.

This contact occurred just twenty hours before the victim's body is found bisected and posed in the vacant lot. (I conducted an in-person interview with Meryl McBride [long retired] in 2001, and she verified the facts on her encounter with Short and her three "companions," "two men and a woman.")

This was the strangest interview I have ever done; the Black Dahlia killer's son is a cop, interviewing another cop, Meryl McBride, some fifty-five years later who was the last known witness to see the victim Elizabeth "Black Dahlia" Short alive.

(**SKH Note** - In the January 6, 1946, Chicago abduction/murder of little Suzanne Degnan, we also have neighbor witnesses placing "two men and a woman" at the victim's residence. See below excerpt from *Most Evil I*):

> Police now believed that the killer may have taken the child out the front door when the neighbor's boxer dogs first started barking at 12:25 a.m.
>
> Mary and Thomas Keegan, third-floor resident tenants at the Degnan house, awakened between 1:30 and 2:00 a.m. when the boxer dogs began barking a second time. They heard loud voices on the sidewalk. Two men were arguing. Fifteen minutes later, they heard a man and a woman talking out front. Overheard, the woman say, "This is the best-looking building in the neighborhood and the best-looking couple."
>
> Over the years, as relates to the BDA investigation, many of my readers have questioned me, asking, "Who do you think the woman was? Do you think it could have been your

mother?" My response was always the same. "No. It could be anyone. Maybe Ellen the maid?" Or, "We will never know."

That was and has been my position for the past fifteen years.

Based on what I now know, I have come to the slow, reluctant conviction; the "mystery woman" was, in fact, my mother. Simply put, my love for my mother prevented me from seeing the truth of it.

The evidence pointing to the fact that Dorothy Huston Hodel was a full-blown Bonnie Parker to George's Clyde Barrow (albeit, likely much more unwilling than the original Bonnie) has been building over the years and crested with my most recent solving (see the standalone TrueCrime book, *In The Mesquite*) of a 1938 West Texas double homicide of a mother and daughter.

That crime, one of Texas's most horrific torture murders (cigarette burns to body identical to Elizabeth Short's) where the victim's bodies were deliberately posed in the desert, remains "unsolved."

This unexpected "hard truth" has been soaking into me for the past three or so weeks.

How do I see this impacting our miniseries?

Dorothy "Dorero" Hodel, I expect, is going to be portrayed as she was. A beautiful, intelligent, and highly literate intellectual. Hedonistic, seductive, and bisexual. (George and Dorero making love with one of the DA's later Dahlia star witnesses, the black and beautiful, 19-year-old Mattie Comfort.) Alcoholic and arrested three times for "Child Neglect," causing her three sons to be placed in protective custody as she is sent to jail for six months. But, always getting her children back and resuming "The Gypsy Years."

Then we have the accomplice scene where George calls her to his secretary Ruth Spaulding's downtown LA apartment where my mother sees Ruth unconscious, but alive and breathing.

George gives her the damning scripts that Ruth has written "naming names and crimes" and orders Dorothy "to take them home and burn them without reading them." She complies. (This act alone makes her an accomplice and forever under George's control.)

As far as the miniseries is concerned, I think the way to go on this is to show the Ruth Spaulding scene as it was. However, maybe best to keep "the mystery woman" just that.

In the San Diego door knock, we see a woman but never see her face or hear her voice. In the following week with LAPD officer McBride and Elizabeth Short and the two men and a woman exiting the bar confrontation, we see it is George and probably Fred Sexton and a woman, but again, we never see her face or hear her voice. Let the viewers wonder who she is? They are smart, and likely many will think it could well be Dorothy, but we keep it a mystery.

We can discuss further as things progress, but I just wanted you to know where my head has been these past few weeks on this.

Just when I thought it was safe to go back into the water.

Steve

~

The preceding letter was never meant to be made public.

Having just completed *The Early Years (Part 1 & 2)* that further document my father's crimes, the detective in me feels bound to present this additional linkage.

What we have learned in my father's crimes from the Twenties and Thirties only adds to the likelihood that "the mystery woman"—an accomplice to many of George Hodel's crimes—may well have been Mrs. Hyde, my mother's dark side.

Consider the following:

Dorothy Jean Hodel, aka Mrs. Hyde, is the only woman with a *long history* with George Hodel.

She was his original girlfriend in Los Angeles in 1924-25. (Before Huston falls in love with her.)

She marries George's good friend, John Huston, in '26.

Dorothy is the likely "go-between" with George and Fred Sexton in the 1926 McPherson kidnap/hoax where she and the two men obtain "the services" of the blind Long Beach attorney, Russell McKinley, in their attempt to extort money from Sister Aimee and her church.

In Dorothy's 1921 short story "Star Dust and Rent Money," written in her Benjamin Franklin HS yearbook, she is "Rose," who is forced to sell her child as a "slave" to pay the rent.

Then five years later, "Rose" will have her revenge and becomes one of the three kidnappers ("two men and a woman") in the ransom note demand sent to the church "for Sister Aimee's release."

After divorcing Huston, she begins again dating George Hodel. She is likely the "30-year-old Brunette" seen as one of the kidnappers, "two men and a woman" in the 1938 double murder of Hazel and Nancy Frome outside El Paso, Texas.

Dorothy becomes pregnant with my older brother Michael, born in 1939, and marries George Hodel in Sonora, Mexico, in 1940.

On September 27, 1944, Dorothy awakened to read the LA newspapers' headlines of the "accidental death of Aimee Semple McPherson."

Knowing that her husband, George, is treating McPherson and has likely overdosed her, Dorothy flees the residence, and goes directly to her attorney and files for divorce on the same day as the "accidental overdose" (think murder) is discovered.

In her 1949 conversation with her stepdaughter, Tamar Hodel, Dorothy implicates herself by admitting that she was an accomplice in the 1945 "overdose death" of George Hodel's secretary, Ruth Spaulding.

My mother admitted that after being called to the apartment and receiving George's orders to "destroy and burn these manuscripts that Ruth has written," she took them home and burned them.

Dorothy was probably with George Hodel and Fred Sexton as the woman in the "two men and a woman" heard outside the private residence, late at night just before the kidnap/murder of little Suzanne Degnan in January 1946.

The woman in the "two men and a woman" who did a late-night door knock at the residence in San Diego searching for Elizabeth Short, but then ran from the porch to their car and drove off.

Again, that same woman who just one week later, after the San Diego incident, was seen with two men leaving the DTLA bar by officer Meryl McBride on January 14, 1947.

The woman with Elizabeth Short in hand on the very eve of her kidnap/murder when officer McBride stopped and questioned the foursome and asked Elizabeth, "Are you all right?" In the company of the "two men and a woman," Short responded, "Yes, I'm going to meet my father at the bus station."

As I see it, my mother's dark-sister side, Mrs. Hyde, is the only woman who would have had this *twenty-nine-year-relationship (1921-1950) with my father*.

The only woman in his life that would have been frozen by horrific fear to remain silent.

First, for her own life, then in the late Thirties forward, out of fear for her children's lives. Dorothy KNEW her husband "was capable of anything," and it was not theoretical knowledge.

Instead, it was real knowledge. A been-there-seen-that kind of knowledge.

As I indicated earlier, this could well have been a *Stockholm Syndrome* situation, the probability of which is reinforced dramatically by my discovery of and publication of "The Huston Letters."

Those heartbreaking letters to John, which were never intended to be read by another living soul, demonstrate our mother's mental/psychological state of terror and fear for herself and her three sons back in the late Forties and into early 1950.

I expect the only time she began to feel a little safer was once our father was out of the country and living in the Territory of Hawaii, then on to Asia.

Of course, the son in me, who loved and still loves his mother, would like to believe that I am totally "off base" on the possibility that she could be an actual accomplice to some of my father's crimes.

But, the detective in me, in looking and reviewing "Just the Facts," *does* believe that her Mrs. Hyde was the "mystery woman," who kept reappearing at the scene or in the background as perhaps a reluctant "Bonnie Parker" to George Hodel's more than willing "Clyde Barrow."

Mr. and Mrs. Hyde, a dark-sided double marriage of convenience—both lifelong companions to the good Dr. Jekyll and his beautiful wife, Dorothy Jean.

~ ~ ~

Finally, I would like to pay my respects to the families of all the victims that I believe were slain by my father and his main accomplice, Fred Sexton.

As we have learned, those crimes span FIFTY YEARS.

I can do nothing to lessen the pain in my own heart and in the hearts of the hundreds of family members of those victims—the Next Of Kins.

Most of the victims' family members are long gone now. They never knew who killed their loved one.

So let me speak to the grandsons and granddaughters, the great-nieces and great-nephews, and their children in hopes of at least providing some bit of "closure."

I sincerely believe that *knowing who killed their kin at least offers some small bit of solace.*

I here provide the names of all of "The Victims," (both slain and those that survived their attack).

And with a heavy heart, I reach out and embrace each living relative with my deepest sympathy and apology for the SINS OF MY FATHER.

To all the victims, I say, REST IN PEACE.

1. Father Patrick Heslin, 8/5/21
2. William Desmond Taylor, 2/1/22
3. Nina Martin, 8/23/24
4. May Martin, 8/23/24
5. Francis Conlon, 8/26/30
6. Lois Kentle, 8/26/30
7. Virginia Brooks, 2/11/31
8. Louise Teuber, 4/19/31
9. Dolly Bibbens, 4/23/31
10. Hazel Bradshaw, 5/2/31
11. Maude Detweiler, 8/28/31
12. Dr. Leonard Siever, 12/12/33
13. Mary Adams, 3/4/34
14. Celia Cota, 8/18/34
15. Doris Dazey, 10/4/35
16. Thelma Todd, 12/16/35
17. Ruth Muir, 8/1/36
18. Madeline Everett, 6/26/37
19. Melba Everett, 6/26/37
20. Jeanette Stephens, 6/26/37
21. Hazel Frome, 4/3/38
22. Nancy Frome, 4/3/38
23. Ora Murray, 7/26/43
24. Aimee Semple McPherson, 9/27/44

25. Georgette Bauerdorf, 10/11/44

26. Ruth Spaulding, 5/9/45

27. Josephine Ross, 6/3/45

28. Frances Brown, 12/10/45

29. Suzanne Degnan, 1/7/46

30. Elizabeth Short, 1/15/47

31. Jeanne French, 2/10/47

32. Laura Trelstad, 5/11/47

33. Marian Newton, 7/16/47

34. Lillian Dominguez, 10/2/47

35. Gladys Kern, 2/14/48

36. Louise Springer, 6/13/49

37. Mimi Boomhower, 8/18/49

38. Jean Spangler, 10/7/49

39. Jane Doe, 2/18/50

40. Ray Davis, 4/11/62

41. Cheri Jo Bates, 10/30/66

42. Lucila Lalu, 5/28/67

43. Betty Jensen, 12/20/68

44. David Faraday, 12/20/68

45. Darlene Ferrin, 7/4/69

46. Mike Mageau, 7/4/69 (survived)

47. Cecelia Shepard, 9/27/69

48. Bryan Hartnell, 9/27/69 (survived)

49. Paul Stine, 10/11/69

Author's Postscript

By the summer of 2001, some twenty-years ago, my investigation had advanced to the point where I had discovered that my father was not just responsible for the murder of Elizabeth "Black Dahlia" Short.

By then, I knew he was a serial killer and had committed some dozen murders in and around Hollywood from the years 1943-1950 when he fled the United States.

I documented these crimes in *Black Dahlia Avenger*, designating them as the "Los Angeles Lone Woman Murders."

But there were more.

As I began researching my father's early life and going deeper into the Rabbit Hole, I asked myself, "When did he begin his serial killing?"

I told myself, it must have been earlier than his first "Lone Woman Murder" in 1943.

In 1943 he was thirty-six years old, the VD czar and the Department Head of the Hygiene Section of the L.A. County Health Department.

It was hard for me to imagine him getting out of bed, stretching his arms at age 36 and saying to himself, "I think I will begin a life as a serial killer now."

So when did he begin?

I began an historical review of some of LA's "unsolved murders" from decades earlier, examining their unique MO and Crime Signatures. The clues I uncovered convinced me that George Hodel could well be responsible for some of these "high profile" whodunits.

I was determined to follow these new leads but knew that would require a follow-up book to *Black Dahlia Avenger* which was finished and scheduled to publish in April 2003.

Below (left) is the front cover of the hardback edition which was soon to be a *New York Times Bestseller*.

Below (right) is my nomination certificate from Mystery Writers of America as "Best Fact Crime Book".

After already having done considerable research, and with the April publication date looming, I approached Richard Seaver, my New York editor/publisher at *Arcade Books*, and made a special request.

I asked Dick to include a "Reference Number" at the end pages of *Black Dahlia Avenger*.

To his credit, he agreed.

Shown below is a scan of page 463 of the 2003 ed. of *Black Dahlia Avenger: A Genius for Murder.*

Author's Postscript

I HAVE JUST COMPLETED THE FINAL REVISIONS of this manuscript. Within the past few months, new evidence and new information, new thoughtprints have been found. I will follow those leads from without, as I continue to be guided from within.

Steve Hodel
December 2002
Hollywood, California

REFERENCE NO.:
2244–WALDTBEASRFTDSMT–SD3036–LFVLDHMWACRMCDBBTBCK–CM2446–MMRGPS–BHBR44

Above Reference No. Enlarged Below

REFERENCE NO.:
2244–WALDTBEASRFTDSMT–SD3036–LFVLDHMWACRMCDBBTBCK–CM2446–MMRGPS–BHBR44

The reason for my wanting to include this "reference number" was that I wanted to document in 2003 the further serial crimes I believed that my father might have committed in his "early years."

The "Reference No." was a cipher of sorts. It was first a guide for me to follow-up on GHH's suspected other crimes. Second, it was similar to staking a claim, so future crime prospectors would know I had already been there and was working the claim.

Here now is the key to that reference number, which was in truth a code of the names of suspected victims that I had amassed and intended to investigate beginning in 2003.

I thought "The Early Years" book would follow *BDA* in a year or two.

I had no idea that five books would precede it, and that *The Early Years* would require two books: *Part 1* and *Part 2*.

2244—WALDTBEASRFTDSMT—SD3036—LFVLDHMWACRMCDBBTBCK—CM2446—MMRGPS—BHBR44

The "Reference No." code had four elements separated by an "em dash" (—). The first three are composed of a date range and the initials/names of the case victims. The fourth element was a placeholder.

2244—WALDTBEASRFTDSMT

SD3036—LFVLDHMWACRMCDBBTBCK

CM2446—MMRGPS

BHBR44

Here is the key to that 2003 code. The number **2244** denotes the date range of the crimes by taking the last two numbers in the year **1922** and combine them with the last two numbers in the year **1944**.

2244 = 1922-1944
SD3036 = San Diego 1930-1936
CM2446 = Child Murders 1924-1946

The capital letter codes refer to the first initial of the victim's first and last names and are placed in concentric order, i.e., the first victim William Taylor's initials WT become the first and last letters in the letter code, **WALDTBEASRFTDSMT**, for example:

WALDTBEASRFTDSMT

~ ~ ~

WT - William Taylor
AM - Aimee McPherson
LS
DD - Doris Dazey
TT - Thelma Todd
BF
ER
AS

Author's Note - Where the victim's bold initials appear beside their name in bold, those victim's cases have been investigated and documented in one or more of my books. Victims' initials in regular font with no name attached indicate cases that have been investigated and documented but as yet have not appeared in one or more of my books and/or intentionally remain unnamed by me at this time.

SD3036 = San Diego 1930-1936

LFVLDHMWACRMCDBBTBCK

Lois Kentle
Francis Conlon
Virginia Brooks
Louise Teuber
Dolly Bibbens
Hazel Bradshaw
Maude Detweiler
Wesley Adams (Mary)
Celia Cota
Ruth Muir

~ ~

CM2446 = Child Murders 1924-1946

MMRGPS
MS - Martin Sisters
MP
RG

Last in the above "Reference No." sequence is BHBR44.

2244—WALDTBEASRFTDSMT—SD3036—LFVLDHMWACRMCDBBTBCK—CM2446—MMRGPS—BHBR44

BHBR44 = Beverly Hill Bank Robbery 1944

ACKNOWLEDGMENTS

The "Early Years" has been a "slow burn" in the sense that this two-book set has been smoldering over the past two decades becoming:

The Early Years - Part 1 and Part 2.

A thoughtprint here, a puzzle piece there, here a "clew," there a "clew," everywhere a "clew" "clew"

Unlike most of my other books, which were very much a team effort with significant contributions coming from my readers-worldwide emails, these final books have been a solitary process for the most part.

It has mostly been a review and condensing of hundreds of print articles from the dailies and old magazines dating back nearly one hundred years.

For these past many months, I have been in solitary confinement.

With one exception—Robert J. Sadler, my man in Dallas.

In addition to being a prolific author of a true-crime book and 20 mystery novels, Robert has served as my Editor, Design Artist, and Formatter-In-Chief on both of "The Early Years" books.

And as if that weren't enough Stetsons for one man to wear, he has also been my ride-along partner (yes, he was a Dallas Police Officer too) and covered my literary back when I tended to stray off the proverbial path. (Pun intended.)

So, THANK YOU, ROBERT!

Robert J. Sadler
https://www.robertjsadler.com/

~

Most of all, I want to take the opportunity to thank and send my deep LOVE and APPRECIATION to my two sons, Michael Sean and Matthew Roger, for their patience and understanding as they watched (with what must have been a difficult yet non-interfering concern), as their father conducted this twenty-year pursuit of the truth, which could very well be considered my obsession.

MUCH LOVE TO BOTH MY SONS AND THEIR BEAUTIFUL FAMILIES.

Steve Hodel
May 9, 2021
Los Angeles, California

www.stevehodel.com
www.stevehodel.com/blog
email: steve@stevehodel.com

Final Author's Note - For those interested in discovering and reading Dr. Hodel's other serial crimes and my follow-up investigations linking him to them, here is a list of my books and their recommended reading order:

Steve Hodel's: 6 True-Crime Books (in reading order left to right)

- in reading order -

Black Dahlia Avenger
Most Evil
Black Dahlia Avenger II
Most Evil II
Black Dahlia Avenger III
In The Mesquite
The China Letter

(by Dr. George Hodel - Introduction by Steve Hodel)

and now

The Early Years - Part 1 & Part 2

Sadler's Note —

Steven K. Hodel, thank you for your years of friendship and for allowing me the opportunity to be involved in the production of *The Early Years - Part 1 & 2*.

Steve, may your truth-telling here (as in your other books) set you free from any personal angst or from anyone's perceived or implied covalent bonds or guilt-by-association your intrepid investigative revelations may have evoked.

As amazing, stunning and horrifying as *The Early Years - Part 1 & 2* were, they were acknowledged and followed by more killings. As both warning and prediction GHH wrote in lipstick:

"there will be more"

and there were—see the reading order, page 431.

and there were—see the reading order, page 431.

rjs 10/30/2021

Some of the
Press and Book Reviews for
Black Dahlia Avenger I, II & III — Most Evil I & II

T BONE BURNETT, Oscar, Grammy and Golden Globe Award-winning musician-songwriter; Music Director, *True Detective* says:

"From this distance, there is no doubt that George Hodel committed/ performed theatrical murders in several cities over several decades. That a mad doctor's son grew up to be a detective and solved a master criminal's surrealist crimes—and it was his father—is mind-blowing. But, there it is. My deepest and sincerest respect for [Steve's] fearless and brilliant investigation into a profound darkness that [he has] brought into a penetrating light."

~~~

STEPHEN R. KAY, L.A. Co. Head Dep. District Attorney (07/2001) said:

"The most haunting murder mystery in Los Angeles County during the 20th century has finally been solved in the 21st century."

~~~

MICHAEL CONNELLY, *New York Times* Bestselling author of *The Harry Bosch Series* wrote:

"Los Angeles is the construct of its mythologies good and bad, fact and fiction. The legend of Elizabeth Short is one of the most enduring. But now Steve Hodel has come to put the Black Dahlia painfully to rest. With the tenacity and patience of the veteran homicide detective he once was, Hodel goes from odd coincidence to rock solid conclusion. Taking us on the intriguing and unsettling journey every step of the way. (Steve) Hodel's investigation is thoroughly and completely convincing. So too is this book. As far as I am concerned, this case is closed. Elizabeth Short's legend is now shared with a killer who has been pulled from the shadows of time and into the light. Everybody counts or nobody counts, and that includes the people shrouded in our myths. Steve Hodel knows this. And now we do, too."

~~~

DAVID THOMSON, *New York Times* Book Review wrote:

"George Hodel, I think, is fit company for some of noir's most civilized villains—like Waldo Lydecker in *Laura*, Harry Lime in *The Third Man*, or even Noah Cross in *Chinatown*."

Epilogue

As I approach my eightieth birthday in November 2021, *The Early Years Part II* will most likely be my final investigation into my father's serial crimes.

My plan now is to pack up and move back to Bellingham, Washington, and spend my remaining years with my family. I want to be near my two sons and two grandchildren.

As many of my readers know, my investigation began with my father's death, nearly twenty-three years ago in May 1999.

It began with a simple transpacific telephone call to my half-sister, Tamar Hodel, in Hawaii, just two of his eleven children expressing and exchanging pride in their father and his many accomplishments.

In that conversation we shared and reflected on "the great man's passing and what a wonderful and most remarkable life he had lived." Then, as we were ending our call, the thunder rolled, and the lightning struck with Tamar's offhand comment of just two dozen words.

> "Well, you know our father was a suspect in the Black Dahlia Murder. Oh, he didn't do it, but the police thought he did."

Thus began my Telemachian quest in search of my father and the Truth so I might clear his and our family name from any suspicion.

My quest is now complete.

I found my father!

But, my discovery was not the noble Ulysses, a father disguised in beggar's clothes.

No!

Instead, I found a Darth Vader, masked as "a healer" dressed in fine *British Tweed* and wearing three-hundred-dollar *Bally* shoes.

By day, a highly respected medical doctor. Also, a psychiatrist and one of the world's leading experts in Market Research. Indeed, "a man of the world."

By night, a monster beyond belief. A nihilist and sadist in the extreme. An urban terrorist and serial killer who stalked the city streets for fifty years, taking at least fifty lives, by my count.

The Early Years Part II is my eighth book and completes my investigation spanning nearly twenty-three years.

The frustrations with law enforcement have been many.

During the past two decades, I have made repeated appeals and requests to LAPD (my LAPD) to "test for DNA."

I have offered time and time again to provide my father's complete DNA profile for comparison. I did this on at least three separate occasions: first to Chief William Bratton, then to his replacement, Chief Charlie Beck, and most recently to Beck's replacement, Chief Michel Moore.

Chief Bratton's public comment in November 2004 was the most stunning.

> "I just told our Cold Case Squad guys to give it up. (Stop investigating the Black Dahlia case.) "I'm more concerned about the nine (9) murders we had last week than one going back that many years. I know that is problematic for some people who would like to see it solved. But what would you have to write about if it was solved? Better it go unsolved. There are more and more books being written about it all the time." (Stunned silence from the crowd for ten seconds.)

Chief Bratton's comments were followed through the decades by Chief Beck, then echoed by Chief Moore and the assigned detectives at LAPD Robbery/ Homicide Division, all professing the same mantra:

> "We are too busy currently with unsolved murder cases and are unable to take the time to examine and prove or disprove Hodel's findings."

I seriously doubt that LAPD will ever be willing to conduct any DNA testing on the "Black Dahlia Murder" or any of the dozen or so "Lone Woman Murders."

Why not?

The answer is obvious.

If LAPD conducted and obtained suspect DNA and it matched that of Dr. George Hill Hodel, they would confirm the 1950 coverup.

They would validate that their (our) two greatest LAPD heroes, Chiefs William Parker and Thad Brown, were responsible for allowing a serial killer to remain free and continue his savage murders well into the Sixties.

Had Chiefs Parker and Brown done their duty in the 1950s the 1966 Riverside victim Cheri Jo Bates, the 1967 Manila victim Lucila Lalu, and the seven "Zodiac" crimes in the San Francisco Bay Area in 1968-69 would not have occurred. Those many victims might all be alive today.

I have decided to take a highly unusual action before closing the books. As my last investigative offering, a parting gift if you will, I make my father's, (Dr. George Hill Hodel), DNA profile public.

I offer this to both the reading public and to law enforcement departments, agencies, and the police officers **who do care.**

Along with his below DNA profile, I have provided the names of forty-nine suspect cases for potential DNA testing.

My request to law enforcement, (specifically, San Diego PD and SO, Riverside PD, Vallejo PD, Napa SO, San Francisco PD, Pasadena, Santa Monica and Long Beach PDs, and Manila Metropolitan PD) is to pull your Cold Case Files, check for what physical evidence remains, and if it still exists, have your criminalist test it for Touch DNA and compare. (See complete list of forty-nine victims on page 421-422.)

No real investigation is required—just a few simple phone calls.

Most Sincerely,

Steve Hodel
Detective III LAPD Hollywood Homicide (ret.)

Author Steven Kent Hodel

Circa 1950   2021

George Hill Hodel Full DNA Profile

Locus	CCA0972-0134-E04a1
D8S1179	13, 15
D21S11	{28, 33.2}
D7S820	No Results
CSF1PO	No Results
D3S1358	16, 17
TH01	6, 8
D13S317	9, ---
D16S539	12, 13
D2S1338	17, ---
D19S433	14, 16
vWA	14, 17
TPOX	8, 9
D18S51	11, ---
Amelogenin	X, Y
D5S818	13, 13
FGA	20, 23

Note to technicians:

D18S51 Lacks intensity required to make "certainty" call, but shows as **- 22**

CSF1PO- Lacks intensity required to make "certainty" call, but shows as **- 13**

Note to my readers:

Despite my first wife Kiyo's claims that "You're not your father's son. Your father was film director Rowland Brown," the **DNA profile** (on page 437) **confirms I am the biological son of Dr. George Hill Hodel**.

Son and Father - Fifty-One Years Apart

1943   1994

Printed in Great Britain
by Amazon